DICKENS AND CARLYLE
The Question of Influence

DICKENS AND CARLYLE
The Question of Influence

WILLIAM ODDIE

LONDON
The Centenary Press
MCMLXXII

First Published 1972, *by The Centenary Press,*
11–14 *Stanhope Mews West, London SW*7, *and*
printed by A. Brown and Sons, Perth Street West,
Hull, in 11*pt Bembo.*

This book is dedicated
TO MY FATHER
with love

Contents

Contents

Preface

THIS book, based on a doctoral thesis of about twice its length, is as short as I have been able to make it. Though it is the first published full-length study on the subject of Carlyle's influence over Dickens, it will not be the last; it is in fact surprising that a topic as vitally important as this one should have had to await for so long the widespread attention now being given to it, the results of which will, it is to be hoped, appear over the next year or so. This book, therefore, is not intended as a definitive treatment (though so far as I know, it contains most of the known facts directly relevant to the question of The Sage's effect on the Novelist; I have reluctantly decided not to treat as fully as I would have liked certain connected topics, such as Carlyle's feelings about Dickens). The last word on the subject is, in any case, unlikely to be uttered before the completion of two mountainous tasks now in progress, the sifting and publication of the complete letters both of Dickens and of Carlyle. These indispensable scholarly labours, however, will not be acheived in the foreseeable future, and some reasonably extended study of the subject is already long overdue.

My thanks are due to many people, who have helped me at various stages in the writing and publication of this book. My most over-whelming debt is to Professor Philip Collins, of whom it is tempting to say that he has forgotten more about Dickens and the Victorian period than some scholars ever learn, were it not for the fact that he seems never to have forgotten anything. To him I am indebted for so many suggestions of fact and method, and for the detection and avoidance of so many wrong turnings, that it would be difficult to imagine what this book would have been like without his guidance; it would certainly have been very different, and its inadequacies (for none of which he is in any way responsible) even more marked. My thanks are also due to Dr. Michael Slater, without whose kindness and encouragement this book might well not have appeared, who allowed me, while I was still engaged on my own preliminary researches, to read his thesis on *The Chimes*, parts of which have now, happily, been published; I concur with nearly all his conclusions, and have not infrequently drawn on them. My thanks are also due to him in his capacity as editor of *The Dickensian*, for permission to use material first published in that journal, from my article *Dickens and the Indian Mutiny*. I would like to acknowledge the help of Professor Jack Simmons of Leicester University, who gave me an afternoon of his time to discuss various topics related to this one, and who suggested several invaluable lines of enquiry, and of Dr. Sheila Smith of Nottingham University, who also contributed a most useful discussion. I am grateful to David and Elizabeth Challen who kindly read the proofs, and to whom I am indebted for a number of penetrating suggestions. My wife not only read the proofs, but also typed out most of the book. Finally I would like to thank the New York Public Library and the Victoria and Albert Museum for their permission to use unpublished manuscript material.

Introduction

'THAT man,' wrote Caroline Fox of Dickens in 1841, 'is carrying out Carlyle's work more emphatically than any . . .'[1] The novel that inspired this judgement was *The Old Curiosity Shop*, and her reasons for coming to such a conclusion reflect a view of Carlyle that was to become increasingly rare during his lifetime. Dickens, continued Caroline Fox, 'forces the sympathies of all into unwonted channels, and teaches us that Punch and Judy men, beggar children, and daft old men are also of our species, and are not, more than ourselves, removed from the sphere of the heroic.' This seems, perhaps, a curious point of comparison to us, though at this point in time Carlyle was regarded as being kindlier than his later reputation might suggest. The two men's names were again linked, some ten years later, in a way which reflects a change that had already taken place in the critical atmosphere surrounding Carlyle's works. 'It is certain,' wrote *Fraser's Magazine* in 1850,

> . . . that no one has been more instrumental than Dickens in fostering that spirit of kindly charity which impels a man to do what he can, however narrow his sphere of action may be, to relieve the sufferings and to instruct the ignorance of his brethren; while Carlyle, on the other hand, treats all such efforts with lofty disdain, and would call them mere attemps to tap an ocean by gimlet-holes, or some such disparaging metaphor.[2]

Trollope's implied contrast of Dickens (portrayed as 'Popular Sentiment') and Carlyle ('Pessimist Anticant') in *The Warden* can be seen to underline this judgement. Carlyle and Dickens were clearly seen by their contemporaries as being writers very different in temperament and outlook. The comparison between them (though it was certainly made from time to time) was not an inevitable one for the Victorian mind, even when (as I shall argue) Dickens saw himself—demonstrably in *The Chimes* and *Hard Times*—as conveying Carlylean ideas.

[1] Fox, C., *Memories of Old Friends*, London, 1882, 117.
[2] 'Charles Dickens and David Copperfield', *Fraser's Magazine*, XLII (1850), 709.

1

The debt of the novelist to the sage has, perhaps, been more readily acknowledged by recent critics than it was at the time. 'His influence upon Dickens was profound,' writes Professor Ford;[1] Humphry House suggests that Dickens 'took a good deal . . . from Carlyle';[2] and Professor Tillotson believes that the evidence for the response to Carlyle, not only of Dickens but of other novelists, 'is overwhelming'.[3]

The similarities between Dickens's view of his world and Carlyle's are certainly, at times, very striking, and one is led to wonder why they were not more commonly acknowledged during Dickens's lifetime. The two writers both had an enormous public—their works were often advertised together, in tandem, and together they headed Chapman and Hall's list of best sellers for years—and though their writings might be imagined to appeal to rather different kinds of reader, they must frequently have been housed in the same bookcase. One reason for the relative infrequency of contemporary attributions to the sage of some of the more Carlylean ideas in Dickens's novels is to be found, perhaps, in the nature of Carlyle's massive influence, not over Dickens merely, or even over literary circles, but over his whole age. Carlyle became influential, not because his message constituted a discovery of new and unsuspected truths, but because at a moment in English history when men were bewildered and fearful of the future, he put the problems of the period—and especially of the late 'thirties and early 'forties—into words whose meaning could not be mistaken, and implied, by his personality rather than by any new revelation that, like Oedipus, he somehow possessed the strength and vision needed to guide his countrymen through their darkness. But the problems already existed. Carlyle articulated uncertainties that were already felt: perhaps this is why few saw any need, both during and after the height of his reputation, to attribute any such attempt as Dickens's to examine these uncertainties, to his reading of Carlyle. More instinctively than we can, they referred Dickens's understanding of society to its source, rather than to a literary intermediary, no matter how eminent.

If Dickens had a mentor, nevertheless, it was certainly Carlyle. In their personal relations, he extended to him a respect, amounting to reverence, for which there is no parallel in his attitude to any other of his contemporaries. We have evidence for his knowledge of *The French Revolution* (which was intimate), and for his acquaintance with *Chartism* and *Sartor Resartus*,[4] and textual indications for the effect on

[1] Ford, G. H., *Dickens and his Readers*, London, 1955, 88.
[2] House, H., *The Dickens World*, London, 1960, 51.
[3] Tillotson, K., *Novels of the Eighteen-forties*, London, 1961.
[4] For *FR*, see Forster, 505. For *SR*, see *UCT*, 358, and "Where we stopped growing", *HW*, VI (1853), 361. Dickens had a copy of *Chartism* in 1840, and lent it to John Overs. Overs sent Dickens in return a long critique of Carlyle's work, which is to be published by Dr. Sheila Smith of Nottingham University.

certain of his novels of these three works, and of *Past and Present*.[1]
We have reason to believe, in other words, that Dickens knew at least
fairly well the four works that can be seen as constituting the summit
of Carlyle's mature achievement, and that these works had a discernible affect on his writings. We can also observe at least two points
in Dickens's career at which he almost certainly saw himself as writing
under Carlyle's influence, a fact which he attempted to bring to
Carlyle's attention at the time. We have no such evidence for Dickens's
admiration of any comparable figure; as Professor Collins suggests,
'Dickens was not well acquainted with the philosophers, nor even with
the "thinkers" or "sages" of his day, except for Carlyle.'[2] Dickens
made no secret of his respect for the Prophet of Chelsea, and his son
Henry recalled long afterwards that Dickens 'used to say—and indeed
he has said it to me—that the man who had influenced him most was
Thomas Carlyle.'[3]

That it is important to establish the existence of, and to attempt in
some way to describe, the literary relationship of two figures so
centrally important to the culture of their times, seems to me to be
obvious enough. What is, or ought to be, equally obvious, is that in
doing so we are dealing with the works of a novelist whose response
to his age was such that the vitality of his novels does not compellingly
need to be explained by any other frame of reference than that supplied
by his own direct experience of his world. To point to Dickens's
admiration for Carlyle, to summarise their respective social philosophies, to point to the similarities, and then to pronounce without
any qualifying framework that something called 'influence' exists is
surely not helpful, though this is precisely the procedure adopted in
one widely cited account of the relationship, by a scholar rightly held
in some esteem. Dickens certainly admired, even revered, Carlyle;
but so did very many other Victorians. His admiration for Carlyle,
indeed, allows us to see, once more, Dickens as the common man
writ large: the reasons why Dickens felt Carlyle to be important were
very similar to those which established Carlyle in the eyes of most of
his contemporaries—as opposed merely to his intellectual admirers—
as a major prophetic figure. But admiration, even veneration, for
Carlyle did not always mean the total—or even partial—acceptance
of his outlook; nor, at the same time, did the promulgation of
'Carlylean' views, on the 'Condition of England Question' (or almost
any other question) mean, necessarily, that Carlyle's works had had

---

[1] For *FR*, see pp. 61ff below; for *SR*, see pp. 58 and 117-8 below, for *Chartism*, see
pp. 52, 109, and 143 below; for *PP*, see pp. 114ff below.
[2] Collins, Philip, 'Dickens's Reading', *Dickensian*, LX (1964), 143.
[3] Dickens, H., 'A Chat about Charles Dickens', *Harper's Magazine* (European Edition),
LXVIII (1914), 189. Henry continues, nevertheless, that 'this somewhat surprised
me. I could understand this in connection with his book, *A Tale of Two Cities*,
but not when taken in its general sense. I gathered, however, that what he most
admired in Carlyle was his sincerity and truth'.

anything to do with their genesis. Hence, despite the fact that Carlyle's influence over Dickens has become a truism of Dickensian criticism, it has seemed to me right, before proceeding to more general speculation, to attempt to establish, by a detailed examination of the two works for which we have the most textual and circumstantial evidence, that the thing exists. A reasonably sceptical survey of the 'Carlylean' themes and material in *Hard Times* and *A Tale of Two Cities* does, I think, accomplish this; it also helps us to indicate the limits of the phenomenon, and the way in which Dickens draws on Carlyle's work to complement and inform parallel sources of information.

Dickens was certainly 'influenced' by Carlyle, though the assertion has been made more often than it has been effectively demonstrated. What also needs to be decided, I think, is how this influence can be seen to operate, and how useful it is to know about it. It will not be helpful if the discovery that Carlyle was an important and creative influence over Dickens's development as an artist leads us to expect influence where it simply does not exist, or where it exists only in an inessential way. This is, for instance, a process that seems to me to be demonstrated by assertions that Carlyle was an important influence over Dickens's prose style, particularly in the later novels. Suggestions of influence are, I think, of dubious value unless some care is taken over their assertion; the great danger is that they tend to reduce the importance of the writer's own powers, to make him appear less the centre of his own creative world than an intelligent critical interest in a particular work might otherwise suggest. To demonstrate the influence of one writer over another is a proceeding fraught with danger, if for no other reason than that it demands a valid critical understanding of the workings of not one, but two creative imaginations, which should ideally be shown as mutually self-revealing, but may well in practice be the reverse. Professor Marcus, for instance, suggests that the references to clothes throughout *Oliver Twist* (Oliver's moving from the criminal underworld to middle-class safety and back again being always dramatised by a change of clothing) show that Dickens may have recently read *Sartor Resartus*, with its exposition of Carlyle's 'philosophy of clothes'.[1] Two replies can be made to such a suggestion. Firstly, that *Sartor Resartus* had only appeared in England in its serialisation in *Fraser's Magazine* (1833-4), at a time when Carlyle was virtually unknown to the general public, and was not republished in book form until 1838. Dickens, therefore, unless—as seems improbable—he had read *Sartor* in *Fraser's* or in an American edition of 1836 or 1837, is very unlikely to have read *Sartor Resartus* by the time he wrote *Oliver Twist*, the serialisation of which began in 1837. A private reprint from the Fraser's serialisation was published in 1834 for Carlyle's friends, but this is not an edition

---

[1] Marcus, S., *Dickens from Pickwick to Dombey*, London 1965, 80.

Dickens was likely to have known. Carlyle's friendship with Forster—a probable channel for much of Carlyle's influence over Dickens—began in the late 'thirties, and became fairly close only during the 'forties; Dickens himself did not meet Carlyle until 1839. It is not always so easy, however, to argue against such suggestions of influence on circumstantial grounds, and the important objection to this one is critical, and hence, to some extent, a question of personal judgement. I do not see Dickens's references to clothes in *Oliver Twist* as having any real affinities with the symbolism of Carlyle's 'philosophy of clothes', and if I am right, the effect if not the intention of such a suggestion of influence (if it is taken to its logical conclusion) is to foster a critical misjudgement of Dickens's novel. What I, at any rate, take to be a simple example of novelistic 'stage business' is, by an effort of—I think—mistaken critical imagination, raised to the awful level of 'philosophy' and 'symbolism'. There is a similar danger in attributions to a Carlylean source of Dickens's social theory. Dickens's feelings about society came in the first place from life and not from books about it, and unless an examination of Carlyle's undoubted effect on Dickens in this field takes account of how essentially Dickensian the 'Carlylean' elements in his social thinking remain, they reduce our understanding of the personal involvement on Dickens's part that it required, and are likely to contribute towards a misapprehension of its content.

What we need to ask here, is not only whether such influence existed, but how it operated; how much of Dickens's awareness of his society would have remained unrealised without Carlyle? How much Carlylean influence over, say *Hard Times*, is real, and how much apparent? How much of Carlyle's influence over Dickens, even when Dickens clearly saw himself as writing under the Prophet's shadow, rested on a complete understanding of the intellectual and spiritual bases of Carlyle's *oeuvre*, and how much on an unconscious moulding of the sage in Dickens's own image? 'These,' in Carlyle's words, 'are Questions'. To attempt an answer to them we need to understand, at least in part, not simply the undoubted and extensive parallels, especially in the second half of Dickens's career, that exist between his works and social theory and Carlyle's; we need to point out, too, other strands in Dickens's understanding of the questions involved, and to show that Carlylean thought in Dickens's novels, where it is alleged, is *distinctively* so, and was unlikely to come from other sources. I agree with Professor Collins that, though Dickens himself acknowledged his debt to Carlyle, he 'was incurious about the processes of his [own] thought and art', and that 'To assert that Dickens was influenced by Carlyle here or there, that he would not have written thus if he had not read Carlyle, is often tempting but rarely safe.'[1]

---

[1] Collins, P., *Dickens and Education*, London, 1963, 216.

Though I will on a number of occasions make precisely this perilous assertion, it is also the case that in every instance where I have found Carlyle's influence over Dickens, I have also found an alternative, and often (as I hope to show) more fundamental reason why he should have been thinking along 'Carlylean' lines.

Carlyle's effect on Dickens's thinking was a forming and shaping one, I think; it did not operate as a simple transference of ideas from one mind to another. This may sound rather like Professor Cazamian's view, that 'L'influence de Carlyle a précisé et fortifié ses propres tendances et leur a souvent donné leurs formules.'[1]   But Cazamian's conclusion is not, I think, entirely adequate, though it is certainly nearer the truth than the idea of Dickens (as a gaping *ingénu* soaking in wisdom at the master's feet) which is conveyed by some suggestions of Carlyle's influence over him.   This influence is a complex and (though of fundamental importance) to some extent a shifting phenomenon, which—like Dickens's personality—continuously resists anything but the most general formulation.   That such formulation must necessarily be fairly explicit here is, in a way, regrettable, and I have tried as much as possible to avoid pinning examples of this elusive butterfly down on a specimen board.   I have certainly not been successful in this: all the same, I hope that fleeting glimpses will emerge of the species in its natural habitat.

---

[1] Cazamian, I, 216 n.

CHAPTER ONE

Carlyle and the Victorians

'I BELIEVE it will be generally admitted,' wrote George Saintsbury in 1895, 'that there is nowadays no more distinct sign of a man's having reached the fogey, and of his approaching the fossil, stage of intellectual existence than the fact that he has an ardent admiration for Carlyle.'[1] The decline in Carlyle's stock was already obvious to most people by his death in 1881, and his irrelevance to the times was pointed by the contrast with a younger writer who also died that winter. 'The common season of their departure,' the *Contemporary Review* noted, 'records a revolution of thought. Thomas Carlyle and George Eliot, though separated by the interval of a bare generation, represented two intellectual eras . . . [Carlyle] belongs to a phase of development that we have already left far behind us. With all the characteristic tendencies of the day he was out of sympathy, with most of them he was out of relation. His figure stands out clearly only in the light of the past.'[2]

There were, nevertheless, many who could still remember the sway over men's minds exercised by the prophet of Chelsea at the height of his powers, and no-one would have found it hard to believe—as Lytton Strachey did fifty years later—'that real red-hot lava ever flowed from that dry neglected crater . . .'[3] Certainly, Dr. Leavis is profoundly wrong to suggest that 'if Carlyle is to get some attention . . . it might reasonably be given by way of an essay on the debt the young Mill may be imagined to owe him.'[4] The inadequacy of such a view can only be conveyed by an appeal to Carlyle's own age,

---

[1] Saintsbury, G., *Corrected Impressions*, London, 1895, 41-2.
[2] 'A Study of Carlyle', *Contemporary Review*, XXXIX (1881), 584.
[3] Strachey, L., *Portraits in Miniature*, London, 1931, 198.
[4] Leavis, F. R., Introduction to *Mill on Bentham and Coleridge*, London, 1950, 14-15.

to what Dickens in another context called 'the tremendous testimony of men living at the time'. Mill, it is clear, was by no means the only important figure to come under Carlyle's spell at some stage in his career, and the way in which many notable figures looked (or appeared to look) to Carlyle for guidance was noted by more than one contemporary observer.[1] 'Rarely if ever in the history of literature,' it was possible to claim by 1850, 'has such a phenomenon been witnessed as that of his influence . . . one can hardly take up a book or a periodical without finding in every page some expression or some mode of thinking that bears the mint-mark of his genius.'[2] This is a far-reaching claim; but that it would have been very widely accepted at the time it was made is beyond doubt.

The reasons for Carlyle's enormous influence, particularly during the late 'thirties and 'forties, emerge, without too much critical prodding, from the vast mass of contemporary reactions to Carlyle and his writings that are available to us, particularly from the periodical press. Like Dickens after the appearance of The Pickwick Papers, Carlyle became a literary household word in 1837, on the publication of The French Revolution. He was forty-two and virtually unknown, and had behind him, among other works, a large body of essays on German literature, a Life of Schiller, a translation of Goethe's Wilhelm Meister, the two important essays, 'Signs of the Times' and 'Characteristics', and Sartor Resartus, which though virtually ignored in its first appearance in Fraser's Magazine, was to become one of the most popular and lasting of all his works. The French Revolution's almost immediate success was probably due in the first place to an enthusiastic article in the Westminster Review, by John Stuart Mill. What most impressed Mill was the imaginative power by which Carlyle breathed life into his inert materials; ironically, in showing appreciation of this quality above all others, Mill defined better than anyone else could have done, not only one of the facets of Carlyle's mind which was to appeal most strongly to the Victorian imagination, but also an issue which was to distinguish Mill and his school in the public mind (and in Carlyle's own) from the prophet of Chelsea. Matthew Arnold, writing in 1848 of an article by Carlyle, makes something like Mill's

---

[1] His effect on some men of eminence, for instance, was noted, in 1851 by Hogg's Instructor, which mentioned, among novelists, Bulwer, Kingsley, Thackeray and Dickens; among politicians, Charles Buller and John Bright; among scientists, Hugh Miller (the geologist) and Samuel Brown (the chemist); among Christian teachers, 'philosophers' and scholars, Thomas Chalmers, Edward Irving, Thomas Irskine, F. D. Maurice and Dr. Arnold; and among poets, Tennyson. By all these men, recorded Hogg's, in spite of the differences between their various opinions and his own, he has been 'heartily, lovingly honoured. Each of them, from his own throne, has recognised, if not a higher, a more central one on which Carlyle sits'; all, continued the writer, had at some time stepped from his own sphere into Carlyle's, expecting and receiving guidance. ('Portrait Gallery: Thomas Carlyle', Hogg's Instructor, N.S. VII (1851), 81).
[2] "Latter-Day Pamphlets. Edited by THOMAS CARLYLE", North British Review, XIV (1850), 4.

point: '. . . the thoughts extracted and abstractly stated are every newspaper's', he wrote: 'It is the style and feeling by which the beloved man appears.' And Arnold places his admiration for Carlyle's 'style and feeling' by an opposition: 'How short could Mill write Job?'[1]: this is unfair but understandable, and sits interestingly by Mill's own isolation of the same framework of discrimination in his review of *The French Revolution*:

> Never before did we take up a book calling itself by that name, a book treating of past times, and professing to be true, and find ourselves actually among human beings. We at once felt, that what had hitherto been to us mere abstractions, had become realities; the 'forms of things unknown', which we fancied we knew, but knew their names merely, were, for the first time, with most startling effect, 'bodied forth' and 'turned into shapes'. Other historians talk to us indeed of human beings; but what do they place before us? Not even stuffed figures of such, but rather their algebraical symbols; a few phrases, which present no image to the fancy . . .[2]

Many years later, Mill was to compare himself with Carlyle in a way which not only reinforces the 'fact' versus 'fancy' distinction between himself and Carlyle, but which clarifies 'style and feeling', not simply as a way of making dull facts come to life, but as a means of perception, a channel, almost, for revealed truth: even in the years of their friendship, wrote Mill in his *Autobiography* (1873):

> I did not . . . deem myself a competent judge of Carlyle. I felt that he was a poet, and that I was not; that he was a man of intuition, which I was not; and that as such, he not only saw many things long before me, which I could only when they were pointed out to me, hobble after and prove, but that it was highly probable he could see many things which were not visible to me even after they were pointed out.[3]

This power of intuitive imagination was, perhaps, the single factor without which Carlyle's astonishing reputation would never have been established, and on which, throughout his career, it rested as firmly as on what he actually said; denials of his originality, even among his admirers, were frequent throughout his career, and probably represent the consensus of contemporary opinion. 'There is not much novelty of matter,' said the *British and Foreign Review* of *Chartism*:

> Indeed we do not know that we have found a single thing in it absolutely new. But the power of painting, the vividness with which each separate element is worked up into the general picture, the brilliancy of colouring, and the force with which the whole view is made to strike the imagination,

---

[1] Arnold, M., *Letters to Clough*, ed. Lowry, H., Oxford, 1932, 75.
[2] *Mill's Essays on Literature and Society*, ed. Schneewind, J. B., New York, 1965, 186-7.
[3] Mill, J. S., *Autobiography*, Oxford, 1924, 149.

are exactly such as we have been accustomed to admire in Mr. Carlyle's writings. We look upon this little book therefore, appearing at such a time as this, to be a very valuable one; not because it gives us views or information which we were absolutely without before, but because it combines the whole subject into a living form, and graphically as well as forcibly places it before our eyes.[1]

The reviewer is obviously talking about something more than a highly coloured popular presentation of an already apparent malaise; it is Carlyle's capacity for the 'combination of the whole subject into a *living form*' that is found so valuable, and which, perceived by his contemporaries in works directly relevant to the social and the spiritual dilemma of the late 'thirties and the 'forties, was to project Carlyle into the central position he enjoyed during this period. Carlyle's work conveyed the impression of a living and strongly individual intelligence, somehow projected through the printed page that mysterious phenomenon, *charisma*. After the publication of *The French Revolution*, it soon became clear to the reading public that a 'very remarkable man'[2] had appeared on the scene, obviously gifted with a more than common insight, and cast in a high prophetic mould. 'His earnestness of belief,' wrote the *Dublin Review* in 1838, 'his sincerity of heart are beautiful and soul possessing. His learning is immense; his industry untiring; his shrewdness, his powers of detecting the truth amid masses of error, quite extraordinary.'[3]

Though many people were not so starry-eyed as this, most accorded respect, if not total approval. And although there was, even at this date, a feeling on the part of some readers that Carlyle was vague, ignorant, or wrongheaded on some points of importance, a mystique seems to have arisen around him and his writings as his wider reputation was established, which included the idea that, like an Old Testament prophet, he was somehow set apart, separated from the ordinary run of mankind by his burning contact with ultimate truth: 'his criticisms,' wrote *Fraser's*, 'are breathings of a high devout soul feeling always that here he has no home, but looking as in a clear vision, to a city that hath foundations.'[4]

The clarity of vision, the apparent certainty of his voice, and the authority it successfully claimed for itself made somehow irresistible Carlyle's analyses of both the immediate and sometimes terrifying social realities of the 'thirties and 'forties, and also the more intangible problems of the period, the collapse of traditional religious belief, the difficulty of evolving a new framework of certainty around a rapidly changing industrial society. Carlyle dealt with both the

[1] 'Chartism and Church Extension', *British and Foreign Review*, XI (1840), 2.
[2] 'Carlyle's works', *Dublin Review*, V (1838), 350.
[3] *Ibid.*, 358.
[4] 'Thomas Carlyle's French Revolution', *Fraser's Magazine*, LXVI (1839), 96.

spiritual problems of the individual, and the social consciousness of the times, and related them to each other indissolubly by seeing both in terms of an underlying world spirit. Teufelsdröckh's spiritual collapse, in Book II of *Sartor Resartus*, is the account of an individual crisis of self-confidence, and, by implication, an epitome of the affliction of a whole society; his private agony is translated by a public symbol, the machine, the emblem of a new world and of the disappearance of an old one:

> I had, practically, forgotten that [the men and women around me] were alive, that they were not merely automatic. In the midst of their crowded streets and assemblages, I walked solitary . . . Some comfort it would have been, could I, like a Faust, have fancied myself tempted and tormented of the Devil . . . but in our age of Down-pulling and Disbelief, the very Devil has been pulled down, you cannot so much as believe in a Devil. To me the Universe was all void of Life, of Purpose, of Volition, even of Hostility: it was one huge, dead, immeasurable Steam-engine, rolling on, in its dead indifference, to grind me limb from limb.[1]

Teufelsdröckh has already indicated part of the cause of his despair, of his sense of loss, and hinted at a possible regeneration:

> Had a divine Messenger from the clouds, or miraculous Handwriting on the wall, convincingly proclaimed to me *This thou shalt do*, with what passionate readiness . . . would I have done it . . . Thus, in spite of all Motive-grinders, and Mechanical Profit-and-Loss Philosophies, with the sick ophthalmia and hallucination they had brought on, was the Infinite nature of Duty still dimly present to me . . .[2]

Teufelsdröckh's mood here, as Professor Houghton suggests,[3] is to some extent that of the age, suddenly bereft of its traditional beliefs, and parched by the emotionally barren inheritance of the 'men of the eighteenth century' conveyed by their modern legatees, the Benthamites, whom Teufelsdröck, of course, is attacking here. Carlyle's appearance was obviously seen by many as almost heaven-sent; here, at last, was a man in earnest: 'Is it not . . . strange', wrote the *Westminster Review*, 'that in such a world, in such a country, and among those light-hearted Edinburgh Reviewers, a man should arise and proclaim a creed; not a new and more ingenious form of words, but a truth to be embraced with the whole heart, and in which the heart shall find, as his has found, strength for all combats, and consolation, though stern not festal, under all sorrows?'[4]

Again and again during the 'forties, as Professor Burn says,[5] we come back to Carlyle. 'In and from 1840,' wrote David Masson,

---

[1] *SR*, 126.
[2] *Ibid.*, 125.
[3] Houghton, W., *The Victorian Frame of Mind*, Yale, 1957, 64.
[4] 'Carlyle's works', *Westminster Review*, XXXIII (1839), 3.
[5] Burn, W. L., *The Age of Equipoise*, London, 1964, 66.

who was twenty in 1842, 'Carlyle's name was running like wildfire
through the British Islands . . . there was the utmost avidity for his
books wherever they were accessible, especially among the young
men; phrases from them were in all young men's mouths and were
affecting the public speech.' His house 'was already looked at . . . as
the home of the real king of British Letters.'[1]   The catch-phrase of
the decade, the Condition of England Question, was, appropriately,
coined by him. Again, one asks why he should occupy this central
position. His emphasis on immaterial values, conveyed by his own
peculiar brand of prophetic imaginative white-heat, can be seen as
obviously relevant to the times and provides one answer; but this
does not entirely account for the feeling conveyed by his writings, not
simply of topicality, but of breathless urgency. One factor was certainly the political instability of the late 'thirties and early 'forties:
to many Englishmen, it seemed far from improbable that England
was on the verge of revolution. The subject of Carlyle's first best-
seller was that of the century's great shaping myth-event, and the
publication of The French Revolution in 1837 was a piece of inspired
timing; some people undoubtedly saw the book as a direct warning
of what might happen all too easily here: 'we need scarcely recommend
this book and its timely appearance,' wrote Thackeray in a review for
The Times, 'now that some of the questions solved in it seem almost
likely to be battled over again.'[2]

The possibility of revolution if the Condition of England Question
was not solved, implied by The French Revolution, was made explicit
by Carlyle in Chartism and Past and Present, both of which refer repeatedly to France before the revolution in their evocations of the
condition of modern England. The point was not lost. 'Well may
Mr. Carlyle point to the French revolution', wrote the British and
Foreign Review of Chartism. Nothing of the kind was to be feared in
England, of course, 'not because the cases are absolutely dissimilar,
but because the hearts of the great body of the English nation are still
sound . . . ' And the writer was convinced, that once the true state of
things was known, many people would be ready to remedy it; nevertheless, 'ere this knowledge be brought home to people's minds', he
continued, 'much pressure of want and misery, much sullenness of
discontent, many a deed of violence and bloodshed, must probably be
endured. Would that men would calmly look at the evil before such
dreadful dangers force it in its worst form upon their attention!'[3]
This indicates again something of the function of Carlyle's writings
about society; although they were not always original in themselves,

[1] Masson, D., Carlyle personally and in his writings, London, 1885, 67.
[2] Thackeray, W. M., 'The French Revolution, by T. Carlyle', The Times, Aug. 3
    1837.
[3] British and Foreign Review (1840), op. cit., 13–14.

they do seem to have crystallised a latent public opinion on the conditions of the working class.[1] Carlyle's appeal to the ruling classes acted in two directions; he appealed to their consciences by showing them in a 'living form' what actually was, and to their sense of self-preservation by bringing before their imagination what might be if they remained inactive. The great social problem of the decade, the relationship between rich and poor, the rulers and the ruled, would beyond doubt have been seen very differently without Carlyle's apocalyptic, questioning voice, though he may have overdone the Perils of the Nation a little; this certainly reduced his credibility from the 'fifties onwards.

Another factor in this relative decline was the sudden realisation of his public, with the appearance of *Latter-Day Pamphlets*, of elements in his character that now seem to us very obvious, and which (with hindsight) are shown clearly enough in earlier writings. The general reaction to the *Pamphlets* is fairly clearly relevant to the question of Carlyle's relationship with Dickens: the unprecedented hostility which greeted them even lead at the time to suggestions that Carlyle's influence would now rapidly disappear.[2] But although it was now impossible for some of Carlyle's radical and philanthropic admirers to paper over the cracks between their admiration for Carlyle's high prophetic seriousness and their own beliefs, it soon became clear that his influence had been tested by fire, and had survived the ordeal. To profess an admiration for Carlyle after the publication of the *Latter-Day Pamphlets* was certainly no evidence of a reactionary temperament; five years after their appearance, George Eliot (an interesting test case) could write, though admitting that many questioned the 'exaggerations' of the *Pamphlets* and were very far from accepting the idea of government by a Carlylean hero, that '. . . for any large nature, those points

---

[1] The frequency with which Engels, in *The Condition of the Working Class* (1845), quotes lengthy passages from Carlyle not only in support of his own arguments but of his factual assertions as well, demonstrates perhaps the freshness and authority that Carlyle's pronouncements on the Condition of England Question had for his early readers.

[2] One writer described, in the *Eclectic Review*, the effect it had on a radical friend who burst into his rooms one evening:

Horror was depicted in his countenance—the fire of a righteous indignation flashed from his eyes—he wore the aspect of a man but just escaped from the hellish clutch of the furies, or some over-exciteable enthusiast whose bubble Utopia had suddenly collapsed—whose anxiously-watched mountain had brought forth a mouse. 'I have come, sir,' began my friend, 'to ask you to help me to unmask a traitor—to put down a man who has betrayed the people's cause . . . Look, sir, read'—he continued, throwing down a neat, but unpretending looking pamphlet—'there, sir, is the death-warrant of the popularity of Thomas Carlyle, signed by Thomas Carlyle himself. He has done for himself now, sir. The mask of liberalism is torn off, and he proclaims himself to have been all along a mere Tory in disguise.'

[XXVII (1850), 353-4]. See also, *Christian Observer*, L (1850), 496; *Athenaeum* (1850), 228; and *Punch*, XVIII (1850), 107.

of difference are quite incidental.'[1] Her estimate of Carlyle's appeal
is not out of place in this decade; when John Morley went up to
Oxford in 1856, there were still 'bands of Carlylites' there, passing
'many an hour of strenuous idleness', discussing 'the imperative duty
of work'.[2] Coming from such a source, George Eliot's view of
Carlyle's influence should carry some weight as a reply to Dr. Leavis's.
And both its date (1855) and its matter tell us something about the
real long-term effect of the *Latter-Day Pamphlets* themselves:

> It is an idle question to ask whether his books will be read a century hence:
> if they were all burnt as the grandest of Suttees on his funeral pile, it would
> be only like cutting down an oak after its acorns have sown a forest. For
> there is hardly a superior or active mind of this generation that has not
> been modified by Carlyle's writings; there has hardly been an English book
> written for the last ten or twelve years that would not have been different
> if Carlyle had not lived. The character of his influence is best seen in the
> fact that many of the men who have the least agreement with his opinions
> are those to whom the reading of *Sartor Resartus* was an epoch in the history
> of their minds. The extent of his influence may be best seen in the fact that
> ideas which were startling novelties when he first wrote them are now
> become common-places. And we think few men will be found to say that
> this influence on the whole has not been for good.[3]

George Eliot's analysis of the *modus operandi* of Carlyle's influence
points to one factor in its survival after 1850, and, incidentally, suggests
why Dr. Leavis may be temperamentally disqualified from understanding it at any period: 'It is not as a theorist', she wrote, 'but as
a great and beautiful human nature, that Carlyle influences us.'[4] This
is discouraging for anyone trying to 'extract' a 'system of thought or
body of wisdom,'[5] and however we might assess the intellectual
stringency of Carlyle's writings, it is obvious that if we are to approach
an understanding of what he meant to his age, and certainly to Victorian poets and novelists—including Dickens—we must be prepared
to deal in counters less definite than Dr. Leavis will accept.

Despite George Eliot's emphasis on Carlyle as a 'great and beautiful
human nature', one element in his temperament, as observed by his
contemporaries in his writings, seems to suggest one reason why we
might be surprised that Dickens should have admired him as much
as he did. Carlyle was a kind man, and as a personal friend Dickens
would have every opportunity of observing this for himself. But he
also showed, in his writings, a fascinated sympathy with a kind of

[1] Eliot, G., 'Passages selected from the writings of Thomas Carlyle . . . By Thomas
Ballantyne', *Leader*, VI (1855), 1034-5, reprinted in *Essays of George Eliot*, ed. Pinney
T., London, 1963, 214.
[2] Morley, J., *Critical Miscellanies*, first series, London, 1871, 196.
[3] Eliot, G., *op. cit.*, 213-4.
[4] *Ibid.*, 214.
[5] Leavis, *op. cit.*, 14.

savage destiny; the spirit of truth that Carlyle perceived in the universe, tearing through falsehood and deception, and establishing itself in political terms only through the rule of the Hero, had no respect for individual human beings. At his worst, Carlyle seems almost to reveal in himself a kind of suppressed blood-lust; his doctrine of submission to Destiny sometimes reveals itself in dark forms. 'The Highland wife, with her husband at the foot of the gallows', relates Carlyle in *Chartism*, apparently with grim approval, 'patted him on the shoulder . . . and said amid her tears: "Go up, Donald, my man; the Laird bids ye". To her it seemed the rights of Lairds were great, the rights of men small, and she acquiesced'.[1]

It was Carlyle's fatalistic denial of the difficulty of individual moral decision that some Victorians found hard to accept. As the *Christian Observer* protested, Carlyle's pamphlet on 'Model Prisons' was, apart from any other consideration, altogether too facile; '. . . nothing is easier than to write in this way', expostulated the reviewer, 'because nothing is easier than to declaim on one side of an intricate subject, carefully keeping the other side out of view. For ourselves, we think the subject so intricate that we do not desire to enter upon it here . . . '[2] One was either in tune with the universe, said Carlyle, or one was not; one obeyed its laws, or one disobeyed them. There was no other course. This point of view distressed the philanthropic christianity of some of his readers, the agnostic humanism of others. Carlyle was seen as Roman, rather than Greek, as conveying the spirit of the Old, rather than the New Testament. 'The qualities he admired with his whole soul', wrote Leslie Stephen, 'were force of will, intensity of purpose, exclusive devotion to some worthy end.'[3] Despite *Sartor*, it is in the distinction between Hebraism and 'sweet reasonableness', as Professor Tillotson suggests, that we can isolate one of the radical differences between Arnold and Carlyle.[4] Carlyle had knocked a window from the blind wall of his century, said R. H. Horne; but he noted that 'some men complain of a certain bleakness in the wind which enters at it . . . '[5]

Bleakness or not, Carlyle's influence nevertheless remained powerful, even over those who valued 'sweet reasonableness', and for one over-riding reason: 'his influence in stimulating moral energy', as John Morley wrote, 'in kindling enthusiasm . . . and in stirring a sense of the reality on the one hand, and the unreality on the other, of all that men can do or suffer, has not been surpassed by any teacher now living'. Or as the *Westminster Review* pronounced in 1850:

[1] *Chartism*, 68-9.
[2] *Christian Observer* (1850), *op. cit.*
[3] Stephen, L., "Thomas Carlyle" *Cornhill Magazine*, XLIII (1881), 351.
[4] Tillotson, K., *Mid-Victorian Studies*, London, 1965, 217.
[5] Horne, R. H., *A New Spirit of the Age*, London, 1844, II, 256.

. . . he has raised the moral tone of the age, and awakened a noble spirit of strength and courage amongst the young men of the present generation, which far transcends anything they will actually show to the world. The influence he has had on the *manliness* of the age cannot be sufficiently estimated. It is true that he gives no prescriptive rule of life, but he is, as it were, the voice of the trumpet inciting to the battle and enduing men with the resolutions to 'do with all their might' whatever they may find appointed.[1]

The idea of action and 'moral tone' cannot be separated from what now seems to us a more attractive characteristic of his writings, his anti-mechanistic romantic emphasis on the imagination. As one popular writer put it:

> In some respects, he is a great poet, and pierces the marrow of a thought with the keen vision of a Seer. He sometimes lays open, in a few brief sentences, a whole realm of thought to the thinker. He is eminently suggestive. He incites the minds of others to action. He wields that great power over others, which the *earnest* man invariably exercises.[2]

It was Carlyle's effect on the earnestness of his age, rather than his authoritarianism, that most disquieted Lytton Strachey.[3] The idea of 'moral tone' still contains the twentieth century's popular notion of the Victorian age, and in this sense of the word, Carlyle is the most Victorian figure of them all. Strachey failed to realise that Carlyle's attack on 'Victorianism' was infinitely more searching and more deeply felt than his own could ever be; nevertheless, Carlyle's effect on the seriousness and on the manliness (two inseparable qualities) of the Victorians was probably considered, by the end of his career, to be his most important contribution. Carlyle, thought Harriet Martineau, had 'infused into the mind of the English nation a sincerity, earnestness, healthfulness and courage which can be appreciated only by those who are old enough to tell what was our morbid state when Byron was the representative of our temper, the Clapham Church of our religion, and the rotten-borough system of our political morality'.[4] Certainly, many educated and sensitive minds attributed 'the blessed change' (as Harriet Martineau went on to call it) at least partially to Carlyle's influence. For Matthew Arnold, though, Carlyle 'was always "carrying coals to Newcastle", . . . preaching earnestness to a nation that had it by nature, but was less abundantly supplied with other things'.[5] One of the 'other things' to which Arnold is referring here underlines how paradoxical was Carlyle's appeal to some literary

[1] 'Religious Faith and Modern Scepticism', *Westminster Review*, LII (1850), 397.
[2] 'Notices of New Works: Latter-Day Pamphlet No. 1', *Eliza Cook's Journal* (1850), 398.
[3] Strachey, 186-7.
[4] Martineau, I, 387.
[5] Quoted by Tillotson, K., 148.

people. It was his creative powers, his liberating imaginative genius, to which Arnold and other writers most readily responded, qualities which were the negation of the inflexible and the insensitive, in a word of Philistinism. But Carlyle himself, especially in his later years, was the most powerful of all its champions. Carlylean earnestness seems to have been a bewildering and versatile phenomenon, a Jekyll and Hyde of Victorian intellectual, or anti-intellectual, life. At its best, it was seen as the product of his contempt for formulae, and of his 'suggestiveness'; at its worst, as it is for Arnold here, it was an instrument of the terrible inflexibility and intolerance that became increasingly characteristic of his mind.

CHAPTER TWO

The Personal Relationship

CARLYLE'S position as a prophet of Victorian 'earnestness' indicates the most obvious divergence between his mentality and Dickens's. The antithesis irresistably proposes one of the most unavoidable questions to be answered by an investigation of their relationship: how could such a personality as Dickens's be so attracted by such an opposite? In the end, the question has to be modified before something like a real answer can be attempted. Both Dickens and Carlyle were certainly more complex and less static than this particular discrimination suggests. Nevertheless, the contrast indicated by their respective positions in the Victorian popular imagination does present one of our most fundamental problems. Carlyle himself gives a convenient starting point: 'His theory of life was entirely wrong', Gavan Duffy reports him saying of Dickens, in the mid-forties:

> He thought men ought to be buttered up, and the world made soft and accommodating for them, and all sorts of fellows have turkey for their Christmas dinner. Commanding and controlling and punishing them he would give up without any misgivings in order to coax and soothe and delude them into doing right. But it was not in this manner the eternal laws operated, but quite otherwise. Dickens had not written anything which would be found of much use in solving the problems of life.[1]

Carlyle's attitude to Dickens was warmer, and more complicated, than this and Dickens himself came to believe more in 'commanding and controlling and punishing' than Carlyle realised; but this oversimplification does contain much of the truth about the two men and their relationship and also about the way in which their contemporaries

[1] Duffy, Sir C. G., *Conversations with Carlyle*, London, 1892, 75.

regarded them. Dickens's famous policy statement for a periodical he once thought of starting sums up one aspect (arguably the most important) of the novelist's meaning for his age: 'Carol philosophy, cheerful views, sharp anatomisation of humbug, jolly good temper; papers always in season, pat to the time of year; and a vein of glowing, hearty, generous, mirthful, beaming reference in everything to Home, and Fireside'.[1] This is just as 'Victorian' as Carlyle's spartan austerity, and represents a response to his times as vital and as authentic, for Dickens, as does 'the eternal nature of Duty', for Carlyle. This is the 'early' Dickens speaking, of course, and the contrast, even at this date (1845) was already not as clearcut as this; but it certainly contains enough of the truth (and for the whole period of their relationship) to be worth considering, for the moment, as it stands.

Part of the explanation for the apparent paradox of Dickens's devotion to Carlyle, lies, of course, in the fact that their relationship was not simply a literary, but also a personal one. Many Victorians reacted to the magic of Carlyle's personality on the evidence of the printed page; Dickens reacted to it as well, at first hand: when he told Forster that he would go 'at all times farther to see Carlyle than any man alive',[2] he was speaking of him as a person, for whom he had affection, and not simply as an influential literary figure. And although, in company, Carlyle was much given to denunciatory monologues, especially as he grew older, there is as much emphasis, in many eye-witness accounts, on his exuberance and his collossal laughter. Dickens's personal attitude to Carlyle, in the 'forties and 'fifties at any rate, was an engaging mixture of devotion and exuberant gaiety; the novelist's natural high spirits seem, if anything, to have been stimulated, rather than crushed, by the Prophet of Chelsea. Percy FitzGerald gives us the tone of several reminiscences of their personal relations, in his memory of 'Boz "playing round" the sage as Garrick did round Johnson—affectionately and in high good humour and wit, and, I could well see, much pleasing the old lion'.[3] This blend of devotion and high spirits is demonstrated conveniently enough in two accounts of a meeting between them that took place in 1849. In May, Dickens gave a dinner, to celebrate the launching of David Copperfield, the first number of which was in the booksellers' windows, and Carlyle overcame his distaste for 'leg of mutton eloquence' sufficiently to attend it. He was accompanied by his wife and by the young David Masson, who was then unknown enough to feel it 'promotion to get into such company'. The other guests, apart from Carlyle and his wife, included Thackeray, Samuel Rogers, Mrs. Gaskell, John Kenyon, and, of course, the ever-present Forster. Masson's clearest memory

[1] Forster, 378.
[2] Ibid., 839. Undated.
[3] FitzGerald, P., Memories of Charles Dickens, London, 1913, 91.

was of the warmth of their reception, of Dickens's unusual cordiality.
He

> . . . seemed particularly rejoiced at the sight of them and hurried to greet
> Carlyle, and shook him very warmly by the hand, saying several times how
> glad he was to see him, and putting many questions in a filial way about his
> health, till at last Carlyle laughed and replied, in the very words of Mrs.
> Gummidge in the third chapter of *David Copperfield;*—'I know what I am. I
> know that I am a lone lorn creetur', and not only that everythink goes
> contrary with me, but that I go contrary with everybody.' The pat quota-
> tion made Dickens entirely happy, he laughed and laughed,—it was a treat
> to see him . . .[1]

Forster's recollection of the incident is very similar:

> . . . it was a delight to see the enjoyment of Dickens at Carlyle's laughing
> reply to questions about his health, that he was, in the language of Mr.
> Peggotty's housekeeper, a lorn lone creature and everything went contrary
> with him.[2]

Dickens had to drag himself away to receive another guest who had
just arrived, but their conversation must have been slightly one-sided;
Dickens 'was always "edging to be within hearing" of Carlyle,—it
was easy to see who was the hero of the evening to *him*'.[3] This 'filial'
hero-worship conveys the tone of Dickens's and (not insignificantly)
of Forster's personal attitude to Carlyle, from the late 'forties (and
probably sooner) onwards. Percy FitzGerald, who saw them together
several times, noted 'the devout and affectionate bearing of both men
to the "sage of Chelsea", and his solemn good humour shown to both
in return'.[4]

Dickens's Carlyle, then, was possibly more in keeping with 'Carol
Philosophy' than the Carlyle of the Victorian popular imagination,
or the Carlyle of reality, for whom 'turkey for their Christmas dinner'
was, certainly by the 'fifties, not only irrelevant, but anathema.
Partly, this inconsistency was due to a curious split in Carlyle's own
personality, which made one side of him capable of being stimulated,
quite unhypocritically, by Dickens's warmth and vitality, a spontaneous reaction which soon became engulfed by a deeply entrenched
Calvinistic recoil against such foolishness; this was a negative impulse
that increasingly extended, not only to Dickens, but to all imaginative
writers. Dickens, probably, never saw this side of Carlyle's feelings
about him; he only observed the liberating and cheering effect he
himself had on the old sage and, perhaps, unconsciously incorporated

[1] Recounted by Masson to Wilson, D. A. W., *Carlyle at His Zenith*, London, 1927, 88.
[2] Forster, 528.
[3] Wilson, *op. cit.*, 88.
[4] FitzGerald, 84.

him, in his own image, into his world. Dickens's fascination with
people and their idiosyncrasies scarcely needs pointing out, and Carlyle
had all the necessary qualifications: he was a compelling raconteur,
a man of great laughter, of overpowering and individual personality,
the subject of innumerable anecdotes. Dickens himself took pleasure
in 'irresistible' imitations of his broad Annandale speech at the dinner-
table and elsewhere,[1] a sign that Carlyle's personality had engaged
Dickens's novelist's imagination, a faculty which we cannot separate
from his actor's interest in details of characterisation.

Carlyle's own feelings about Dickens and about his writings alter-
nated curiously, for over forty years, between condescension, even
contempt, and an affectionate warmth tinged strongly with genuine
respect. His attitude to Dickens's writings was bewilderingly inconsistent: on the publication of *Pickwick*, he wrote to Stirling that 'thinner
wash, with perceptible vestige of a flavour in it here and there was
never offered to the human palate';[2] and yet he told someone else
that he 'sat almost a whole day reading it', and a few years later, at a
public reading of the trial scene, his enjoyment was quite simply
uncontrollable:

> I thought Carlyle would split, and Dickens was not much better. Carlyle
> sat on the front bench, and he haw-hawed right out, over and over again
> till he fairly exhausted himself. Dickens would read and then he would stop
> in order to give Carlyle a chance to stop. Of course the whole crowded
> audience were in the same mood and the uproar was tremendous. I
> laughed till my jaws ached, and I caught myself involuntarily stamping . . .
> His acting was splendid. It cannot be exceeded. Carlyle had a young com-
> panion with him, and, speaking to him in answer to some remark, said:
> 'He is a wonderful creature with a book' . . . When Mr. Dickens came on
> the stage the two saluted with a nod and between the readings Mr. Carlyle
> was taken out to meet him.[3]

Carlyle certainly responded to the comic Dickens; equally certainly
he felt ashamed of himself afterwards for having done so.[4]   Reading
Carlyle's comments on Dickens's writing, throughout the novelist's
career, one gets the strong impression of Carlyle, the great prophet
of manly, self-reliant earnestness, escaping from his own terrible
austerity into a warmer and more human world. Jane Carlyle 'would

1   DeWolfe Howe, M. A., *Memories of a Hostess*, Boston, 1922, 141; Yates, E., *Recollec-
    tions and Experiences*, London, 1884, 166-7.
2   Carlyle, T., *Letters to Mill, etc.*
3   Pike, J. S., 'Dickens, Carlyle and Tennyson', *Atlantic Monthly*, CLXIV (1939), 811.
    The young companion was the sculptor, Thomas Woolner, and in the interval,
    he and Carlyle were taken out to meet Dickens backstage for brandy and water.
    'Carlyle took his glass and nodding to Dickens said "Charley, you carry a whole
    company of actors under your hat".' (Woolner, A., *Thomas Woolner, R.A.*,
    Sculptor and Poet, London, 1917, 232-3.)
4   See, for instance, a somewhat defensive letter, written to Froude the following
    evening: *Life in London*, 1884, II, 270.

laughingly relate what outcry there used to be on the night of the week when a number was due, for "that Pip nonsense!" and what roars of laughter followed, *though at first it was entirely put aside as not on any account to have time wasted over it.*[1] A quarter of a century earlier, he had explained his willingness to sit by the fire reading *Pickwick*, rather than more serious works: 'the reason is', he confessed, 'we are very indolent, very wearied and forlorn, and read oftenest chiefly that we may forget ourselves'.[2] One thing is almost certain: even when Carlyle took pleasure in Dickens's novels, he rarely or never perceived in them (except possibly on one occasion[3]) any common purpose, or even the existence of any serious concern with the state of society. Dickens was simply an entertainer; it would never have occurred to Carlyle to think of him as an ally in the great fight against the 'hearsays and the cants and the grimaces' of the age; 'Oh for a thousand sharp sickles in as many strong right hands,' he wrote to Browning in 1847;

> ... I poor devil have but one rough sickle, and a hand that will soon be weary ... Dickens writes a *Dombey and Son*, Thackeray a *Vanity Fair*; not *reapers* they, either of them! In fact, the business of the rope-dancing goes to a great height ...[4]

If Dickens had known exactly what Carlyle thought of his writing, it would probably have come as a profound shock. There is little doubt that he was very anxious for Carlyle's good opinion of his work, and not simply as an entertainer: Dickens, on several occasions, went to some pains to indicate to him his claims to be taken seriously, as one of the 'thousand sharp sickles' that Carlyle longed for, and on one occasion even brought *Pickwick* into the effort: when Dickens invited him to attend one of his readings, he suggested that if Carlyle would come on an evening when the trial scene was to be read, he would 'find a healthy suggestion of an abuse or two, that sets people thinking in the right direction'.[5] But if Dickens tried to bring even his most unashamedly comic writing to Carlyle's attention for its social import, Carlyle, for his part, probably saw only comedy in Dickens's most serious attempts to come to grips with his society. Of his reaction to *Hard Times*, certainly Dickens's most 'Carlylean' novel, we seem to have no record, though, since the book was dedicated to him, there must presumably have been one. But all his

---

[1] Forster, 737n. My italics.
[2] *Letters to Mill, etc.*, 206.
[3] In 1855 he conveyed to Dickens his approval (with its inevitable qualification) of the latest number of *Little Dorrit*: 'Recommend me to Dickens', he wrote to Forster, 'and thank him a hundred times for "the circumlocution office", which is priceless after its sort! We have laughed loud and long over it here; and laughter is by no means the supreme result of it—Oh heaven!' Forster collection, undated.
[4] *Letters to Mill, etc.*, 281-4.
[5] *Letters*, III, 348, 13 April, 1863.

comments on *Dombey*, which was certainly written under his own shadow, seem to indicate, incredibly, that he was quite unaware either of any point of contact with his own thinking, or even of any serious intention in the book: *Dombey and Son* was, at worst, mere 'rope-dancing', at best, a cheerful relief from a wretched and cynical world. Seen against Carlyle's steadfast incomprehension of the seriousness of his intentions, there is something slightly pathetic about Dickens's attempts to bring himself to his attention as an earnest social critic. He began the effort with *The Chimes*, which as Dr. Michael Slater has suggested,[1] was certainly the first significant stirring of the 'later' Dickens, the prelude to the second half of Dickens's career. It was also the first work in which Dickens consciously saw himself as working in Carlyle's tradition, and he took good care that Carlyle should observe his allegiance for himself. In October 1844 before the story was completed, he wrote to Forster from Genoa, to suggest that he should read the finished tale to a 'little circle' assembled for the purpose. There is no doubt about whom the guest of honour, perhaps even the *raison d'être* of this group, was to be: 'Shall I confess to you', Dickens wrote, 'I particularly want Carlyle above all to see it before the rest of the world, when it is done; and I should like to inflict the little story on him ... with my own lips ...'[2]   The next month, he was writing again, to say that the story was finished, and to repeat his request for Forster to organise a small private reading: 'Don't have anyone, this particular night, to dinner, but let it be a summons for the special purpose at half-past 6. Carlyle, indispensable, and I should like his wife of all things: *her* judgement would be invaluable.'[3]

There seems to be no record of Carlyle's reaction to this reading of *The Chimes*; the 'grave attention'[4] of his expression that Forster noticed (vouching for its accuracy) in Maclise's drawing of the occasion, might equally well be simple boredom. But Carlyle certainly has the seat of honour, at Dickens's right hand, and here the drawing could be seen to fit, if nothing else, Dickens's feelings towards Carlyle. *The Chimes* is Dickens's first attempt at producing a fictional work pervaded throughout by (rather than dealing locally with) social issues, and it is possible to see a clear line of descent, partly via *Dombey and Son*, between *The Chimes* and *Hard Times*. It was this now controversial novel that produced, implicitly and explicitly, Dickens's most thorough-going and unmistakable statement of his allegiance to the Sage. 'My dear Carlyle', Dickens wrote from Boulogne, in July 1854:

1   See Introduction, to Penguin English Library, *Christmas Books*, Vol. I., vii—xxiv, and "Carlyle and Jerrold into Dickens: A Study of *The Chimes*," repr. upto *Dickens Centennial Essays*. Ed. Nisbet, A. and Nevius, B., London, 1971, 184—204.
2   Forster, 355.
3   *Ibid.*, 356.
4   *Ibid.*, 363.

I am going, next month, to publish in one volume a story now coming out in *Household Words*, called *Hard Times*. I have constructed it patiently, with a view to its publication altogether in a compact cheap form. It contains what I do devoutly hope will shake some people in a terrible mistake of these days, when so presented. I know it contains nothing in which you do not think with me, for no man knows your books better than I. I want to put in the first page of it that it is inscribed to Thomas Carlyle. May I?[1]

This is plain enough, though (so far as we know) it produced no answering gleam of recognition from Carlyle, and a comparison of his statements about Dickens's work before and after 1854 shows no perceptible change in his attitude. Whatever Carlyle's reaction to *Hard Times*, however, Dickens's next pervasively (though very differently) 'Carlylean' novel, *A Tale of Two Cities*, appears to have given him pleasure; at any rate, he wrote to Dickens to say so, and Dickens took a boyish delight in telling people of his approval. It seems possible, however, that as well as pleasing Dickens, the note also exacerbated his dissatisfaction with the novel's mode of publication, since, as a letter written some months later indicates, it probably referred to the shortcomings of publication in weekly serial form. This may well explain some (though by no means all) of Dickens's exasperation with the brief episodes. 'The small portions thereof, drive me frantic;' he wrote to Forster in March 1859, after the first episode had appeared, 'but I think the tale must have taken a strong hold . . . A note I have had from Carlyle about it has given me especial pleasure.'[2] Of course, Dickens had never liked weekly serial publication, but Carlyle's reference to it (possibly made in this note) obviously struck home; some six months later, he wrote to a lady admirer, thanking her for a complimentary letter about the serial, and adding 'I hope you will be confirmed in that opinion when you can better perceive my design in seeing it all together, instead of reading it in what Carlyle (writing to me of it, with great enthusiasm) calls "teaspoons".'[3] Carlyle was still reading the weekly parts in October and wrote to Forster ' . . . when you go to Dickens, our best regards. *A Tale of Two Cities* is wonderful.'[4] Dickens was pleased by this message, but his reply shows that his own dissatisfaction with weekly publication was still being made worse for him by the comment Carlyle had made months before about 'teaspoons': this very possibly explains his anxiety to let Carlyle see the overall plan of his novel without further delay. Four days after Carlyle sent his message, through Forster, Dickens wrote to him: 'Forster is here, and has given

[1] *Letters*, II, 567, 13 July, 1854.
[2] Forster, 730.
[3] *Letters*, III, 119, 28 Aug., 1859.
[4] Forster Collection, 26 Oct., 1859; reprinted, Sanders, *op. cit.*, 222.

me your message concerning the *Tale of Two Cities*—which has heartily delighted me. It will be published some three weeks hence in one dose, after having occasioned me the utmost misery by being presented in the "tea-spoonful" form. Nevertheless, I should like you to read what remains of it, before the Many-Headed does, and I therefore take heart to overwhelm you with the enclosed proofs. They are not long . . .'[1]

Whatever judgement Carlyle allowed himself of Dickens's novels, there can be do doubt of the warmth of their personal relationship. Dickens's personal regard for Carlyle began in his gratitude for the assistance he received from him at a difficult time. During his first visit to America, Dickens had taken the opportunities offered to him to air his views on the subject of international copyright. He himself suffered an enormous loss of income as a result of pirated American editions, and his crusading blood was aroused. He had already made one public speech against it when in February 1842, he spoke out again at a public dinner in New York. 'I wish you could have heard how I gave it out', he wrote to Forster; 'My blood so boiled as I thought of the monstrous injustice that I felt as if I were twelve feet high when I thrust it down their throats.'[2] No sooner had he made his speech when such an outcry began, 'as an Englishman can form no notion of'. But he refused to be cowed, and wrote to Forster, asking him to gather signatures for a letter, protesting against the absence of international protection for writers, from as many English men of letters as possible. In response to Forster's appeal, Carlyle sent a separate letter of protest. 'Dickens deserves praise and support', he wrote to Forster in a covering note, 'but the claims of authors seem to me so infinitely beyond what anybody states them at, or what any congress will hear of, that I can seldom speak of them without getting into banter, or a tone inconveniently *loud*, which is worse.'[3] His letter, together with one signed by, among others, Lytton, Tennyson, Hood, Leigh Hunt and Samuel Rogers, appeared in the *New York Evening Post* in May 1842. The two letters were accompanied by one from Dickens, which makes it clear which of them he considered to carry the most weight, in spite of the number and importance of the signatures Forster had collected for the other. Dickens may have already noted Carlyle's reputation in America; by 1842 Carlyle was almost as well known in America as in England, and Dickens noticed in Boston how wide, through Emerson, his influence was.[4] 'I would beg to lay particular stress upon the letter from Mr. Carlyle,' Dickens wrote, 'not only because the plain and manly truth it speaks is calculated, I should conceive to arrest attention and respect in my country,

[1] *Letters*, III, 131, 30 Oct., 1859.
[2] Forster, 219.
[3] Forster Collection, 26 March, 1842.
[4] *AN*, 57.

and most of all in this, but because his creed in this respect is, without the abatement of one jot or atom, mine.'[1] Writing to C. C. Felton twelve days later, Dickens gave what are perhaps revealingly different reasons: 'I anticipated objection to Carlyle's letter. I called particular attention to it for three reasons. Firstly, because he boldly *said* what others *think*, and therefore deserves to be manfully supported. Secondly because it is my decided opinion that I have been assailed on this subject in a manner which no man with any pretensions to public respect or with the remotest right to express an opinion on a subject of universal literary interest would be assailed in any other country . . .'[2] Carlyle himself was not primarily concerned about Dickens's personal predicament, but it was this contribution to his campaign that probably sowed the seeds in Dickens's mind of an affection that was to grow with time, and lasted until his death twenty-eight years later: 'This brave letter', as Forster says, 'was an important service rendered at a critical time, and Dickens was very grateful for it. But as time went on, he had other and higher causes for gratitude to its writer. Admiration of Carlyle increased with his years; and there was no one whom in later life he honoured so much, or had a more profound regard for'.[3] Their relationship was certainly sent off to a happy start by the international copyright affair. Dickens was grateful to Carlyle; and Carlyle, on his side, was impressed enough by Dickens's campaign to write a congratulatory letter to him on his return to England. Dickens's reply seems to refer, not simply to the effect on him of Carlyle's support, but also to what he knew of Carlyle's writings.[4] 'My dear Carlyle,' he wrote:

I have been truly delighted by the receipt of your most welcome letter. You will believe me, I know, when I tell you that having always held you in high regard for the manliness and honesty with which you have exercised your great abilities, there are few men in the world whose commendation, so expressed, would so well please me.

I am going down into Cornwall for a few days. When I return, I shall come to Chelsea to report myself. For as we are to know each other *well* (which I take to be clearly recognised as a fact in perspective, by both of *us*) the sooner we begin, the better.

Ever believe me
Heartily yours
Charles Dickens.[5]

1   *Letters*, I, 447, 30 April, 1842.
2   *Ibid.*, I, 456, 21 May, 1842.
3   Forster, 227.
4   Dickens was already personally acquainted with both Carlyle and his writings. He had met him for the first time at a gathering in Lord Stanley's house in 1839, and seems to have become friendly with him before his departure for America. He was certainly familiar by this time with at least the arguments of *Chartism*; he had lent a copy to John Overs, and received a detailed commentary on this work in return. In reply, he told Overs that 'I have received, and read, your notes on the Chartist book, some of which I will shew to Mr. Carlyle as I am sure he would be glad to see them' (Pilgrim *letters*, II, 141; 27 Oct., 1840.)
5   MS., New York public library, 26 Oct., 1843.

Carlyle, in 1842, was nearing the height of his fame, and Dickens's reference here to his 'manliness and honesty' is a useful link between his own admiration for Carlyle, and the Prophet's wider reputation as one whose peculiar abilities, whose 'steadfastness' and 'courage', enabled him, almost magically, to see truth through a mass of falsehood and to present it in a 'living form'. Dickens, if he was not already, like many others, partially under the spell of the Carlylean prophetic aura, was soon to become so. By 1843,[1] Carlyle's social teachings had begun to have their effect, and in December of the following year (after having read it to Carlyle) Dickens published *The Chimes*, which he had just composed with such great difficulty, in Italy. 'Several months before he left England,' Forster 'noticed in him the habit of more gravely regarding many things before passed lightly enough; the hopelessness of any true solution of either political or social problems by the ordinary Downing-street methods had been startlingly impressed on him in Carlyle's writings; and in the parliamentary talk of that day he had come to have as little faith for the putting down of any serious evil, as in a then notorious city alderman's gabble for the putting down of suicide.'[2] How much this change was brought about, not simply by Carlyle's writings, but also by his personal influence, is difficult to tell. Carlyle was a famous and voluble talker, and certainly later and perhaps already Dickens was observed listening to him with respect. Espinasse contrasted him, in this respect, with Thackeray: 'Personally, Carlyle preferred Dickens, who always treated him with deference, to Thackeray, who often opposed to his inopportune denunciations of men and things at miscellaneous dinner-parties some of that persiflage which was more disconcerting to Carlyle than direct contradiction.'[3] By the mid-forties, Carlyle and Dickens had established a warm though not intimate friendship. 'I truly love Dickens', Carlyle could write to Forster in 1844, 'and discern in the inner man of him a tone of real Music, which struggles to express itself as it may, in these bewildered, stupified [sic] and indeed very empty and distracted days—better or worse! This, which makes him in my estimation one of a thousand I could with great joy and freedom testify to all persons, to himself first of all, in any good way.'[4] Beneath all Carlyle's wintry denunciations, this attitude probably persisted throughout their relationship and was more than reciprocated by Dickens himself. Their personal relationship, nevertheless, though it partly helps to explain the attraction of Carlyle's writings for Dickens, also has the effect of diverting our attention from the very real difference between what they separately stood for: despite the obvious mutual affection of the two men, one has the impression that for both,

---

[1] See pp. 108-9 below.
[2] Forster, 347.
[3] Espinasse, 215-6.
[4] Forster Collection [1844].

their relationship engaged only part (for Carlyle, perhaps the least important part) of their personalities. The idea of a tragic, even a reactionary Dickens, does not, really modify the paradox very much; as we have seen, Dickens himself responded to a Carlyle rather more cheerful than the one perceived by most of his readers, and Carlyle, like many other Victorians, certainly did not look for a despairing, socially engaged Dickens, even when it stared him in the face. Carlyle's writings may have contributed to the increasingly reactionary attitudes adopted by Dickens as he grew older, but as I hope to show, there were usually other factors besides Carlyle's influence at work; and they were nearly always (sometimes despite superficial appearances) more important for Dickens than Carlyle's teachings. Despite the frequent, and occasionally very close, convergences of their attitudes, the differences between the two men, their writings, their attitude to human life, remain overwhelmingly more important than the similarities. One has the impression that both men saw in the other what they *wanted* to see, a selectivity that extended itself, partly, to their writings. The more one looks at their relationship, both personal and literary, the more it takes on every appearance, for both Carlyle and Dickens, of a case of mistaken identity. Nevertheless, Carlyle's influence on Dickens has become, rightly I think, a truism of modern scholarship. Why *should* Dickens have responded to Carlyle? This remains a key question. The contrast in their attitudes to the problems of existence, to what for want of a better word must be called the 'religious' dimension of life, suggests their most crucial difference. Carlyle was a transcendentalist, formed by the Old Testament and then by German idealism, a romantic built on a base of Scottish Calvinism; he believed in the division of the world's population into the elect and the non-elect, and in the existence of a pantheistic spirit of truth, that surged and bubbled like molten lava beneath a thin crust of earthly forms, and which must (as he showed it in *The French Revolution*), continually burst through and consume its containing membrane of falsehood, destroying it like the God of the Old Testament, and creating new and truthful forms. Dickens was a vague believer in the Sermon on the Mount, whose moral beliefs were formed in the first place by his child's bitter sense of personal injustice and deprivation, and by the New Testament. Carlyle believed, at root, in a God of vengeance; Dickens believed (perhaps more emphatically at the beginning of his career) in a God of mercy, who pitied and raised up the suffering and the oppressed. Carlyle's father was an unorthodox Scottish dissenter, a grim, silent man, 'strictly temperate, pure, abstemious, prudent and industrious.'[1] Carlyle's admiration for him shows how great was his influence on his son:

---

[1] Froude, J. A., *Thomas Carlyle: A History of the First Forty Years of his Life*, London, 1882, I, 7.

More remarkable man than my father I have never met in my journey
through life; sterling sincerity in thought, word, and deed, most quiet, but
capable of blazing into whirlwinds when needful, and such a flash of just
insight and brief natural eloquence and emphasis, true to every feature of
it as I have never known in any other. Humour of a most grim Scandinavian
type he occasionally had . . . No man of my day, or hardly any man, can
have had better parents.[1]

Dickens's father was amiable and feckless, and probably his religious
belief, such as it was, was vaguely Anglican. He, too, had a decisive
effect on his son's character, both by his responsibility for the trauma
of the blacking warehouse, and by his engaging and comic eccentricity:
his son's attitude to him later in life was a complex amalgam of affection and resentment, and he became the model, successively, for Mr.
Micawber and for William Dorrit.[2]   The contrast between James
Carlyle and John Dickens, and more importantly, between the attitude
they evoked in their sons, can be seen to delineate approximately the
gulf between the Prophet and the Novelist.

Nevertheless, Carlyle possessed three overriding qualities which
Dickens himself differently epitomised, and to which it is not amazing
that he responded in Carlyle.   And they are all facets of his genius
that not only Dickens, but his age, valued most in Carlyle; here as
so often, Dickens reflected the public assessment. As I have suggested,
the three great hallmarks of Carlyle's prophetic utterances (to which
his public could and often did respond separately from the actual
content of what he said) were seen by the Victorians to be, briefly,
his anti-mechanistic imaginative vision; his vitality; and his honesty,
his undying hatred of falsehood and cant.

The effect of these qualities on Dickens can only be shown fully at
some length, but the biographical evidence we possess can certainly
be seen to fit this suggestion. Perhaps Carlyle's attack on cant is his
most obvious link with Dickens, even with the Christmassy Dickens:
embedded in the list of benevolent virtues he proposed in 1845 for an
unrealised periodical, between 'cheerful views' and 'jolly good temper',
is 'sharp anatomisation of humbug'.   The substructure of meaning
implied by Dickens's 'humbug' is certainly not the same as that contained by Carlyle's 'cant', but the two ideas are near enough for all
practical purposes, and Dickens's mind was not one to be concerned
with such underlying distinctions. The international copyright affair
shows both of them embattled together against one egregious humbug,
and Carlyle's famous reference, in *Past and Present*, to 'Schnüspel the
distinguished novelist', though certainly condescending, nevertheless
confers on him the greatest of Carlylean accolades: for Carlyle,

---

[1] *Ibid.*, 11.
[2] See my 'Mr. Micawber and the redefinition of experience', *The Dickensian*, LXIII
(1967), 100–110.

Dickens was 'genuine', he was not a 'sham'.[1] From his first recorded personal statement about Dickens in 1840, to his heartfelt and touching statements of his grief at the younger man's death in 1870,[2] this judgement underlies all Carlyle's wildly inconsistent feelings about Dickens. The adjectives 'cheery' and 'genuine' recur again and again, often together, in Carlyle's remarks on the popular novelist. And for Dickens, this opinion was reciprocated tenfold. Carlyle was distinguished by his 'manliness and honesty'; and his qualities were set apart from those of lesser men by such epithets as 'noble'.[3] This link between the two men goes a long way towards explaining the relevance, for Dickens, of Carlyle's critique of his age.

Carlyle's emphasis on the 'genuine', his persistent (and in the end almost routine) attack on cant, goes with his honesty and his real, but not always obvious, hatred of injustice; it also links with his hatred of mechanistic thinking and his imaginative genius, his power of transforming the mere data of life into what appeared to be the living truth. These two qualities are at the very root of Carlyle's considerable influence on the two most Carlylean novels Dickens wrote, *Hard Times* and *A Tale of Two Cities*: despite all their differences in kind and in content, it is the quality and operation of Carlyle's imaginative vision that (though very differently) provides the great link between the two novels. The romantic distinction between fact and fancy (seen in a way to which Carlyle is obviously relevant) is the clearest underlying theme of *Hard Times*; and Dickens himself suggests the relevance of this distinction to the extensive body of historical material in *A Tale of Two Cities*, for which *The French Revolution* provided the source. To an American hostess, over dinner, he once described the effect of the book on him:

> C.D. told me that the book of all others which he read perpetually and of which he never tired, the book which always appeared more imaginative in proportion to the fresh imagination he brings to it, a book for inexhaustiveness to be placed before every other book, is Carlyle's 'French Revolution'.

One of the things that made him go through its pages again and again was his fascination with the imaginative fusion by which Carlyle transformed disjointed historical statistics into something complete and living. When Dickens was writing *A Tale of Two Cities*, he asked Carlyle to let him have some of the books which he had used when writing his history. Carlyle sent him a large quantity of books

---

[1] 'Oh, if all Yankee-land follow a small good "Schnüspel the distinguished Novelist" with blazing torches, dinner-invitations, universal hep-hep-hurrah, feeling that he, though small, *is* something, how might all Angle-land once follow a hero-martyr and great true Son of Heaven!' PP. 55.
[2] Forster Collection.
[3] Forster, 341.

from the London Library, and (as he claimed) Dickens ploughed faithfully through them:

> . . . the more he read the more he was astounded to find how the facts but passed through the alembic of Carlyle's brain and had come out and fitted themselves each as a part of one great whole, making a compact result, indestructible and unrivalled, and he always found himself turning away from the books of reference and re-reading this marvellous new growth from those dry bones with renewed wonder.[1]

The points of, as it were electrical, contact between the two writers are certainly as striking as the perhaps more frequent points at which this contact broke down. To see how the Carlylean current flowed, and to judge how much of its effect was real, and how much apparent, we must turn our attention to two novels: *Hard Times*, perhaps his only true 'social novel', and *A Tale of Two Cities*, perhaps the most popular and the most a-typical of all the writings of the second half of Dickens's career. Before we do this, however, we must attempt to answer an important question. If Dickens was indeed so fascinated by the creative workings of Carlyle's mind, above all in *The French Revolution*, we might expect that Carlylean influence on Dickens would manifest itself, among other ways, by its effect on his use of language. Is this the case? And if so, in what way does the process take place?

[1] DeWolfe Howe, M., *Memories of a Hostess*, Boston, 1922, 191.

CHAPTER THREE

Carlylean Diction: A Cautionary Note

THAT passages can be found in Dickens's writing which show obvious stylistic traces of his reading of Carlyle, is beyond dispute. This fact necessarily poses the question of the extent of the phenomenon, and of the critical weight we should attach to it. In 1845, the *Christian Remembrancer* went so far as to claim, of *The Chimes*, that 'a good deal of the diction is a palpable borrowing from Carlyle';[1] in our own times, Professor Ford has suggested (a different and more weighty proposition) that 'Carlyle's influence on the later style of Dickens's novels is easily seen.'[2] Such conclusions have not been common, but the fact that at least one contemporary observer and at least one outstanding modern Dickens scholar have felt able to advance them, suggests that they cannot be ignored. Dr. Michael Slater has, I think, dealt adequately with the charge of the *Christian Remembrancer*, and there is no need to repeat his arguments here; his conclusion, 'that Dickens had too strongly individual a style for it to be more than momentarily submerged beneath that of his mentor', seems to me to be clearly correct, and the fleeting and occasional nature of Carlyle's stylistic effect, on a work so heavily influenced by Carlyle's ideas, rules out, I think, any suggestion of a consistent link between a Carlylean style and Carlylean ideas or material in Dickens's writing.

One such passage occurs, for instance, in *Martin Chuzzlewit*, and provides one of the earliest examples of a particular Carlylean mannerism that appears from time to time in Dickens's writings: the habit of apostrophising some kind of absurdity or social evil in the form of an abstract representation of those who commit it:

[1] 'The Chimes . . . By Charles Dickens', *Christian Remembrancer*, IX (1845), 303.
[2] Ford, 90.

33

Oh late-remembered, much-forgotten mouthing, braggart duty, always owed, and seldom paid in any other coin than punishment and wrath, when will mankind begin to know thee! When will men acknowledge thee in thy neglected cradle, and thy stunted youth, and not begin their recognition in thy sinful manhood and thy desolate old age! Oh ermined Judge whose duty to society is, now, to doom the ragged criminal to punishment and death, hadst thou never, Man, a duty to discharge in barring up the hundred open gates that wooed him to the felon's dock, and throwing but ajar the portals to a decent life! Oh prelate, prelate, whose duty to society it is to mourn in melancholy phrase the sad degeneracy of these bad times in which thy lot of honours has been cast, did nothing go before thy elevation to the lofty seat, from which thou dealest out thy homilies to other tarriers for dead men's shoes, whose duty to society has not begun! Oh magistrate, so rare a country gentleman and brave a squire, had you no duty to society, before the ricks were blazing and the mob were mad; or did it spring up, armed and booted from the earth, a corps of yeomanry, full-grown![1]

Dickens's use of what we might term the 'prophetic vocative' to appeal to various representatives of upper-class power to remember their duty to society, and the emphasis on the word 'duty' itself, are both obviously Carlylean. So too, is another, typical mannerism, the rhetorical question demanding the answer 'yes', and as here, and as often in Carlyle, underlining a failure in responsibility. The emphasis here on looking to root causes rather than to symptoms is also Carlylean, and this passage was written at a particular time, at which, there are other reasons for supposing, Dickens's thought was demonstrably under the influence of Carlyle.[2]

The usefulness of detecting a quasi-Carlylean style in this passage lies mainly in the fact that it supplies supporting evidence for a suspicion that Carlylean ideological influence (in this case elsewhere) was operating on Dickens's mind at the time; we can scarcely claim that the style of this passage is Carlylean in any other sense than that it deploys certain mannerisms in a certain way—the rhythm, texture, and use of language here have nothing in common with Carlyle's. But the detection of 'Carlylean' mannerisms is not always useful in even this marginal way; a Carlylean echo is by no means always connected with a Carlylean idea. Pip's narrative voice, addressing Joe Gargery in recollection ('O dear good Joe . . . O dear good faithful tender Joe'[3]) may well, for instance, be an example of his use of a stylistic mannerism he learned, as it were, at Carlyle's knee; but it is very obviously not an indication of Carlylean influence in any other respect. And even when there is evidence of Carlyle's influence on the thought, even on the imagery of a passage, the style—perhaps more often than not—remains firmly that of Dickens. The most striking

[1] *MC*, 497-8.
[2] See pp. 109-10 below.
[3] *GE*, 133.

example of this, is to be found in the scene describing the fall of the Bastille in *A Tale of Two Cities*. As I shall show,[1] there is a very intimate relationship indeed, in imagery and incident, between the text of Dickens's description of this episode and that of Carlyle's. What is very noticeable, however, when we compare the two accounts, is the use by the two writers of almost completely opposed stylistic techniques. One distinctive feature of Carlyle's vivid evocations of mob violence can be observed in his continual momentary withdrawals from the madness of the situation, in his reiterated breaking of the reader's involvement in the excitement of the scene, so that he can impose on him an assessment of what is happening. Often, this is done by a conscious appeal to the 'thought' of the scene rather than to its heat; the tension is suddenly relaxed, there is a calm interlude in the action; we remain involved in the excitement of the action that has been and is to come, and yet our historical sense, our intellectual distance from the scene, are firmly appealed to. The technique is akin, in a way, to that of Brechtian drama; when there is any danger of our over-involvement in the action, a placard appears, we are made aware that we are in a theatre:

> What shall De Launay do? One thing only De Launay could have done: what he said he would do. Fancy him sitting, from the first, with lighted taper, within arm's-length of the Powder-Magazine; motionless, like old Roman Senator, or Bronze Lamp-holder . . . [2]

Even at the climax of the drama, Carlyle's prose demands assessment rather than empathy. Questions are asked; images obtrude themselves on our attention rather than being subordinated to the action:

> Blood flows; the aliment of new madness. The wounded are carried into houses of the Rue Cerisaie; the dying leave their last mandate not to yield till the accursed Stronghold fall. And yet, alas, how fall?[3]

Dickens goes for empathy. Not only here, but throughout the novel, the political situation is ignored. Hence, the massacre of Foulon follows, in Dickens's narration, hard upon the fall of the Bastille, though a week of comparative peace, filled with political manoeuverings (which Carlyle describes in detail) actually separated the two events: Dickens, quite simply, does not want to let down the tension. Much the same point can be made about his prose style; his description of the actual fall of the Bastille, for example, is free from the complex accumulation of qualifications and apostrophes, the deliberately self-conscious imagery, and the perpetual changes of tempo and rhythm

---

[1] See pp. 71ff below.
[2] *FR*, I, 188.
[3] *Ibid.*, 187.

of Carlyle's. Dickens is aiming at a kind of ritual exaltation, which he gains by simple percussive rhythmic effects and by a crude descriptive impressionism:

> Cannon, muskets, fire and smoke; but, still the deep ditch, the single draw-bridge, the massive stone walls, and the eight great towers. Slight displacements of the raging sea, made by the falling wounded. Flashing weapons, blazing torches, smoking waggon-loads of wet straw, hard work at neighbouring barricades in all directions, shrieks, volleys, execrations, bravery without stint, boom, smash and rattle . . . [1]

The details come from *The French Revolution*,[2] but here at any rate the prose is Dickens's. At one point, however, the nearly authentic voice of the prophet breaks through:

> Seven prisoners released, seven gory heads on pikes, the keys of the accursed fortress of the eight strong towers, some discovered letters and other memorials of prisoners of old time, long dead of broken hearts,—such, and such-like, the loudly echoing footsteps of Saint Antoine escort through the Paris streets in mid-July, one thousand seven hundred and eighty-nine. Now, Heaven defeat the fancy of Lucie Darnay, and keep these feet far out of her life![3]

The tones of Carlyle are announced by the use of the historic present, by the chopped, miscellaneous sequence of ideas, under which is buried the grammatical structure (still functioning, but deformed), and by the invocation of the second sentence, not quite authentic, but certainly adding to the general effect of Carlylean insistence. Again, like other Carlylean passages in Dickens, this one is isolated and brief. What it serves to underline, perhaps, is that, in the one moment of Dickens's writing career when we can show his imagination consistently fired by Carlyle's throughout the length of a sustained description of several pages, when we can show such an intimate and consecutive use of Carlyle's own imagery and situations, we can nevertheless only discover his stylistic influence in one brief paragraph, and then manifested in a way which adds little to our awareness of the scene Dickens is re-creating.

Carlyle's stylistic influence on Dickens, then, amounts to no more than the very occasional use of certain mannerisms (notably the apostrophe to a representative type), which are often used in an only superficially Carlylean way. Professor Ford, however, puts forward an hypothesis which, if accepted, would certainly confound this view, in his suggestion that Carlyle's influence on the style of Dickens's later novels 'is easily seen'. Elsewhere, he indicates one novel he

---

[1] *TTC*, 205–6
[2] See pp. 73–4 below.
[3] *TTC*, 210.

appears to be thinking of particularly: *Bleak House*. Professor Ford refers to the increased versatility of Dickens's mature prose style, 'which flows almost effortlessly in *Copperfield* and, in the succeeding novel, takes on a harsh, jabbing, Carlylean rhythm, as broken-backed and discordant as the bleak London world it reflects'.[1] This, if it were true, would certainly suggest a much more comprehensive and consistently realised stylistic debt to Carlyle than I have argued exists: the rhythm of Carlyle's prose is very distinctive indeed, and if that of Dickens's prose in *Bleak House* can be seen as in any sense Carlylean, this would certainly be a strong argument in favour of Professor Ford's view. The novel's opening chapter provides the most famous example of the kind of prose Professor Ford presumably means:

> Fog everywhere. Fog up the river, where it flows among green aits and meadows; fog down the river, where it rolls defiled among the tiers of shipping, and the waterside pollutions of a great (and dirty) city. Fog on the Essex marshes, fog on the Kentish heights. Fog creeping into the cabooses of collier-brigs; fog lying out on the yards, and hovering in the rigging of great ships; fog drooping on the gunwales of barges and small boats. Fog in the eyes and throats of ancient Greenwich pensioners, wheezing by the firesides of their wards; fog in the stem and bowl of the afternoon pipe of the wrathful skipper, down in his close cabin; fog cruelly pinching the toes and fingers of his shivering little 'prentice boy on deck.[2]

For the purposes of comparsion, here is a passage from *The French Revolution*—the work of Carlyle for which we have the most conclusive evidence of Dickens's close knowledge—selected at random:

> While the unspeakable confusion is everywhere weltering within, and through so many cracks in the surface sulphur-smoke is issuing, the question arises: Through what crevice will the main Explosion carry itself? . . . In every Society are such chimneys, are Institutions serving as such: even Constantinople is not without its safety-valves; there too Discontent can vent itself,—in material fire; by the number of nocturnal conflagrations, or of hanged bakers, the Reigning Power can read the signs of the times, and change course according to these.[3]

One thing emerges clearly from this comparison, I think: that though the rhythm of Dickens's prose in the passage I have quote may perhaps be described as 'harsh' and 'jabbing', it emphatically cannot be described as Carlylean. Indeed, it becomes clear that the word 'Carlylean' is being used by Professor Ford very loosely, to describe unorthodox prose whose movements are jerky rather than smooth. It will be seen

---

[1] *Ibid.*, 122.
[2] *BH*, 1.
[3] *FR*, I, 61.

surely quite obviously, (as in the comparison between the two writers' descriptions of the fall of the Bastille), that the function, technique, and final effect of the two passages could scarcely be more different. Nor is this particular comparison unfair: the same could be said, I think, of any other two representative passages from *Bleak House* and from *The French Revolution*, or any other of Carlyle's mature works. Despite its differences with the smoothly flowing diction of *David Copperfield*, this example of the style of *Bleak House* is still distinguishable from that of Carlyle by its regularity; the rhythmic contrast is perhaps most easily seen as that which distinguishes public and private expression: if we imagine these two passages in the mouths of their creators, we see Dickens on a platform, reading to a large audience, and Carlyle at the dinner table, delivering himself of one of his long monologues. Carlyle's prose is irregular and questioning, as in private argument: Dickens's—for all its unorthodoxy—has its own regularity, slices itself up, balances and emphasises itself, as if for public performance. Dickens's style here is a conscious *tour de force*; Carlyle's is the natural expression of the material it embodies.

The influence of Carlyle's style on Dickens's, I think, is a very occasional phenomenon which, even where it exists, operates in terms of superficial speech mannerisms, rather than anything more intimately connected with Dickens's identity as a writer. The one reservation we might make in this judgement is in Dickens's use of what I have called the prophetic vocative, which often reflects the hatred of cant and injustice they shared. But Carlyle's stylistic effect on Dickens nearly always takes effect on a very much less important level than his ideological influence. The diction of the two novels for which there is the weightiest evidence of Carlylean influence, *Hard Times* and *A Tale of Two Cities*, is almost entirely unaffected by Carlyle. This, in itself, may suggest a question which we must now attempt to answer: how 'Carlylean', in fact, are these two novels? Does their almost complete lack of Carlylean diction serve to confirm that their debt to Carlyle is more apparent than real? The answer to these questions lies not in the manner, but in the matter of these two novels; and to their matter we must now turn our attention.

Part II

CHAPTER FOUR

Hard Times

THE two novels that provide us with the most detailed and satis-factory evidence of Carlyle's 'influence' over Dickens could scarcely be more different in tone, content, intention, and general effect. The problems of demonstrating Carlyle's effect on them are similarly distinct: whereas, in *Hard Times*, Carlylean ideology permeates con-temporary 'source material', in the *Tale*, a philosophy of history—if the term is permissible in such a context—which is quite clearly, I think, Dickens's own, informs various historical sources, of which *The French Revolution* is almost certainly the most important.

To present Carlyle's function as an historical source is a relatively easy matter, though even this is not without its problems. To demonstrate his influence over *Hard Times*, the vitality of which so intimately derives from Dickens's feelings about his own times and his own knowledge of the scenes and issues evoked in the novel, is a much more dangerous business, though it might at first glance seem simple enough. Carlyle was the foremost anti-rationalist of his age; *Hard Times* is an attack on a kind of extreme and perverted rationalism. This, together with Dickens's famous letter to Carlyle,[1] might be thought enough to establish, at least partially, that *Hard Times* is influenced by Carlyle: the 'Hard Facts' philosophy anatomised in the novel is obviously the 'terrible mistake of these days' that Dickens is writing about to the Sage, and this is fairly clearly what Dickens is referring to when he says 'I know it contains nothing in which you do not think with me'. But, of course, all the letter can justify is a suggestion that Dickens certainly *thought* that he was reflecting Carlyle's

---

[1] For the full text of this letter, see pp. 24-5 above.

41

teachings; whether or not–and if so how much–he actually did so, is another matter.

The novel's attack on 'Hard Facts', by itself is clearly not enough to make it necessary to evoke Carlylean influence as an *indispensable* framework of reference for the novel: what Dickens, and what Carlyle, respectively perceive as the human inadequacy of mere logicality can be seen to differ most simply by observing what Dickens (partly but vitally) opposes to it. Sleary's horseriding epitomises, as nearly as one could imagine, everything Carlyle anathematised in 'modern literature'. If the circus were called 'Sleary's rope-dancing',[1] some critics might be a little more careful about the precise way in which they outline Carlyle's influence on the novel. The horseriding should remind us of Carlyle's dismissal of Dickens as 'a showman whom one gives a shilling to once a month to see his raree-show, and then sends him about his business';[2] and 'rope-dancing' or dancing on the 'slack-Jeff' is, as one would expect of a self-respecting circus, an item in Sleary's programme. *Hard Times* must, obviously enough, be seen in the context of the romantic anti-rationalist tradition, in which Carlyle was certainly one vital link. But to talk, as one commentator does, of Dickens's '*advocacy* of the *Carlylean* sense of wonder'[3] is surely to take semantic imprecision beyond acceptable limits: the contrast between Dickens's sense of wonder and Carlyle's is plain enough, and we will soon get into deep waters if we lose sight of it.

The point must not, of course, be overemphasised. Carlyle's anti-rationalism certainly does present interesting analogies with Dickens's, and it is open to doubt whether the novelist would have pressed as far as this a distinction between his 'sense of wonder' and Carlyle's. This does not invalidate the contrast or its importance for us; it emphasises, though, how large a part was played, in Carlyle's influence on Dickens, by the novelist's misinterpretation of Carlyle's deepest purpose. Carlyle's description of Teufelsdröckh's education (as I shall suggest) is certainly relevant to the educational theme of *Hard Times*. But even if we forget that Dickens is no transcendentalist, *Sartor* contains ample material to emphasise how *Hard Times* itself demonstrates the temperamental difference between them. After describing the narrowness and strictness of Teufelsdröckh's upbringing, Carlyle continues:

> In an orderly house, where the litter of children's sports is hateful enough, your training is too stoical; rather to bear and forbear than to make and do. I was forbid much: wishes in any measure bold I had to renounce; every-where a strait bond of Obedience inflexibly held me down. . . . In which

---

[1]   Cf. Carlye's letter to Browning (*letters to Mill etc.* 281,—4) discussed on p. 23 above.
[2]   Fitzgerald, E., *Letters and Literary Remains*, London, 1889, I, 198.
[3]   Goldberg, 140—1.

habituation to Obedience, truly, it was beyond measure safer to err by excess than by defect. Obedience is our universal duty and destiny; wherein whoso will not bend must break . . . [1]

This reminds us, perhaps, by contrast, of Dickens's attitude to Arthur Clennam's childhood, and, in a different way, of David Copperfield. Perverted rationalism in *Hard Times* has also the distinctly non-Carlylean dimension of monstrous, flower and child-crushing authority. Gradgrind is no Murdstone; but David's partial emancipation by, *inter alia*, the *Arabian Nights* shows that fancy presents an antithesis for Dickens not uniquely to rationalism, but also to power, especially the potentially monstrous power of the adult over the child. 'The Carlylean sense of wonder' may at times seem like Dickens's, and Dickens himself very possibly thought it was: but the difference in emphasis is nevertheless immense.

This is not our only difficulty in connecting Carlyle with Dickens's dislike of rigid formulae—rationalist or otherwise—that stifled spontaneity and flexible human values; we do not have to look far in the undergrowth that forms the 'background' of *Hard Times* before we find that 'the terrible mistake of these days' was not something Dickens *needed* Carlyle's help to discover, whatever we may decide was his effect on Dickens's understanding of it. A handful of relevant quotations to demonstrate its contemporary pervasiveness and the accessibility, at the most popular level, of the running debate it engendered, is easily garnered:

(i) They tell us that the working classes are ignorant, that we don't understand the laws by which capital and labour are regulated. What is there about the matter that we don't understand? We have had a Cobden and a Bright and a number of other men, and Adam Smith's *Wealth of Nations* into the bargain, to explain to us all about political economy; and yet, after all, there is such a mystery about it, that we don't understand it . . . The sooner we can rout political economy from the world the better it will be for the working classes of this country.
(George Cowell, leader of the Preston Strike, reported in *The Times*, Jan. 23, 1854.[2])

(ii) To understand what are the true relations of capital and labour involves the study of a class of abstract truths, easily obscured or perverted to an uneducated people.
(Sir James Kay-Shuttleworth, reported in the *Manchester Guardian*, Jan. 14, 1854.)

---

[1] *SR*, II, ii, 75–6.
[2] See Carnall, G., 'Dickens, Mrs. Gaskell, and the Preston Strike', *Victorian Studies*, VIII (1964).

(iii) It is only in accordance with immutable laws, and is now an admitted political axiom, that Corporate or Government work must necessarily be inferior in quality to the work of individuals.
(Sir Henry Cole, writing about the Department of Practical Art.[1])

(iv) Until men turn their attention to the subject they are little aware how entirely empirical most of their judgements in matters of taste are, and consequently, as to what is correct and just in Decorative Design also. Men are inclined to believe that judgement on objects of taste does not depend on any acknowledged principles nor can be defined by any rules, but is an innate feeling or perception . . . [2]
(Richard Redgrave, the Department's Art Superintendent.)

Dickens is likely (in one case almost certain) to have been familiar with these among other statements on the 'immutable laws' which were alleged to govern such diverse problems as industrial relations and graphic design, when he was writing the parts of *Hard Times* to which they are relevant. The speech of George Cowell which I have quoted was given exactly a week before Dickens arrived to observe the Preston Strike for himself, and it is highly probable that he would read press reports of speeches by the strike leaders during the week before his visit; if he did not read Cowell's speech in *The Times* on the Monday before, he is very likely to have seen the report of it which appeared in the *Preston Advertiser* on the actual day of his arrival. The attack on the abstract generalisations of laissez-faire economics was, in any case, a constant theme of all Cowell's speeches, and in this he certainly represented the consensus of working class opinion.[3]

Cowell's onslaught on the laws of political economy was a reply to two recent speeches attacking the strikers. If Dickens did, as seems very probable, read one of the reports of Cowell's speech, the name of one of the objects of the strike leader's contempt would have strongly arrested his attention. The opening chapters of *Hard Times* (which may have been written when Dickens visited Preston[4]) are in part, as Professor Fielding and Professor Collins have shown,[5] a

---

[1] Redgrave, R. and Cole, H., *Addresses of the Superintendent of the Department of Practical Art*, London, 1853.

[2] *Ibid.*, 72.

[3] In 1860, for instance, a statistician compiling a paper on the rates of wages in the manufacturing areas of Lancashire bewailed the reluctance of operatives to co-operate in furnishing him with information, and 'much regretted to find that some of the leading members of Trades' Unions attempted to deny the existence and operation of the *law* of Political Economy in regard to *Supply* and *Demand* governing the *price* of LABOUR, as well as of all *materials* and *products* . . . ' (Original emphasis.) Chadwick, D., 'On the Rate of Wages in Manchester and Salford, and the manufacturing districts of Lancashire, 1839-59', *Journal of the Statistical Society of London*, XXIII (1860), 22.

[4] In a letter written on 11 March, Dickens claimed that 'the title was many weeks old, and chapters of the story were written before I went to Preston, or thought about the present strike'. (*Letters*, II, 546.)

[5] *Education*, 157, and Fielding, K. J. "Charles Dickens and the Department of Practical Art" MLR, XLVIII (1953) 270-7.

satire on certain recent developments in education. On Wednesday 11 January the author of these developments, Sir James Kay-Shuttleworth, gave a speech at the opening of a trade school at Padiham, which was the occasion of Cowell's attack, and which not only dealt with educational themes—in a way highly relevant to the opening chapters of *Hard Times*—but also contained a full-scale attack (which attracted wide attention[1]) on the Preston Strikers, the nub of which was conveyed by the pronouncement, quoted above, that relations between masters and men should be determined by 'a class of abstract truths'. Dickens was certainly aware of Kay-Shuttleworth's speech (the controversy it aroused was still fresh in the public mind when he arrived in Preston) and a brief extract from it—chosen out of context to reflect something much nearer Dickens's own beliefs—appeared in the *Household Narrative* for January 1854. Curiously enough, Kay-Shuttleworth's speech also contained a reference[2] to the Department of Practical Art, the work of which Dickens had in mind when he wrote the opening chapter of *Hard Times*. The beliefs of the Government Gentleman, as Professor Fielding has demonstrated, are partly a parody of those of Sir Henry Cole, the Department's General Superintendent; Dickens's character seems to owe his credo also to the Department's Art Superintendent, Richard Redgrave, who was responsible for the organisation of a body of itinerant teachers whose duties were to visit schools in possession of the Department's graded drawing examples, and to instruct masters and mistresses in their use. The Government Gentleman is obviously one of these roving instructors, and a lecture given by Redgrave on the work of the Department, and published in 1853, seems very likely to have inspired at least part of his disquisition on interior design which, it will be recalled, ends with the following crushing statement: ' " . . . You must use, . . . for all these purposes, combinations and modifications (in primary colours) of mathematical figures which are susceptible of proof and demonstration. This is the new discovery. This is Fact. This is taste".'[3] This compares interestingly with a pronouncement from Redgrave's lecture:

---

[1] Newspaper reports, in fact, tended to concentrate on his remarks on the Preston Strike. Only the *Manchester Guardian* seems to have given a full report of the entire speech; the *Examiner*, the *Daily News* and the *Morning Post* ignore Kay-Shuttleworth's educational pronouncements, and no report at all appeared in *The Times*. Kay-Shuttleworth's remarks on the strike appeared in the *Manchester Guardian* on 14 Jan, his educational pronouncements (which in the speech actually come first) were published on 18 Jan.

[2] He points out that 'one of the earliest acts of this department has been to concert with the Committee of Council on Education, arrangements for the introduction of the rudiments of the arts of design into ordinary schools'. See also, Cole, H. and A., *Fifty Years of Public Life of Sir Henry Cole, K.B.*, London, 1884, I, 302-3, and Redgrave and Cole, *op. cit.*

[3] *HT*, 6.

. . . colours must be arranged together in specific and absolute quantities
to be agreeable to the eye . . . Thus, in arrangements of the primaries, a
surface quantity of three yellow requires, to be agreeable to the eye, a surface
of five red and eight blue; or three yellow harmonises with its secondary
purple as three to thirteen in surface quantity.[1]

There are, then, two fairly obvious objections to a 'Carlylean'
reading of *Hard Times*. Not only is Dickens's anti-rationalism very
different from Carlyle's; it is also very clear that the novel (perhaps
more than any other in the Dickensian canon) is concerned, almost
journalistically, with a theme of immediate and contemporary relevance. The notion of the imprisonment of human spontaneity by
rigid, formulistic dogma was a topic of the moment and the subject
of some controversy, even as Dickens wrote, and with particular
reference to areas *Hard Times* is closely concerned with; Industrialism,
and the relations between Masters and Men; Benthamite political
economy; and Education. And all these were not only topical, but
were so in such a way that Dickens was either likely or certain to
be aware of them as he wrote *Hard Times*; in some cases, it is beyond
doubt that such topics provided him with the direct impulse for
important parts of the novel.

It may be as well, therefore, before going any further, to set out
the evidence for the claim that Dickens's perception of 'the terrible
mistake' owes anything at all directly to Carlyle's writings. This can,
I think, be done with some confidence. *Hard Times* is the most openly
and consistently didactic of Dickens's novels, and the Hard Fact
philosophies of Bounderby, the Captain of Industry, and Gradgrind,
the Logic-Chopper and Motive-Grinder (we may as well employ the
relevant Carlylean terms) are examined in several ways. Dickens
obviously thought of his didactic purpose as being one that Carlyle
would approve of, and his famous letter to him is the clearest indication, in his own words, of a relationship between their ideas, that we
possess. There exist other letters and anecdotes confirming Dickens's
admiration for Carlyle; here we have a positive profession of belief.
What was Dickens thinking of specifically when he wrote 'it contains
nothing in which you do not think with me'? This is obviously a
matter of conjecture, but it seems possible to surmise that, whatever
else he may have been thinking of as well, Stephen Blackpool was
certainly on his mind when he composed this letter. It was written
on July 13th 1854; the following day, Dickens wrote to Forster. 'I
am three parts mad, and the fourth delirious, with perpetual rushing
at *Hard Times*', he told him; 'I have done what I hope is a good thing
with Stephen, taking his story as a whole; . . . I have been looking
forward through so many weeks and sides of paper to this Stephen

---

[1] Redgrave and Cole, *op. cit.*, 78-9.

business, that now—as usual—it being over, I feel as if nothing in
the world, in the way of intense and violent rushing hither and thither,
could quite restore my balance.'[1]   Whatever we may think of
Stephen's death scene, to Dickens it was obviously important, both in
itself and as part of the total structure of the novel. Writing the same
day to Wills, Dickens reiterated an idea from his letter to Forster:
'The MS now sent, contains what I have looked forward to through
many weeks.'[2]   Obviously, Stephen was only one element in this, but
he was an important one for Dickens. We can at least suggest that
when he wrote to Carlyle that *Hard Times* 'contains nothing in which
you do not think with me', 'this Stephen business' was very clearly
in his mind for other reasons.

Few critics today are entirely happy about Stephen Blackpool, for
obvious reasons, and even among the book's earliest readers there
were those who found him a little difficult to take.[3]   For our limited
purpose, nevertheless, his part of the novel is entirely satisfactory;
his utterances contain, beneath their rude surface, some of the thoughts
on Industrialism which were uppermost in Dickens's mind when he
was writing *Hard Times*; at the same time, they express these thoughts
in the form of the most comprehensively and consistently Carlylean
analysis of society to be found anywhere in his writings. This is worth
emphasising; instead, as so often, of sensing an unelaborated Carlylean
theme or overtone, we are here, for once, dealing with a concrete and
reasonably complex intellectual formulation, covering a fairly wide
area.

Stephen's death scene is a maudlin affair in the best Dickensian
tradition, replete with a vague wash of Dickens's brand of all-purpose
religion: 'Often as I coom to myseln, and found it shinin' on me
down there in my trouble, I thowt it were the star as guided to Our
Saviour's home.'[4]   This is so near to self-parody that it is difficult
to realise that Dickens himself took it very seriously indeed, and
embedded in Stephen's dying words are two ideas that he certainly
thought would be underlined rather than compromised by their
appearance here. His death scenes had always gone down big with his
readers (although the taste for this kind of thing was passing), and
Dickens was probably working on the principle that a man's dying
words had somehow an additional weight. Stephen reiterates two
pregnant pronouncements of which he has already unburdened himself, together with other perilous matter, in his second interview with
Mr. Bounderby: firstly, the idea of protective government action;
Stephen has fallen into a pit, which has been the vain subject of a

---

[1] Forster, 566n.
[2] *Letters*, II, 14 July, 1854.
[3] See, for instance, Yates, E. H. and Brough, R. B., '*Hard Times* (refinished), by
    Charles Diggins', *Our Miscellany*, London, 1857, 143.
[4] *HT*, 208.

public petition, 'as onny one may read, fro' the men that works in pits, in which they ha' pray'n an' pray'n the lawmakers for Christ's sake not to let their work be murder to 'em . . .'[1]   Stephen also laments once more the lack of sympathy between workers and employers. This was a topic of the moment, and not only in the context of the Preston strike. Dickens's old friend, Talfourd, the judge, had died in March 1854. Shortly before his death, Talfourd addressed some remarks on the subject to the grand jury of the Staffordshire Assizes, while deploring the rise in the crime-rate, which he attributed to 'that separation between class and class which is the great curse of British Society'.[2]   Dickens recalled his words when he wrote an obituary of his friend for *Household Words*, and (perhaps unconsciously) interestingly implied that they were uttered on his death bed; he also put into the Judge's dying mouth some of the ideas he himself was then transposing into fictional form: 'Who, knowing England at this time,' he wrote, 'would wish to utter with his last breath a more righteous warning than that its curse is ignorance, or a miscalled education which is as bad or worse, and a want of the exchange of innumerable graces and sympathies among the various orders of society, each hardened unto each and holding itself aloof?'[3]   Who, one might add, indeed?   'In my pain an' trouble', says Stephen, with his own 'last breath' ' . . . I ha' seen more clear, and ha' made it my dyin' prayer that aw' th' world may on'y coom toogether more, an' get a better unnerstan'in o' one another, than when I were in't my own weak seln'.[4]   'If Mr. Bounderby had ever know'd me right—if he'd ever know'd me at aw—he would'n ha' took'n offence wi' me. He would'n ha' suspect'n me,'[5] he says earlier.   Stephen is, above all, a vehicle for the 'two nations' theme, which, for nearly two decades, from *The French Revolution* onwards, had been one of the most constantly reiterated ideas in the Carlylean armoury. Carlyle, of course, did not have a monopoly of the idea; in a very different way, Utilitarian Economists believed in an identity of interests between employers and workers, and the newspapers during the time of the Preston strike were full of the idea that workers and employers should understand each other more; that there was a gulf between the different classes of society was one of the political truisms of the time. It had also been examined by other novelists. It was, of course, Disraeli who coined the famous phrase 'the two nations', and Kingsley and Mrs. Gaskell had also worked the same vein. All these novelists may themselves have been writing under the influence of

---

[1] *HT*, 207.
[2] 'A Memoir of Mr. Justice Talfourd', *Law Magazine*, n.s.XX (1854), 323.
[3] [Dickens, C.], 'The late Mr. Justice Talfourd', *Household Words*, IX (1854), 117-8.
[4] *HT*, 207.
[5] *Ibid.*

Carlyle, Disraeli possibly, Mrs. Gaskell probably, and Kingsley certainly.   Nevertheless, despite the common currency of the theme
(for which Carlyle himself was in any case partly responsible) there
are fairly clear reasons for supposing that for his understanding of
this among other 'Carlylean' notions enunciated by Stephen, Dickens
was directly indebted to Carlyle, and, though he was obviously
enough drawing on his own observation, that Carlyle's influence here
was a shaping one and did not act in a merely peripheral way.   The
most important reason is one of context.   None of the individual
ideas for which Stephen is made a vehicle can be claimed to be ex-
clusively Carlylean; but the combination of them undoubtedly is.
The same argument will serve for other themes in Stephen's analysis,
besides that of the 'two nations', some of which are important to our
assessment of the novel as a whole.   Taken separately, some of these
ideas can be placed intelligibly outside a strictly Carlylean setting;
together they form an interdependent and distinctively Carlylean
corpus of ideas.

The fullest exposition of Stephen's views is given in his second
confrontation with Bounderby.   To make his ideas clearer, I will
paraphrase his utterances in Queen's English, instead of quoting him
in Dickens's dubious Lancastrian.   After refusing to condemn his
fellow workers, Stephen also refuses to place the responsibility entirely
on Slackbridge: 'I am as sorry as you are when the people's leaders
are so bad; it is one of their greatest misfortunes when they can get
no better.'   Bounderby expostulates, but Stephen still refuses to betray
his fellow workers.   Bounderby again tries to make Stephen deliver
what he thinks ought to be a typical operative's speech, for the benefit
of Harthouse: 'What . . . do you people in a general way complain
of?'   Stephen replies, at length, and his reply is worth paraphrasing
in full.   For purposes of analytic convenience, I shall place a reference
letter in parenthesis after each clearly identifiable Carlylean idea:[1]

I was never very good at demonstrating [what is wrong], though I have had
my share of feeling it (A).   We are in a muddle.   Look around this town,
which is so rich, and observe how many people have been born here, to
weave and card and scrape a living, all alike from the cradle to the grave.
Look where we live and in what numbers and with what monotony, and
look how the mills are always working, but never provide us with any
ultimate goal except Death (B).   Look how you think and write and talk
about us, and go with deputations about us to Secretaries of State (C),
and how you are always right and we are always wrong, and never had any
reason in us since our birth.   Look how our problems have grown continually
through the years, from generation to generation (D).   Who can look at
all this and say it is not a muddle?

[1] All references in Stephen's analysis are to *HT*, 111-116.

To this, Bounderby, not unjustly, asks Stephen for his solution. 'I
don't know,' replies Stephen, 'I cannot be expected to. It is not I
who should be looked to for that. It is those who are in authority over
myself and all of us. What do they take upon themselves if not
that?' (E) Bounderby's analysis is different: to transport a few agitators
as an example. Stephen demurs:

> If you were to take a hundred Slackbridges . . . and were to sink them in the
> deepest ocean . . . you would alter nothing . . . the trouble is not made
> by mischievous strangers . . . instead of taking them from their trade, their
> trade should be taken from them . . . just as that clock is not time itself,
> but only an indication of time, so Slackbridge is only a symptom, rather than
> the cause of the trouble (F) . . . I cannot, being uneducated give the solution
> for all this (A) but I can say what is not the solution. Physical power and
> unjust compulsion is not the solution (G), nor is laissez faire ('lettin' alone')
> (H). Let the masses alone, and there will be an impassable gulf between
> you (I), for as long as such misery is capable of lasting (J). Refusal to cherish
> the people in a kindly way is no solution to the problem (K). Above all,
> to consider people in terms of physical energy, and to regulate them like
> arithmetical counters or machines, without any human feelings, or souls
> capable of hope or weariness when all goes in your interests, and to use
> such feelings as a stick to beat them with when you need to, this also will
> not solve the problem (L).

After this, of course, Stephen is dismissed, and goes his way towards
his fate.

What is Carlylean about this analysis? Firstly, perhaps, we can
note that it is put into the mouth of an inarticulate worker (A);
although Stephen talks at great length, and gives what we might
think a very fluent analysis of the workers' situation, we are meant to
take at its face value his opening remark to Bounderby, ' . . . I were
never good at showin' o't, though I ha' had'n my share in feelin' o't'.
The impenetrable rudeness of his speech serves to camouflage the fact
that, on paper, he is far from incoherent. The general effect conveyed
by Stephen reminds us of one standard Carlylean *dramatis persona*;
Bounderby and Harthouse, Stephen's audience, remind us of two more.
The three of them, taken together, are as Carlylean a trio as we will
find anywhere in nineteenth century fiction:

> Mark on that nose the color left by too copious port and viands; to which
> the profuse cravat with exorbitant breastpin, and the fixed, forward, and
> as it were menacing glance of the eyes correspond. That is a "Man of Busi-
> ness"; prosperous manufacturer, house-contractor, engineer, law-manager;
> his eye, nose, cravat have, in such work and fortune, got such a character :
> deny him not thy praise, thy pity. Pity him too, the Hard-handed, with
> bony brow, rudely combed hair, eyes looking out as in labor, in difficulty
> and uncertainty; rude mouth, the lips coarse, loose, as in hard toil and life-
> long fatigue they have got the habit of hanging:—hast thou seen ought

more touching than the rude intelligence, so cramped, yet energetic, un-
subduable, true, which looks out of that marred visage . . . . Or what kind of
baking was it that this other brother mortal got, which has baked him into
the genus Dandy? Elegant Vacuum . . . . The doom of Fate was, Be thou a
Dandy! Have thy eye-glasses, opera-glasses, thy Long-Acre cabs with
white-breeched tiger, thy yawning impassivities, pococurantisms . . . [1]

Each notion enunciated by Stephen is either essentially or peripherally
part of the Carlylean 'system'. His inarticulateness, though it is
apparently like Othello's, contradicted by the printed evidence, is
an essential part of his persona. His inability to speak in his own
interests (A) goes with his inability to give an answer to Bounderby's
request that Stephen should say 'how you would set this muddle to
rights'. His answer, like Carlyle's, is 'give me a leader' (E). Like
Carlyle, he suggests the doctrine of laissez-faire as a root cause of the
gulf between employer and employed (H, I); like Carlyle he points
to the responsibility of employers for the human needs of their
employees (I, K) and suggests that the relations between them should
be based on spiritual rather than on material, formulistic considerations
and self-interest (L). Stephen echoes Carlyle's concern about the
monotony and the spiritual debility of Industrial society (B), and his
insight that the problem is a deep-rooted one (D), not to be cured by
attempts to suppress its symptoms (F). He agrees with Carlyle that
coercion of the working classes, without just understanding of their
needs, will achieve nothing (G). Like Carlyle, too, Stephen emphasises
that this problem is not one which can be solved by Parliamentary
methods, by 'deputations to Secretaries of State' (C): it has grown
'from generation to generation'; the root problem of the working
classes as Carlyle puts it in *Chartism* is 'weighty, deep-rooted, far-
extending; did not begin yesterday; will by no means end this day
or tomorrow'.[2]

In a way, this is the most Carlylean point of all, and it is elaborated
in Stephen's remarks on Slackbridge. Perhaps Stephen indicates here
an important general point of contact between Carlyle and Dickens,
in pointing to the fatuousness of dealing with symptoms rather than
with causes; though this is obviously a fundamental Dickensian perception, Dicken's expression of it in *Hard Times* is plainly influenced
by Carlyle:

[1] *PP*, 125-6.
[2] *Chartism*, 37.

Hard Times	*Chartism*
'We'll indict the blackguards for felony, and get 'em shipped off to penal settlements.' . . . . 'Sir,' returned Stephen . . . 'If yo was t'tak a hundred Slackbridges . . . an' was t' sew 'em up in separate sacks . . . yo'd leave the muddle just wheer' tis. . . . 'tis hopeless and useless to dream o' takin them fro their trade, 'stead o' takin their trade fro them! . . . . Put that clock aboard a ship . . . an' the time will go on just the same.[1]	What will execration; nay at bottom, what will condemnation and banishment to Botany Bay do for it? Glasgow Thuggery, Chartist torch-meetings, Birmingham riots, Swing conflagrations, are so many symptoms on the surface; you abolish the symptom to no purpose, if the disease is left untouched.[2] Is the condition of the English working people wrong . . . ? A most grave case, complex beyond all others in the world; a case wherein Botany Bay, constabulary rural police, and such like, will avail but little.[3]

That we should judge by the root causes of phenomena rather than by their symptoms is, clearly enough, a belief held by both Carlyle and Dickens (though it is not a central theme of *Hard Times* itself) and is a vital source of the creative energy of both writers. Equally clearly this idea, seen by turn in a Carlylean and a Dickensian context, undergoes a distinct change in meaning. For Dickens, it is part of a general fund of passionate decent-mindedness, part of the impulse to expose hypocrisy and cant. For Carlyle, it is this and something besides; associated with the idea of causes and symptoms is Carlyle's whole philosophy of truth and falsehood: the truth is a kind of volcanic force, which can be kept down by a crust of falsehood only for so long. Eventually, the truth will blast a way through; physical force, for instance, unless justly applied, is useless in the long run:

> Conquest, along with power of compulsion, an essential universally in human society, must bring benefit along with it, or men, of the ordinary strength of men, will fling it out.[4]

And:

> Injustice, infidelity to truth and fact and Nature's order, being properly the one evil under the sun . . . our grand question as to the condition of these working men would be: Is it just?[5]

Injustice is a kind of 'falsehood' that cannot last.

---

[1] *HT*, 115.
[2] *Chartism*, 37.
[3] *Ibid.*, 38.
[4] *Ibid.*, 63.
[5] *Ibid.*, 64.

This kind of thing takes us a long way outside the boundaries inside which we are accustomed to see Dickens's mind working. Such thinking depends, not simply on an attitude to 'society', but on an attitude to 'the universe' as well. Sooner or later, social problems, no matter how immediate, always become problems of existence for Carlyle. Dickens is not very convincing when he starts to speculate about the infinite, and when he writes about his society, it is not usually the prelude to some such statement as 'sooty Manchester, it too rests upon the Great Abysses'. Nevertheless, *Hard Times* contains one or two hints of what may be the partly-digested influence of such thinking. Stephen attacks capitalists for their failure to provide "onny dis'ant object—ceptin awlus, Death',[1] and seems to hint at the Carlylean notion of the impossibility that a transgression of 'Nature's order' can endure (J) when he says that if the employers leave the people alone, there will be a 'black unpassable world betwixt yo', just as long or short a time as sitch-like misery can last.'[2] A more unequivocal transposition from industrial society to The Immensities occurs at the beginning of Book I, chapter 11:

> So many hundred Hands in this Mill; so many hundred horse Steam Power. It is known, to the force of a single pound weight, what the engine will do; but, not all the calculators of the National Debt can tell me the capacity for good or evil, for love or hatred, for patriotism or discontent, for the decomposition of virtue into vice, or the reverse, at any single moment in the soul of one of these its quiet servants, with the composed faces and the regulated actions. There is no mystery in it; there is an unfathomable mystery in the meanest of them, for ever.—Supposing we were to reserve our arithmetic for material objects, and to govern these awful unknown quantities by other means![3]

Even this is a long way short of a full-blown Carlylean statement; Carlyle's critique of Mechanism is only partially that it and the ways of thinking analogous to it have no 'unfathomable mystery', that mechanistic thinking is inadequate to sum up human motivations and vitality. This is, of course a point he made early in his career; attacking Benthamite political philosophers in *Signs of the Times* he criticised them as Mill was to criticise Bentham, for an inadequate view of human nature. They

> . . . deal exclusively with the Mechanical province; and occupying themselves in counting up and estimating men's motives, strive by curious checking and balancing, and other adjustments of Profit and Loss, to guide them to their true advantage: while, unfortunately, those same 'motives' are so innumerable, and so variable in every individual, that no really useful

[1] *HT*, 114.
[2] *Ibid.*, 116.
[3] *Ibid.*, 53.

conclusion can ever be drawn from their enumeration . . . . Consider the
great elements of human enjoyment, the attainments and possessions that
exalt man's life to its present height, and see what part of these he owes to
institutions, to Mechanism of any kind; and what to the instinctive, un-
bounded force, which Nature herself lent him, and still continues to him.[1]

This is, in essence, a large part of Dickens's case in *Hard Times*; nevertheless, this is far from demonstrating that the opposition between
Hard Facts and Spontaneous vitality, between Heart and Head, in
the novel, is a Carlylean one. In one way this passage is untypical of
Carlyle's more influential later work, in its slightly surprising emphasis
on 'human enjoyment': this seems far more like Dickens's creed.
And it does not touch on the real nub of Carlyle's critique of the
philosophy of the machine age, one of the great pillars on which his
massive influence was built: 'Mechanism' does not simply destroy
vitality (in the narrowest sense of the word), it also destroys a man's
whole capacity for assent. It undermines, not simply his capacity for
enjoyment, but his reason for existing.

It is Dickens's partial transmission of this essential Carlylean perception that allows us, I think, to say not only that certain of Carlyle's
writings had their effect on *Hard Times*, but that unless Dickens had
digested and been 'influenced' by them, the novel would have been
very different, and almost certainly less successful. Carlyle's influence
on *Hard Times*, that is to say, (and having made a claim of such a
fundamental nature, it may be as well that there should be no mistake
about what is proposed) is formative and not merely accidental, and
has to do, not merely with confirming an existing suspicion about a
tendency of his society, but with the profundity of vision and the
'insistence'—to borrow Dr. Leavis's term—that informs the whole
novel, and makes it one of Dickens's major achievements.

Such an assertion of course, depends on our adoption of a particular critical interpretation of *Hard Times*. We will not find it
necessary, for instance, to make even the most distant comparison
with any of Carlyle's writings, if we really believe, with Dr. Holloway,
that Dickens's intention in the novel is merely to assert that 'all work
and no play makes Jack a dull boy'.[2]   This contention seems to me to
have been convincingly rebutted by Dr. Leavis:

> The fact is that 'all work and no play' in Dr. Holloway's use of the phrase
> is . . . grossly reductive. Years before *Hard Times*, and years before *Dombey
> and Son*, too, Dickens was insisting that 'play' as a need is intimately bound
> up with 'wonder', imagination and creativity, and that any starving of the
> complex need is cruel, denaturing and sterilising, and may be lethal.[3]

1   'S of T', 474.
2   Holloway, J., '*Hard Times*: A History and a Criticism', in *Dickens and the twentieth
    century*, London, 1962, 169.
3   Leavis, F. R. and Q. D., *Dickens the Novelist*, London, 1970, 210.

Dickens's examination of Utilitarianism, as Dr. Holloway suggests,[1] is certainly not searching (does it claim to be?) and Dr. Leavis's contention that it is, conveyed by his chapter-heading—'*Hard Times*: The World of Bentham', is surely extravagant.[2] But Dr. Holloway's representation of Dickens's understanding of the 'terrible mistake', as a kind of Arts man's distrust of figures, though easy to make plausible by short quotations taken out of context (no novelist can be more easily distorted by this practice) completely fails to take account of the total effect of Dickens's use of the 'addition, subtraction, multiplication and division' theme. Certainly, Dr. Holloway's criticism covers much of Dickens's intellectual formulation of the theme of *Hard Times*; what it fails to convey, though, are the reverberations this formulation sets up—and was meant, with conscious art, to set up—in the book's human relationships, reverberations which powerfully transmit its essential wisdom. Dickens's attitude to statistics (of which, more in a later chapter) is cited by Dr. Holloway in support of his general thesis, and it is certainly easy enough to find examples in *Hard Times* of a slightly childlike distrust of 'tabular statements' *per se*. But that Dickens's critique of statistics and of rationalism itself, also operates on a more profound level than this can surely be observed throughout the novel by those who have eyes to see:

> ... I would advise you ... to consider this question, as you have been accustomed to consider every other question, simply as one of tangible Fact. ... Now, what are the Facts of this case? You are, we will say in round numbers, twenty years of age; Mr. Bounderby is, we will say in round numbers, fifty. There is some disparity in your respective years, but in your means and positions, there is none; on the contrary, there is a great suitability. Then the question arises, Is this one disparity sufficient to operate as a bar to such marriage? In considering this question, it is not unimportant to take into account the statistics of marriage, so far as they have yet been obtained, in England and Wales. I find, on reference to the figures, that a large proportion of these marriages are contracted between parties of very unequal ages, and that the elder of these contracting parties is, in rather more than three-fourths of these instances, the bridegroom.[3]

The whole scene from which this comes is justly indicated by Dr. Leavis as 'a triumph of ironic art',[4] and it concentrates in a vital

---

[1] Dr. Leavis is right, of course, to deny that 'an account of his art that implies marked intellectual powers—a capacity, for example, to read and understand Bentham—is obviously absurd' (Preface, p. ix). No one disputes that Dickens was well able to read Bentham; but this hardly demonstrates that he actually did, or if he did that such reading was *directly* relevant to *Hard Times*. Until textual or other evidence for such a suggestion is available, it will surely seem more likely that *Hard Times* refers to a general atmosphere of neo-Benthamite theory and practice, and to the widespread popular debate engendered by it and available equally to those who had and had not read Bentham.

[2] Leavis, *op. cit.*, 187.

[3] *HT*, 75.

[4] Leavis, *op. cit.*, 198.

E

way what is arguably the book's real theme: not simply that Hard
Facts are dull, or cruel, or humanly inadequate; but that a life ruled
entirely by logical considerations is perverted and undermined at its
very roots; Louisa, quite simply, marries Bounderby because she does
not care whether she lives or dies. Her single weary question 'what
does it matter?' indicates the dimension of the Hard Facts theme that
is so noticeably missing from Dr. Holloway's account of *Hard Times*,
a deficiency which, inevitably, produces a serious misjudgement of
the novel's scope. Sleary's horseriding, as he says, is the main vehicle
of the 'all work and no play theme'; but even the circus also sym-
bolises other elements in what Dickens 'champions' against Gradgrind;
'the sacredness of the heart's affections' is the ideal that we might
suggest, together with Dr. Leavis's 'Lawrentian' vitality, as conveying
perhaps the most important part of its meaning.

This, of course, is not even slightly Carlylean in itself; nevertheless,
the pattern involved in a clear connection between the encapsulation
caused by lack of love, or simply of human contact, and the related
indifference to life inseparable from the tyranny of unyielding
mechanistic ideals, shown as culminating in a spiritual crisis, provides
Hard Times with its just dramatic culmination in Louisa's (surely not
hollowly 'melodramatic') collapse, and in Gradgrind's very movingly
realised loss of faith. And this is a dramatic configuration that evokes,
almost unavoidably, a comparison with perhaps the best known part
of Carlyle's best known work: once we have accepted a Carlylean
framework of reference for *Hard Times*, Louisa's story (taken together
with Gradgrind's) recalls irresistibly that of Teufelsdröckh in *Sartor
Resartus*. Teufelsdröckh, too, suffers from an education based on Hard
Facts. 'We find', says Carlyle, 'that his Greek and Latin were
"mechanically" taught; Hebrew scarce even mechanically; much else
. . . no better than not at all. So that, except inasmuch as Nature was
still busy; and he himself "went about, as was of old his wont, among
the Craftsmen's workshops, there learning many things"; and farther
lighted on some small store of curious reading, in Hans Wachtel the
Cooper's house . . . —his time, it would appear, was utterly wasted.'[1]
There is in *Sartor* the same contrast as in *Hard Times* between the
educational values implicit in such mechanistic pedantry and that of
the wisdom of everyday life (here, as in *Hard Times*, *humble* everyday
life) and of Nature. Dickens's views on education have a complex
genesis, of course, and Professor Collins goes no further than to suggest
Carlyle's views as being analogous with those of Dickens in *Hard
Times*.[2]   Nevertheless, it seems worthwhile tentatively to hazard the
theory, given other parallels between the two works, and the existence
in the novel of a demonstrably and intentionally Carlylean structure
of ideas, that Teufelsdröckh's education should be seen as forming,

[1] *SR*, 80–81.
[2] *Education*, 214–6.

directly rather than indirectly, part of the background of the educational satire of *Hard Times*. Certainly, Teufelsdröckh's description of his own education outlines almost exactly the same romantic opposition between the sterility of Hard Facts, and the mysterious vital power of Nature, that is the main theme of the book:

> 'My Teachers', says he, 'were hide-bound Pedants, without knowledge of man's nature, or of boy's; or of aught save their lexicons and quarterly account-books. Innumerable dead Vocables (no dead Language, for they themselves knew no Language) they crammed into us, and called it fostering the growth of mind. How can an inanimate, mechanical Gerund-grinder, the like of whom will, in a subsequent century, be manufactured at Nürnberg out of wood and leather, foster the growth of anything; much more of Mind, which grows, not like a vegetable (by having its roots littered with etymological compost), but like a spirit, by mysterious contact of Spirit; Thought kindling itself at the fire of living Thought? How shall *he* give kindling, in whose own inward man there is no live coal, but all is burnt out to a dead grammatical cinder?'[1]

Like Louisa, Teufelsdröckh has (though rather differently) an abortive love affair; like her, he suffers from a sense of isolation from other human beings and an incapacity to see any meaning in life; for both, this is caused by an emotional debility induced by a rationalist upbringing; and for both it leads to a spiritual crisis. Teufelsdröckh's collapse occurs in Book II of *Sartor*, perhaps the best-known part of Carlyle's most famous book, and even if we did not have other reasons[2] for asserting Dickens's knowledge of this work, Louisa's story, it might be thought, would suggest it without any other supporting evidence.

Harthouse is the living embodiment of Louisa's incapacity for assent, and he strengthens both this vital theme and (I think) my identification of *Sartor* as a possible literary source. Even when we have made ample allowance for literary tradition and contemporary reference,[3]

---

1 *Ibid.*, 81.
2 The year before the publication of *Hard Times*, Dickens referred directly to Book II, Chapter iv, of *Sartor Resartus* (Teufelsdröckh's crisis occurs in Book II, Chapter vii) in a *Household Words* article, describing adolescence as 'that perplexing state of immaturity when Mr. CARLYLE, in mercy to Society, would put him under a barrel for six years' (*HW*, VI (Jan. 1, 1853), 361; *SR*, 98). Another reference to *Sartor* occurs in *AYR*, June 5, 1867, repr. in *UCT*, 358).
3 What to do with high-born young men without either training or inclination for work was a topical question while Dickens was writing *Hard Times*, and on 27 January, 1854 a leader on the subject appeared in *The Times*. The writer ironically imagines the ruminations of a wielder of patronage deciding on a career for such a dilettante:
    We have not much interest with peers, so he shall be secretary to an MP. There is not much trouble involved in the pursuit. It is astounding, after a three months' manipulation of blue books, how intensely wise a man may appear in the eyes of those who do not affect that class of literature. There is no responsibility . . .
    Harthouse, of course, 'coached himself up with a blue-book or two' (p. 95) and 'with a discreet use of his blue coaching, came off triumphantly, though with a considerable accession of boredom' (p. 99).

Harthouse, as I have suggested, is clearly recognisable as that most pervasive Carlylean caricature figure, the Dilettante; he also seems to refer specifically to Book II of *Sartor Resartus*. Here is Dickens on Harthouse:

> And yet he had not, even now, any earnest wickedness of purpose in him. Publicly and privately, it were much better for the age in which he lived, that he and the legion of whom he was one were designedly bad, than indifferent and purposeless. It is the drifting icebergs setting with any current anywhere, that wreck the ships.
> When the Devil goeth about like a roaring lion, he goeth about in a shape by which few but savages and hunters are attracted. But, when he is trimmed, smoothed, and varnished, according to the mode; when he is aweary of vice, and aweary of virtue, used up as to brimstone, and used up as to bliss; then, whether he take to the serving out of red tape, or to the kindling of red fire, he is *the very Devil*.[1]

In both content and imagery, this is very reminiscent of a famous passage in *Sartor Resartus*, and there is an almost visible shift to a neo-biblical, 'Carlylean' style in the second paragraph as Dickens warms to his theme. This is how Carlyle deals with the same idea:

> Some comfort it would have been, could I, like Faust, have fancied myself tempted and tormented of the Devil; for a Hell, as I imagine, without Life, though only diabolic Life, were more frightful: but in our age of Down-pulling and Disbelief, *the very Devil* has been pulled down, you cannot so much as believe in a Devil.[2]

This is substantially the same idea, and it is explored by Dickens in language which is reminiscent enough of this passage to make it worthwhile to suggest that it may have directly provided Dickens with the impulse behind his heavy statement on the Harthouses of this world. Referring to his isolation, Carlyle's hero, Teufelsdröckh, has referred to his 'devouring' his own heart 'as the tiger in the jungle'. This reminds us of Dickens's 'Roaring Lion' and an earlier passage from this chapter of *Sartor* reminds us of Louisa. Teufelsdröckh's sense of the purposelessness of life is intimately linked with his separation from other living beings: 'was there, in the wide world, any true bosom I could press trustfully to mine?',[3] he mournfully asks himself. Louisa begins to gain a sense of the meaning of life as she finds a refuge in Sissy's affection:

---

1   *HT*, 137. My emphasis. Note Dickens's use here of the Carlylean term 'red-tape'. Cf. Dickens's article, "Red-Tape," published the year after the appearance of *L-DP* (Feb 5, 1851) repr. *MP*, 295–302.
2   *SR*, 126. My emphasis.
3   *Ibid*.

'Forgive me, pity me, help me! Have compassion on my great need, and let me lay this head of mine upon a loving heart!'
'O lay it here!' cried Sissy. 'Lay it here, my dear.'[1]

Harthouse represents incapacity for faith in one distinctively Carlylean way, and he may refer directly to *Sartor Resartus*. He certainly embodies another, rather different Carlylean emphasis. Not only does he represent the lack or collapse of belief and its generic relationship with Mechanism; he is also, and as a function of this, shown as being one partner in an even more unmistakably Carlylean alliance: the entente between Dilettantism and Mammonism, taken in conjunction with the overlapping but separable connection between incapacity for assent and Mechanism, firmly establishes Harthouse as a Carlylean figure. Harthouse (Dilettantism and loss of faith), Gradgrind (logic-chopping rationalism), and Bounderby (Mammonism) can be seen as three figures in a distinctively Carlylean demonology. Dickens indicates part of Harthouse's meaning at the beginning of Book II, chapter ii:

> The Gradgrind party wanted assistance in cutting the throats of the graces. They went about recruiting; and where could they enlist recruits more hopefully, than among the fine gentlemen who, having found out everything to be worth nothing, were equally ready for anything?
> Moreover, the healthy spirits who had mounted to this sublime height were attractive to many of the Gradgrind school.... They became exhausted in imitation of them; and they yaw-yawed in their speech like them; and they served out, with an enervated air, the little mouldy rations of political economy, on which they regaled their disciples.[2]

This passage shows Dickens attacking mere rationalism with the tools, and the metaphors of Carlylean allegory; it neatly epitomises, too, how Dickens, in the rest of the book, can be seen to fit his own reading of the opposition between fact and fancy into a Carlylean conceptual framework. Dilettantism here, it will be seen, is not quite a Carlylean vice; or, rather, there is something about it that belongs, if anywhere, to a period in Carlyle's career about twenty years before the appearance of *Hard Times*, to the writing of *Sartor Resartus*: Carlyle's ideas of Dilettantism or of Mechanism do not normally include the notion that one of their besetting sins is 'cutting the throats of the graces', an activity to which Carlyle himself became more and more addicted as he grew older.

This reminds us once more of the very different functions, for the two men, of the imagination, and it is worth stressing again that one vital ingredient in Dickens's onslaught on mechanism in *Hard Times*

---

1 *HT*, 172.
2 *Ibid.*, 94–5.

remains unmodified by the book's grim and insistent analysis
Throughout the book, Sleary's circus remains separate, encamped
outside Coketown, a fantastic Dickensian alternative to this unyielding
Carlylean reality. Its values permeate through, by Sissy's agency:
to suggest, however uncertainly, some kind of regeneration, Dickens
must fall back on his own resources. Gradgrind's rejection of his
own mechanistic creed reminds us of Teufelsdröckh; but it must also
be related to Scrooge's conversion, and to the whole Dickensian
philosophie de Noël. That Dickens wholeheartedly accepted his role
as a purveyor of imaginative escape from a harsh industrial world is
clear enough, and is interestingly illustrated by an account of a public
reading, given in Birmingham, while he was already at work on
Hard Times: 'He has not left an unconverted Scrooge in the great
Hardware Metropolis', reported *The Times*. Dickens had made a
point of insisting that seats should be available for working men:

> ... it was indeed a spectacle of some novelty, and not devoid of high interest,
> to see 2,000 people, whose lives are one long round of material toil, resigning
> themselves during long hours that never sped more swiftly to the pleasures
> of the imagination and the present influence of genius. They formed an
> eagerly attentive and delighted audience, catching up with their applause
> every stroke of humour and melting at each touch of pathos, sensitive to
> all the changing emotions which it is the object of fiction to evoke, and
> yielding a ready homage to that magic power which, by the bonds of
> sympathy, 'makes the whole world kin'.[1]

Here, certainly, is part of the meaning of *Hard Times*; but, just as the
values of Coketown persist (despite Gradgrind's conversion and
Bounderby's discomfiture) so Dickens's quasi-Carlylean vision remains
overpoweringly the book's strongest shaping force. That Stephen's
story and meaning (the divorce theme apart) were—and probably
consciously—conceived in a Carlylean mould and to illustrate a
Carlylean perception, is beyond any doubt; that Louisa's education,
consequent indifference to life, and ultimate spiritual crisis owe much
to Dickens's reading of Carlyle—though this is difficult to establish
definitively—seems hardly less clear. Together, these two narratives
determine (despite the weakening effect of Stephen's supine resignation) the vision and total structure of *Hard Times*, and the limiting
boundaries inside which the novel's special character as a powerfully
ordered work of art establishes itself. 'The book contains nothing in
which you do not think with me'? Perhaps not; but in no other major
novel is Dickens's reverence for the Prophet of Chelsea so pervasively
and deliberately proclaimed.

---

[1] *The Times*, 2 Jan., 1854.

CHAPTER FIVE

A Tale of Two Cities

DICKENS'S admiration for *The French Revolution* is well known. According to Froude, he carried a copy of it everywhere when the book first appeared in 1837;[1] by 1851, he himself claimed to have read it five hundred times.[2] Chesterton's judgement, that Dickens 'read nothing about the French Revolution at all except for Carlyle'[3] is understandable enough and (though usually with reservations) has generally been broadly endorsed by later and better-informed commentators. When we transfer our attention from Dr. Manette and Sidney Carton to the storming of the Bastille and the September Massacres, the confusion evident in discussions of the novel's plot-sources is conspicuous by its absence. *The French Revolution*, as Professor Monod puts it, is 'la source historique essentielle du *Tale*'.[4] After paying due regard, perhaps, to Mercier's *Tableau de Paris*, most critics who consider the question are almost unanimous in their assumption that it was to Carlyle's masterpiece that Dickens went for his historical 'background material'. There has certainly been little attempt, that I am aware of, to take the search any further than the sources that Dickens himself mentions, in a letter to Forster,[5] and in the preface of *A Tale of Two Cities*.

As Professors Butt and Tillotson suggest of *Barnaby Rudge*, 'Dickens's use of his historical sources ... has never received the detailed consideration it deserves ...'[6] This is also true of the *Tale*, and I shall attempt no more here than to indicate the complexity of the problem and the

---

1   Froude, J. A., *Thomas Carlyle: His Life in London*, London, 1884, I, 93.
2   Forster, 505.
3   Chesterton, G. K., *Appreciations and Criticisms of the Works of Charles Dickens*, London, 1911, 193.
4   Monod, S., *Dickens Romancier*, Paris, 1953, 502.
5   See, for instance, Böttger, 55.
6   Butt and Tillotson, 85.

importance of Carlyle's contribution. There are undoubtedly other sources for the *Tale* than the ones I shall discuss, and the size simply of the collection of books on the French Revolution possessed by the London Library in 1859, which would fit nicely into 'two cartloads',[1] suggests that whoever undertakes to fill the blanks left by previous studies has a large task ahead of him. There is a mass of unrelated detail that cannot be traced to any of the sources which have so far been considered in published accounts, and which it is outside the scope of this inquiry to track down.

Carlyle is certainly a major historical source for the *Tale* and, as I say, the fact has been generally recognised. Some critics make a further, related suggestion, again inspired partly by Dickens's preface, with its reference to the 'philosophy' of the *French Revolution*: Carlyle's books give Dickens, not only his historical facts, but his theory of history, too. 'La Thèse du Romancier', asserts Professor Monod, 'est toute entière contenue dans l'ouvrage de Carlyle . . . '[2] Curt Böttger says very much the same thing: *A Tale of Two Cities* is 'in seiner Revolutionshandlung eine popularisierung der Carlyle'schen Ideen-welt'.[3]

We have, then, two related but separable conclusions to examine: that Carlyle was an important historical source; and that the 'philosophy' (the word is Dickens's own, so we may as well continue to use

[1]   At Dickens's request, Carlyle sent him a number of books from the London Library to help him with the historical background of *A Tale of Two Cities*. As I have described in Chapter Two, Dickens later told an American hostess how he had worked through Carlyle's sources, and had marvelled at the new imaginative fusion he had achieved. On this occasion, Dickens is reported as having said that Carlyle had sent his own books on the French Revolution, but this is fairly clearly a mistake. On 24 March, 1859, Dickens wrote to Carlyle:

> I cannot tell you how much I thank you for your friendly trouble, or how specially interesting and valuable any help is to me that comes from you. I do not doubt that the books received from the London Library, and suggested by you, will give me all I want. (*Letters*, III, 97.)

The contents of the collection of books that might have been sent by the London Library is of obvious interest, if only to demonstrate the multiplicity of sources available. Fairly clearly, Carlyle did not get the Library to send all his own sources, firstly because it did not possess them all, secondly because of their number. Professor C. F. Harrold points out that Carlyle cites more than eight hundred and fifty sources in his footnotes, and assumes that these largely account for his factual knowledge; Dr. Hedva Ben-Israel, however, believes that 'Carlyle used twice as many books as he cited' (Harrold, 'Carlyle's general method in *The French Revolution*', PMLA, XLIII (1928), 1150, and Ben-Israel, 'Carlyle and *The French Revolution*', *Historical Journal*, II (1958), 126). Clearly, Carlyle could not rely on the resources of his own library for such a vast array, though we know that he possessed the *Biographie Universelle*, in which he invested after the destruction of the first draft of Volume I. We know, too, that Carlyle worked on the book for some time in the British Museum. Unfortunately, the London Library's records of borrowings during this period have not survived, and it is therefore impossible to determine exactly which works were suggested by Carlyle for Dickens's use. I estimate (from the London Library's catalogue of 1842, and its supplements of 1852 and 1856, and from the new catalogue of 1865) that in 1859 it possessed around one hundred and ten works on the 1789 revolution.

[2]   Monod, 425.

[3]   Böttger, 45.

it) of *A Tale of Two Cities* derives substantially from that of *The French Revolution*. The implications of the second proposal are clearly more important than those of the first. Dickens's acquaintance with *The French Revolution* was intimate by 1851; if he accepted its philosophy in the *Tale*, which appeared in 1859, why should he not have done so long before this date? If there *is* a relationship between the philosophies expounded in the two books, what is its nature? How susceptible, in other words, *was* Dickens, not simply to Carlyle's localised conclusions, but to the essence, the intellectual and spiritual base of his teaching?

The theory of history (if the phrase isn't too ponderous to describe what is involved here) that Dickens illustrates in the *Tale* is simple enough, and he sums it up for us in his final chapter:

> Crush humanity out of shape once more, under similar hammers, and it will twist itself into the same tortured forms. Sow the same seed of rapacious licence and oppression over again, and it will surely yield the same fruit according to its kind.[1]

Dickens had come to this conclusion about the meaning of the French Revolution over ten years before he wrote these words: in 1848, replying, in *The Examiner*, to a heavy statement from the Bench (designed to confound the Chartists) that 'previous to the Revolution in France, of 1790, the physical comforts possessed by the poor greatly exceeded those possessed by them subsequent to that event', Dickens summarised what he took to be the meaning of the revolution:

> It was a struggle on the part of the people for social recognition and existence. It was a struggle for vengeance against intolerable oppression. It was a struggle for the overthrow of a system of oppression, which in its contempt of all humanity, decency, and natural rights, and in its systematic degradation of the people, had trained them to be the demons that they showed themselves, when they rose up and cast it down for ever.[2]

This is substantially the historical 'philosophy' of *A Tale of Two Cities*. The idea is elementary enough, and of course (as he can scarcely avoid) Carlyle—both implicitly and occasionally explicitly—makes something like the same point in *The French Revolution*. 'Horrible, in Lands that had known equal justice!' he says, of the death of Berthier:

> Not so unnatural in Lands that had never known it. '*Le sang qui coule, est-il donc si pur?*' asks Barnave; intimating that the Gallows, though by irregular methods, has its own.[3]

---

[1] *TTC*, 353.
[2] *MP*, 133.
[3] *FR*, I, 201.

Dickens's view of the revolution as an event with valid causes certainly aroused no surprise on the appearance of the *Tale*; 'it is such very elementary truth', wrote Sir James Fitzjames Stephen, 'that, unless a man had something new to say about it, it is hardly worth mentioning . . .'[1] Dickens's ambiguous mixture of sympathy and revulsion for the mob reflected a traditionally English view of the revolution,[2] which had gained greatly in currency during the general debate that preceded the enactment of the 1832 Reform Bill. It was a view with which, it is a fair guess, Dickens was both familiar and sympathetic as a parliamentary reporter and a young radical in the making. The mildness of the 1830 revolution was compared with the wildness of that of 1789, and interpreted by radicals as a good omen for change in England: reform, it was held, did not necessarily lead to violent upheavals:

> The apologetic argument that the blame for the violence lay with the example and brutalising effect of the old regime greatly gained force. It was said that the violence of a revolution is in proportion to the misrule that preceded it . . .[3]

The Dickensian phrase 'rapacious licence and oppression' suggests a vital distinction: pre-revolutionary France is obnoxious to Carlyle, not so much because it is oppressive, as because it is unreal; its crimes have to do, not in the first place with lack of humanity, but with lack of truth. For Carlyle the French revolution is 'the End of the Dominion of IMPOSTURE (which is Darkness and opaque Fire-damp); and the burning up, with unquenchable fire, of all the Gigs that are in the Earth'.[4] Carlyle's French revolution is the shattering of a crust of falsehood on top of a volcano of truth: that of Dickens, less exotically, is an illustration of the idea that one form of evil and cruelty will, in its turn, produce another. 'Portentous change!', the later Wordsworth could exclaim of Carlyle's version of the revolution, 'When History can appear/As the cool advocate of foul device'[5]; there was never any danger that Dickens might be accused of this kind of sympathy with the revolution. Oppressed the members of the Paris mob may have been, but once they are in full cry, Dickens can see only 'their frenzied eyes;—eyes which any unbrutalised beholder would have given twenty years of life, to petrify with a well-directed gun'.[6] 'That "well-directed",' suggests John Gross, 'has the true ring of outraged, rate-paying respectability while the image seems oddly

---

1   Repr. in *The Dickens Critics*, ed. Ford, G. H. and Lane, L. Cornell, 1961, 44.
2   See Ben-Israel, H., *English Historians on the French Revolution*, Cambridge, 1968, 8.
3   *Ibid.*, 98.
4   *FR*, II, 461.
5   Wordsworth, W., Ed. de Selincourt, E, and Darbishire, H., *Poetical Works*, Oxford, 1947, 130.
6   *TTC*, 249.

out of place in a book which has laid so much stress on the stony faces and petrified hearts of the aristocracy'.[1] Dickens's particular emphasis on the misrule that preceded the first French revolution similarly distinguishes his view of history from Carlyle's, and it is interesting that for material describing aristocratic cruelty, Dickens can go to *The French Revolution* only for scattered details. The gallows, for instance, from which the Marquis's assassin is hanged, is forty feet high;[2] Carlyle relates that two members of a crowd that had marched to Versailles in 1775 with a petition of grievances were hanged on a 'new gallows forty feet high'.[3] For Carlyle, the forty-foot gallows becomes a symbol (reiterated so frequently that Dickens could hardly have missed it) of the failure of France's rulers to understand the needs of the people; for Dickens it becomes, rather differently, a simple illustration of aristocratic nasty-mindedness.

Nevertheless, though the divergences between Dickens's view of the revolution and Carlyle's seem clear enough, it has certainly been widely assumed that their 'philosophies' are, for all practical purposes, identical. The book's most insistent theme, says Professor Fielding, 'was the same as that of *The French Revolution*: that certain conditions must always lead to anarchy and anarchy destroys itself...'[4] Professor Fielding advances a slightly different proposition, when he suggests that, in the *Tale*, 'the doctrine of determinism was derived from Carlyle...'[5] Certainly, the first part of the novel is heavy with hints of historical fatality, with ironic symbols of the ensuing upheaval; the most obvious is the spilt wine-barrel, which gives the opportunity for some (surely not very impressive) intimations of historical inevitability. Carlyle, too, can frequently be seen in the early part of *The French Revolution* to foreshadow the tragedy to come with ironic-prophetic references to the future, and this can be seen to underline his own view of historical causality, which he expresses at one point in metaphors strikingly reminiscent of one of Dickens's journalistic pronouncements on the revolution ('... the harvest that is reaped, has sometimes been sown'[6]):

How often must we say ... The seed that is sown, it will spring! Given the summer's blossoming, then there is also given the autumnal withering: so is it ordered not with seedfields only, but with transactions, arrangements ... French Revolutions ... The Beginning holds in it the End ... as the acorn does the oak ...[7]

[1] In *Dickens and the Twentieth Century*, ed. Gross, J. and Pearson, G., London, 1962, 192.
[2] *TTC*, 163.
[3] *FR*, I, 35 and 38.
[4] Fielding, 199.
[5] *Ibid.*
[6] *RP*, 477.
[7] *FR*, I, 377.

But, of course, Carlyle did not believe in historical inevitability. As Dr. Hedva Ben-Israel points out, Carlyle was quite opposed to the deterministic ideas of Thiers on the French revolution; such a historical viewpoint inevitably reduced the moral responsibility of the individual actors in the drama, by emphasising the fatality of events. Given Carlyle's view of history, and his belief in the shaping power of heroic individuals, it was impossible for him to believe in historical determinism, except in such a heavily qualified form as to make the word meaningless. It was, as he wrote ironically to Mill, 'a wonderful system of ethics . . . every hero turns out to be perfectly justified in doing whatsoever he succeeded in doing'.[1]   Broadly, Carlyle shows the French revolution as something, inevitable in itself (this is as far as his 'determinism' takes him), but which could have been avoided in the form it finally took by individual action: hence the importance he attaches to the untimely death of Mirabeau, one of the great heroes of his history. Dickens, on the other hand, does place a great deal more emphasis on the relentless march of events, and *nowhere* does he suggest that the revolution, or even the Terror, were avoidable; he heavily implies, rather, that they were fated to happen. Dickens may well owe more to Thiers than to Carlyle for this part of his 'philosophy'. Dickens certainly knew his *History of the French Revolution*; in his *Examiner* article of 1848 he gave the following quotation from it (rather, significantly, than one from Carlyle's History) to demonstrate the state of France before the revolution:

> All . . . was monopolised by a few hands, and the burdens bore upon a single class. The nobility and the clergy possessed nearly two-thirds of the landed property. The other third, belonging to the people, paid taxes to the king, a multitude of feudal dues to the nobility, the tithe to the clergy, and was, moreover, liable to the devastations of noble sportsmen and their game. The taxes on consumption weighed heavily on the great mass, and consequently on the people. The mode in which they were levied was vexatious. The gentry might be in arrear with impunity; the people, on the other hand, ill-treated and imprisoned, were doomed to suffer in body, in default of goods. They defended with their blood the upper classes of society, without being able to subsist themselves.[2]

Thiers was known in England as an apostle of determinism, and T.W. Redhead, one of his English translators, found it necessary to defend him, in 1845, against the criticism brought on by 'the view of inevitability, or fatalism, which he inclines to take of many of the atrocities committed during the revolution'; nevertheless, thought Redhead, 'this is an opinion daily gathering ground . . .'[3]   Dickens had no need

---

[1] Ben-Israel, 134, and *Letters to Mill, etc.*, 33–4.
[2] *MP*, 132.
[3] Redhead, T. W., trans., Thiers, M. A., *History of the French Revolution*, London, 1845, viii.

to get his fatalism from Carlyle, since (if we really need to explain in terms of a 'philosophy' what can simply be seen as an effective dramatic idea) he knew Thiers from Schoberl's English translation of 1838, whence comes the extract quoted above.[1]

Dickens's picture of pre-revolutionary France, properly enough, drew critical fire which he later felt it necessary to return. He justified his picture of the French aristocracy by giving his source, Mercier's *Tableau de Paris*, 'scattered up and down the pages of which is full authority for my Marquis'.[2] Mercier can hardly, I think, be said to support Dickens's case[3] and Stephen's judgement, that 'the sort of atrocities which Mr. Dickens depicts as characteristic of the eighteenth century were neither safe nor common in the fourteenth'[4], though arguably itself slightly overstated, remains unanswered. What is relevant to note here is, as I have suggested, not only that Dickens does not and cannot justify his picture of pre-revolutionary France by an appeal to *The French Revolution*, but also that one main reason (among others) for Carlyle's failure to supply—except in a limited way—gory pre-revolutionary details, is his concern to illustrate an idea of the revolution itself which is fundamentally different from that which fires Dickens's imagination in the *Tale*: it is only marginally part of Carlyle's purpose to argue that the downfall of the *ancien régime* was the result of its oppressive nature.

Dickens's idea of the revolution does not, of course, subsume the philosophy of the *Tale* in the same inclusive way as Carlyle's does the philosophy of *The French Revolution*. What is represented by Sidney Carton's self-sacrifice, for instance, certainly has a relationship with Dickens's general feelings about insurrectionary anarchy; as his reaction to the Indian mutiny amply demonstrates,[5] there was a strong natural antithesis in his mind between the notion of revolutionary massacre and that of devotion and self-sacrifice. What

---

[1] Schoberl, trans., I, 20. We can identify Dickens's quotation, despite minor modifications, as almost certainly coming from this translation. In Dickens's quotation, for obvious reasons, the word 'therefore' is omitted from the first sentence ('All was *therefore* monopolised') and his final sentence is slightly different from Schoberl's which reads 'It subsisted therefore by the sweat of the brow; [Dickens omits this] it defended with its blood the upper classes of society without being able to subsist itself'. The rest is identical.

[2] Forster, 731.

[3] Dickens undoubtedly drew some of his material for the Marquis from Mercier (see, for instance, Book III, 'Vie d'un homme en place'), but Mercier cannot justify the Marquis's cruelty, which appears to be Dickens's contribution. The *Tableau de Paris*, for instance, contains a chapter on the carelessness of Parisian coach-drivers, in which Mercier tells us that there was in operation a tariff of financial compensation for injury and death. But this has nothing whatever to do with aristocratic repression, about which Mercier is silent. The book does not, as Professor Davis claims, contain details of atrocities, nor does it touch on the *droit de Seigneur*. (Davis, 243.)

[4] Stephen, 45.

[5] See my 'Dickens and the Indian Mutiny', *Dickensian*, LXVIII (1972), 3–15.

is evident, though Carton certainly conveys a vital part of the 'philosophy' of the *Tale*, is that Dickens's main argument about the meaning of the revolution can be clearly separated from Carton's part of the story. Not only this: Carton undoubtedly conveyed—for Dickens as for his public—a vital element in the book's meaning, one which has continued to move successive generations of readers unsullied by the higher Dickensian criticism. Carton's characterisation and story owe, at several points, a fairly unambiguous debt to *The French Revolution*, and the way in which the debt is incurred is clearly relevant to our wider inquiry.

Carton draws from Carlyle's history both circumstantial detail and ideological nourishment. Carlyle seems likely to have contributed towards the idea of his self-sacrificing substitution, though this was a common theme, and had been used surprisingly often by other writers.[1] Several sources have been suggested for this idea, some with little supporting evidence (such as Bulwer Lytton's almost unreadable *Zanoni*[2]) others—most acceptably Watts Phillips's *The Dead Heart*—with more foundation. Dickens almost certainly knew Phillips's play,[3] and since it contains both the idea of a long, spiritually damaging incarceration in the Bastille (hence the title) and a self-sacrificing substitution to save a loved one from the guillotine, it very probably played its part in Dickens's story. Phillips himself got the substitution idea from Carlyle; in a letter[4] he gave his source as the following incident from *The French Revolution*:

The notable person is Lieutenant-General Loiserolles, a nobleman by birth and by nature; laying down his life here for his son. In the prison of Saint-Lazare, the night before last, hurrying to the Grate to hear the Death-list read, he caught the name of his son. The son was asleep at the moment. 'I am Loiserolles', cried the old man: at Tinville's bar, an error in the Christian name is little; small objection was made.[5]

Whether Dickens was thinking directly, or indirectly, via Phillips, of this account of Loiserolles's self-sacrifice, probably does not matter. But that there was, at some stage, a direct reference to Carlyle's account of this episode, seems extremely likely. In the same chapter of *The French Revolution*, some two pages later, passages occur, describing the last ride of Robespierre, which are almost certainly a source for Carton's final journey:

[1] See 'The Sources of *A Tale of Two Cities*', MLN, XXXVI (1921).
[2] Davis, E., *The Flint and the Flame*, London, 1964, 240.
[3] Dolmetsch, C., 'Dickens and The Dead Heart', *Dickensian*, LV (1959).
[4] Phillips, H. W., *Watts Phillips, Author and Playwright*, London, 1891, 44.
[5] *FR*, II, 423.

Dickens	*Carlyle*
There is a guard of sundry horse-men riding abreast of the tum-brils, and faces are often turned up to some of them . . . The horsemen abreast of [the third cart] frequently *point out one man in it with their swords.* The leading curiosity is, *to know which is he* . . . . Here and there in the *long street of St. Honoré*, cries are raised against him. (354)	All eyes are on Robespierre's Tumbril . . . The Gendarmes *point their swords at him, to show the people which is he.* (II, 425)
	His poor landlord, the Cabinet-maker in *the Rue Saint-Honoré*, loved him . . . (II, 426)

Three more details from Carton's progress to the guillotine are pro-bably from Carlyle. During Madame Roland's imprisonment Carlyle says, she calls 'the beheaded Twenty-two [Girondin deputés] *"Nos amis*, our Friends"—whom we are soon to follow'.[1] The seamstress, whom Carton follows, is the twenty-second victim that day: 'she goes next before him—is gone; the knitting-women count Twenty-Two'.[2] According to Carlyle, Madame Roland herself, on her way to the guillotine, comforted a fellow-sufferer, as Carton does the young girl.[3] Carlyle's description of Madame Roland's death almost certainly triggered off the train of thought which gave us Carton's final speech, and perhaps one of the most memorable and universally-known sentences in English literature. 'Biography', says Carlyle, 'will long remember that trait of asking for a pen "to write the strange thoughts that were rising in her". It is a little light-beam, shedding softness, and a kind of sacredness, over all that preceded: so in her too there was an Unnamable; she too was a Daughter of the Infinite; there were mysteries which Philosophism had not dreamt of!'[4] Carton's final utterance, evidently, fulfils this kind of function: it is clearly meant to shed 'a kind of sacredness over all that preceded'. This page of Carlyle's history is a memorable one, for Dickens or anyone else, and contains Madame Roland's famous utterance, 'O Liberty, what things are done in thy name!' Any doubts as to whether or not Dickens is thinking of Madame Roland are removed by him:

> One of the most remarkable sufferers by the same axe—a woman—had asked at the foot of the same scaffold, not long before, to be allowed to write down the thoughts that were inspiring her. If he had given an utterance to his, and they were prophetic, they would have been these:[5]

Carton's famous last words follow.

[1] *Ibid.*, 355.
[2] *TTC*, 357.
[3] *FR*, II, 355, and *TTC*, 356-7.
[4] *FR*, II, 355.
[5] *TTC*, 357.

Carlyle's 'mysteries which Philosophism had not dreamt of' reminds us how Dickens responded to this Carlylean notion (we merely have to substitute for 'Philosophism' its natural ideological descendant, Benthamite rationalism) in the writing of *Hard Times*, and Carlyle's words emphasise how Dickens failed to make the appropriate Carlylean connection three years later.[1]   That Carton is a 'Carlylean' figure is less obvious than that Harthouse is: nevertheless, with obvious reservations, he is certainly in the Carlylean tradition of the dilettante figure of *Hard Times*.   It is interesting, embodying lack of faith as he does, that he is also a lawyer.   The plot demands it, of course (though not imperatively); nevertheless he reminds us interestingly of a passage in *The French Revolution*, in which Carlyle is discussing the spiritual condition of France before the Revolution.   '. . . there is a new recognised Noblesse of Lawyers', notes Carlyle, and links their rise with that of the *philosophes*: the effect of all this, he says, is that 'Faith is gone out: Scepticism is come in'.   His next remarks might be thought reminiscent of Carton: 'Evil abounds and accumulates; no man has Faith to withstand it, to amend it, *to begin by amending himself*; it must even go on accumulating'.[2]   Carton, too, cannot amend himself, cannot free himself from 'the cloud of caring for nothing, which overshadowed him with such a fatal darkness, [and] was very rarely pierced by the light within him'.[3]   Carlyle's use of the analogous theme in *The French Revolution* indicates, again, how distinct here is his 'philosophy' from Dickens's:

> While hollow langour and vacuity is the lot of the Upper, and want and stagnation of the Lower, and universal misery is very certain, what other thing is certain? That a Lie cannot be believed! Philosophism knows only this: her other belief is mainly, that in spiritual supersensual matters no Belief is possible.[4]

For Carlyle, as I have suggested, it is this spiritual debility of pre-revolutionary France, rather than her rampant injustice, that is the essential cause of the Revolution and of its violence. Philosophism is concerned only with sweeping away falsehood: but,

> . . . the Lie with its Contradiction once swept away, what will remain? The five unsatiated Senses will remain, the sixth insatiable Sense (of vanity); the whole *demonic* nature of man will remain,—hurled forth to rage blindly without rule or rein; savage itself, yet with all the tools and weapons of civilisation: a spectacle new in History.[5]

---

1   Though in the chapter 'Monseigneur in town', Dickens interestingly uses the Carlylean term 'unreality', in connection with Monseigneur's entourage. (*TTC*, 100.)
2   *FR*, I, 15–16.
3   *TTC*, 142.
4   *FR*, I, 16.
5   *Ibid.*

Unlike Carlyle, Dickens is not dealing in this kind of perception; very much like him, however, he is deeply fascinated by 'the whole *demonic* nature of man . . . hurled forth to rage blindly without rule or rein'. Apart, possibly, from the high pathos of Carton's end everyone, as John Gross says, 'remembers *A Tale of Two Cities* above all for the intoxication of its crowd scenes'.[1] This is almost equally true of *The French Revolution*, and the *Tale* demonstrates vividly one reason why Dickens should have read and reread Carlyle's history with such devotion. From the point in the *Tale* at which we leave the placid safety of London for the terrors of insurrectionary Paris, we are plunged, not simply into the taking of the Bastille and the September massacres, but into Carlyle's re-creation of them; we are here, beyond any doubt, in the world of *The French Revolution*. Page after page recalls Carlyle's situations and imagery so vividly that we can say with near certainty that Dickens either knew the relevant passages in Carlyle's history almost by heart, or that he actually had his copy open before him as he wrote.

The extent of Dickens's debt to Carlyle at this point can be ade-quately suggested only by lengthy comparative quotation from both works, and readers who find this kind of thing tedious should skip the next few pages. The first chapter and a half (i.e. the second part of Chapter xxi and the whole of Chapter xxii) of Dickens's *French Revolution* describes the following sequence of events, which I shall number for purposes of closer examination: (1) the arming of the crowd; (2) the seige of the Bastille and its fall; (3) the search for Dr. Manette's document by Defarge; (4) the murder of the Bastille governor and of a soldier by the crowd; (5) the release of seven prisoners and the parade of seven heads through the streets; and (6) the discovery and massacre of old Foulon and then of his son-in-law. All these events have their close equivalent in *The French Revolution*, and with the exception of one episode (the search for Manette's document) occur in this sequence. The whole cycle of events, with this exception, unfolds in Dickens almost exactly as it does in Carlyle, with one important qualification; Dickens omits any reference to the political background of the events he describes: he is not interested in the historical assessments that can be seen as part of the fibre even of Carlyle's most fevered descriptions. Dickens is interested in sustain-ing the tension of his narrative; hence, the week of political manoeuvres (related by Carlyle) which actually separated the fall of the Bastille and the massacre of Foulon, are omitted.

These two chapters, as I have suggested, can be seen as a sequence of six events, all of which have Carlyle as their principal and (with one exception) probably their only source. Since short quotations,

---

[1] Gross, *op. cit.*, 187.

from both Dickens and Carlyle, give an inadequate idea of what is involved, I shall place extracts from the two texts side by side.

(1) *The arming of the mob*

The mob, according to Carlyle, armed itself with weapons from the cellars of the Hôtel des Invalides. Hence perhaps, in Dickens's account, 'every weapon or semblance of a weapon that was thrown up from the depths below'. Common to both descriptions is the fervour of the mob's desire for arms, in Carlyle's words, 'more ravenous than famishing lions over dead prey'; and the general visual effect of Dickens's crowd, in its 'clutching' movement (both descriptions use the word), and its contrast of light and dark, of the 'frequent gleams of light' over the 'vast dusky mass' of the mob, recalls Carlyle's crowd, with its contrast (also involving fire-arms) of 'darkness' and 'fiery light'. 'Saint Antoine', of course, is Carlyle's as well as Dickens's personification of the mob:

A Tale of Two Cities	*The French Revolution*
Saint Antoine had been . . . a vast dusky mass . . . with frequent gleams of light above the billowy heads, where steel blades and bayonets shone in the sun . . .	. . . firelocks are on the shoulders of . . . National Guards, lifted thereby out of darkness into fiery light. (I,183)
. . . all the fingers convulsively clutching at every weapon or semblance of a weapon that was thrown up from the depths below . . .	Patriotism . . . rummaging distractedly for arms. What cellar, or what cranny can escape it? The arms are found . . . More ravenous than famishing lions over dead prey, the multitude, with clangor and vociferation, pounces on them; struggling, dashing, clutching . . . (I,182-3).
. . . over the heads of the crowd, like a kind of lightning . . . muskets were being distributed— so were cartridges, powder, and ball, bars of iron and wood, knives, axes, pikes, every weapon that distracted ingenuity could discover or devise. People who could lay hold of nothing else . . . [forced] stones and bricks out of their places in walls. Every pulse and heart in Saint Antoine was on high-fever strain and at high-fever heat. (204)	. . . heaps of paving stones, old iron and missiles lie piled . . . (I,183)

(2) *The living sea*

The first use by Dickens of water imagery to describe the crowd is in its comparison with a whirlpool. This clearly derives from Carlyle. The crowd then becomes the sea itself, an image which Dickens elaborates for all it is worth. Many details show that Dickens was following Carlyle closely at this point:

A Tale of Two Cities	The French Revolution
As a whirlpool of boiling waters has a centre point, so, all this raging circled round Defarge's wine - shop, and every human drop in the caldron had a tendency to be sucked towards the vortex where Defarge himself, already begrimed with gunpowder and sweat . . . laboured and strove . . . (204-5)	Paris wholly has got to the acme of its frenzy; whirled, all ways, by panic madness. At every street barricade, there whirls simmering a minor whirlpool . . . and all minor whirlpools play distractedly into that grand Fire-Mahlstrom which is lashing round the Bastille. And so it lashes and roars . . . (I, 186)
With a roar . . . the living sea rose, wave on wave, depth on depth, and overflowed the city to that point. Alarm-bells ringing, drums beating, the sea raging and thundering on its new beach, the attack begun. (205)	. . . our National Volunteers rolling in long wide flood . . . (I, 182) . . . how the multitude flows on, welling through every street: tocsin furiously pealing, all drums beating . . . The Suburb Saint-Antoine rolling hitherward wholly, as one man! (I, 184)
. . . the sea cast him up against a cannon . . . . Slight displacements of the raging sea, made by the falling wounded . . . the furious sounding of the living sea . . . (205-6)	Ever wilder swells the tide of men; their infinite hum waxing ever louder . . . (I, 184) Upwards . . . flashes one irregular deluge of musketry . . . (I, 186) And still the fire-deluge abates not . . . (I, 187) . . . the crowd seems shoreless. (I, 188)
. . . suddenly the sea rose immeasurably wider and higher, and swept Defarge . . . over the lowered drawbridge, past the massive stone outer walls, in among the eight great towers surrendered!	Sinks the drawbridge . . . rushes in the living deluge: The Bastille is fallen! . . . (I, 189)

So resistless was the force of the ocean bearing him on, that even to draw his breath or turn his head was as impracticable as . . . in the surf at the South Sea . . .

As we said, it was a living deluge, plunging headlong . . . (I, 190)

. . . 'The Prisoners!' was the cry most taken up by the sea that rushed in, as if there were an eternity of people, as well as of time and space . . . (206)

. . . so tremendous was the noise of the living ocean, in its irruption into the Fortress, and its inundation of the courts and passages and staircases. (207)

And so it goes plunging through court and corridor; billowing uncontrollable . . . (I, 190)

(3) *Dr. Manette's document*

As the fortress is ransacked after its fall, Carlyle says, 'ashlar stones of the Bastille continue thundering through the dusk; its paper archives shall fly white. Old secrets come to view; and long-buried Despair finds voice.[1]   There follows in this account a passage which (as scholars have not failed to note[2]) is undoubtedly the source for the end of Dr. Manette's document, and which may even have prompted the whole idea of its use as a key plot-device:

If it had pleased GOD to put it in the hard heart of either of the brothers, in all these frightful years, to grant me any tidings of my dearest wife—so much to let me know by a word whether alive or dead—I might have thought that He had not quite abandoned them. (315)

If for my consolation Monseigneur would grant me, for the sake of God and the Most Blessed Trinity, that I could have news of my dear wife; were it only her name on a card, to show that she is alive! It were the greatest consolation I could receive; and I should for ever bless the greatness of Monseigneur. (I, 192)

The implications, not simply of the similarity of these two passages but of their respective position in their own sequence of events, are interesting. The immediate equivalent in the *Tale* of the original letter from *The French Revolution* is not the passage so similar to it,

[1] *FR*, I, 192.
[2] See Davis, 244; Böttger, 18, and Falloner, 1–10.

quoted above, but the search for Manette's document by Defarge. The document itself reappears towards the end of the book, to give the plot its ironic twist. Carlyle's letter must be of primary importance to Dickens's strategic deployment of the 'recalled to life' theme: the various sources for this idea fit better into the whole sequence of events implied by the discovery of the letter, than the other way round. The passage from Carlyle looks backward to Manette's incarceration, and forward to the trial of his son-in-law. *The French Revolution* is the only possible source (apart from Carlyle's own source[1]) for the buried alive theme which, because of close textual similarities, is indisputably a source for Manette's document and all it implies, and which also involves both the discovery of a hidden document, *and* the fall of the Bastille. Hence, *The French Revolution* can be seen, not only as a major historical source but, in a sense, as providing a cornerstone of the whole plot.

(4) *The murder of the Bastille governor and of a soldier*

A Tale of Two Cities	*The French Revolution*
Saint Antoine was clamorous to have its wine-shop keeper foremost in the guard upon the governor who had defended the Bastille and shot the people. Otherwise, the governor would not be marched to the Hôtel de Ville for judgement . . . (208-9)	De Launay, "discovered in gray frock with poppy-colored ribbon," is for killing himself with the sword of his cane. He shall to the Hôtel-de-Ville; Hulin, Maillard and others escorting him . . . (I, 190)
In the howling universe of passion and contention that seemed to encompass this grim old officer conspicuous in his grey coat and red decoration, there was but one quite steady figure, and that was a woman's . (209)	Through roarings and cursings . . . (I, 190) Rigorous De Launay . . . (I, 191) [. . . Demoiselle Théroigne, with pike and helmet, sits there as gunneress (cf. Defarge) . . . . Maillard has his Menads in the Champs Elysées . . . . A small nucleus of Order is round his drum; but his outskirts fluctuate like the mad Ocean.) (cf. Madame Defarge) (I, 246)]
She . . . remained immovable close to him when he was got near to his destination, and began to be struck at from behind; remained immovable close to him	Through roarings and cursings; through hustlings, clutchings, and at last through strokes! Your

---

[1] *Mémoires de Linguet et de Dusaulx*, ed. Berville, S.-A. et Barrière, J., Paris, 1821, 292-307.

A Tale of Two Cities	*The French Revolution*
when the long-gathering rain of stabs and blows fell heavy; was so close to him when he dropped dead under it, that, suddenly animated, she put her foot upon his neck, and with her cruel knife— long ready—hewed off his head. (209)	escort is hustled aside, felled down; Hulin sinks exhausted on a heap of stones. Miserable De Launay! He shall never enter the Hôtel-de-Ville: only his "bloody hair-queue, held up in a bloody hand"; That shall enter, for a sign. The bleeding trunk lies on the steps there; the head is off through the streets; ghastly, aloft on a pike. (I, 190-1)

(5) *The seven heads and seven prisoners*

I have quoted this passage on p. 36 (chapter three) to show Carlyle's style breaking through Dickens's normal prose; the corresponding passage from *The French Revolution* runs as follows: 'Along the streets of Paris circulate seven Bastille Prisoners, borne shoulder-high; seven Heads on pikes; the Keys of the Bastille; and much else'.[1] Dickens's phrase 'such, and such like', seems to correspond to Carlyle's 'and much else'. The first three items in Carlyle occur in Dickens, in the same order, and Dickens's 'discovered letters and other memorials' come from the next paragraph in Carlyle's account which we have discussed (in paragraph three) above. In the third paragraph in *The French Revolution* occurs Carlyle's reference to the time and season, as well as a reference to the continued activity in the streets: 'so does the July twilight thicken; so must Paris . . . brawl itself finally into a kind of sleep . . . . patrols go clashing . . . there go rumors; alarms of war, to the extent of "fifteen thousand men marching through the Suburb Saint-Antoine" . . .'[2] is paralleled in the *Tale* by the reference to mid-July, and the 'loudly echoing footsteps of Saint-Antoine'.[3]

(6) *The discovery and massacre of old Foulon and his son-in-law*

This is Dickens's most horrifying description, because of its personal nature. As with other descriptions in Dickens of mob violence, we can see a kind of dual sympathy, with Berthier and Foulon because they are victims and with the mob because of its infectious violence and its righteous anger. It is interesting that in this most lurid and personally-felt of the mob's outrages, Dickens should emphasise the culpability of the victims, though it is difficult to feel at this point that this stress is strongly felt. Partly, of course, it is due to the closeness with which Dickens follows his source, which is (without any doubt here) *The French Revolution*:

1 *FR*, I, 192.
2 *Ibid.*, 193.
3 *TTC*, 210.

A Tale of Two Cities	*The French Revolution*

Haggard Saint Antoine had had only one exultant week, in which to soften his modicum of hard and bitter bread . . . . Madame Defarge . . . sat in the morning light and heat . . . . (211) 'Does everybody here recall old Foulon, who told the famished people that they might eat grass, and who died, and went to Hell?' . . . . 'He is among us' . . . . ' . . . he caused himself to be represented as dead, and had a grand mock-funeral. But they have found him alive, hiding in the country, and have brought him in. I have seen him . . . on his way to the Hôtel de Ville . . . .'
Wretched old sinner of more than threescore years and ten . . . (212)

This Foulon was at the Hôtel de Ville, and might be loosed. Never, if Saint Antoine knew his own sufferings . . . .They were all by that time choking the Hall of Examination where this old man, ugly and wicked, was, and overflowing into the adjacent open space and streets.

'See!' cried madame, pointing with her knife. 'See the old villain bound with ropes. That was well done to tie a bunch of grass upon his back. Ha, ha! . . . let him eat it now!' Madame put her knife under her arm, and clapped her hands as at a play. (213)

The people immediately behind Madame Defarge, explaining the cause of her satisfaction to those behind them, and those again

We are but at the 22d of the month, hardly above a week since the Bastille fell, when it suddenly appears that old Foulon is alive; nay, that he is here, in early morning, in the streets of Paris: the extortioner, the plotter, who would make the people eat grass . . . The deceptive 'sumptuous funeral' (of some domestic that died); the hiding place at Vitry towards Fontainebleau, have not availed that wretched old man . . . . Merciless boors of Vitry unearth him; pounce on him, like hell-hounds: Westward, old Infamy; to Paris, to be judged at the Hôtel-de-Ville! His old head, which seventy-four years have bleached, is bare . . . (I, 199)

Sooty Saint-Antoine, and every street, musters its crowds as he passes;—the Hall of the Hôtel-de-Ville, the Place de Grève itself, will scarcely hold his escort and him. Foulon must . . . be judged . . . without any delay . . . . Delay, and still Delay! (I, 199-200)

. . . they have tied an emblematic bundle of grass on his back . . . in this manner; led with ropes; goaded on with curses and menaces, must he, with his old limbs, sprawl forward; the pitiablest, most unpitied of all old men. (I, 199)

Ought not the truth to be cunningly pumped out of him,—in the Abbaye Prison? It is a new light! Sansculottism claps hands;

A Tale of Two Cities	*The French Revolution*
explaining to others, and those to others, the neighbouring streets resounded with the clapping of hands . . . (213)	—at which hand-clapping, Foulon . . . also claps. 'See! they understand one another!' cries dark Sansculottism, blazing into fury of suspicion . (I, 200)
At length the sun rose so high that it struck a kindly ray as of hope or protection, directly down upon the old prisoner's head. (214)	
The favour was too much to bear; in an instant . . . Saint-Antoine had got him! . . . Defarge . . . folded the miserable wretch in a deadly embrace . . . the cry seemed to go up, all over the city, 'Bring him out! Bring him to the lamp!'	With wild yells, Sansculottism clutches him, in its hundred hands: he is whirled across the Place de Grève, to the '*Lanterne*', Lamp-iron which there is at the corner of the Rue de la Vannerie; pleading bitterly for life,— to the deaf winds. (I, 200)
Down, and up, and head foremost . . . stifled by the bunches of grass and straw that were thrust into his face by hundreds of hands; torn, bruised, panting, bleeding, yet always entreating and beseeching for mercy; now full of vehement agony of action, with a small clear space about him as the people drew one another back that they might see; now, a log of dead wood drawn through a forest of legs; he was hauled to the nearest street corner where one of the fatal lamps swung . . . Once, he went aloft, and the rope broke, and they caught him shrieking; twice, he went aloft, and the rope broke, and they caught him shrieking; then, the rope was merciful, and held him, and his head was soon upon a pike, with grass enough in the mouth for all Saint Antoine to dance at the sight of. (214)	Only with the third rope—for two ropes broke, and the quavering voice still pleaded—can he be so much as got hanged! His Body is dragged through the streets; his Head goes aloft on a pike, the mouth filled with grass: amid sounds as of Tophet, from a grass-eating people. (I, 200)

BERTHIER

Nor was this the end of the day's bad work, for Saint-Antoine so shouted and danced his angry blood up, that it boiled again, on hearing when the day closed in that the son-in-law of the despatched, another of the people's enemies and insulters, was coming into Paris under a guard five hundred strong, in cavalry alone.   Saint-Antoine wrote his crimes on flaring sheets of paper, seized him—would have torn him out of the breast of an army to bear Foulon company— set his head and heart on pikes, and carried the three spoils of the day, in Wolf-procession, through the streets. (215)

Berthier . . . sycophant and tyrant . . . is he not Foulon's son-in-law; and, in that one point, guilty of all? . . . . At the fall of day, the wretched Berthier . . . arrives at the Barrier; in an open carriage; with the Municipal beside him; five hundred horsemen with drawn sabres; unarmed footmen enough . . . Placards go brandished round him; bearing legibly his indictment, as Sanscullotism, with unlegal brevity, 'in huge letters', draws it up. [Berthier is taken to the Hôtel-de-Ville for questioning; refuses to answer questions, demands sleep. He leaves the Hôtel-de-Ville under guard, for the Abbaye prison.] At the very door of the Hôtel-de-Ville, they are clutched; flung asunder, as by a vortex of mad arms; Berthier whirls to-wards the Lanterne . . . he is borne down, trampled, hanged, mangled: his Head too, and even his Heart, flies over the City on a pike. (I, 201)

The chapters that follow in *A Tale of Two Cities* are by their nature much less intimately related to the text of *The French Revolution*. The 'historical' material now reverts to its role as a kind of shaping and informing background to the plot that Dickens has evidently worked out with some care. Obviously fact and fiction cannot be separated: the principal plot owes its first impulse to a clearly identifiable historical source which is vitally linked with scenes in the *Tale* which approach nearer to being a non-fictional account of actual events than anything in the novel. One can, nevertheless, see a continuing rela-tionship with the text of *The French Revolution*, though there is a blurring of focus until Book III; Dickens no longer bases his details so closely on those of Carlyle. At the beginning of Book II, Chapter xxiii, for example, Dickens describes the poverty of the countryside: 'Far and wide lay a ruined country, yielding nothing but desolation. Every green leaf, every blade of grass and blade of grain, was as shrivelled and poor as the miserable people . . . . Habitations, fences, domesticated animals, men, women, children, and the soil that bore them—all worn out'.[1]   In the corresponding passage in *The French Revolution*, however, Carlyle points out that at this time the harvest was good, but that for various reasons, food was not being sold or distributed; this was the cause of the continuing starvation: 'Heaven has at length sent an abundant harvest: but what profits it the poor man, when Earth with her formulas interposes?'[2]   But Dickens continues to be nourished in his imagery and local situations by Carlyle's heightened visions.   The chapter in the *Tale* which describes the arrival of a 'Jacques', whose mission is to set on fire the château of the Evrémondes, seems to owe a good deal to Carlyle's description of 'the general over-turn'.   The mysterious incendiary according to Dickens, is a 'rough figure . . . . a shaggy-haired man, of almost barbarian aspect, tall, in wooden shoes that were clumsy even to the eyes of a mender of roads, grim, rough, swart . . .'[3]   He is obviously one of Carlyle's imagined horde, who sprung up over the whole country to fire the aristocrats' châteaux:

> Fancy, then, some Five full-grown Millions of such gaunt figures, with their haggard faces . . . in woollen jupes, with copper-studded leather girths, and high sabots, starting up to ask, as in forest-roarings . . . this question: How have ye treated us; how have ye taught us, fed us and led us, while we toiled for you? The answer can be read in flames, over the nightly summer-sky. *This* is the feeding and leading we have had of you: EMPTINESS,—of pocket, of stomach, of head and of heart.[4]

Dickens points out the hunger of his 'rough figure' and of the road-mender.   Other details from Carlyle's account, after a sea-change, reappear in the *Tale*.   Among those who must now be wary, says Carlyle, is the tax-gatherer who, 'long hunting as a biped of prey, may now find himself hunted as one . . .'[5]   One of the taxes that have oppressed the people, Carlyle has already told us, is the *Gabelle*,[6] or salt tax.   Hence the appearance of Gabelle, the unjustly accused agent of Darnay, an important (if slightly creaking) mechanism for the future movement of the plot.

Until our next immersion in revolutionary horrors, Carlyle's contribution to the *Tale*'s progress is of this indirect kind.   Gabelle's subsequent arrest leads to the plot sequence culminating in Darnay's arrest and trial, an episode which takes place against the background of the September Massacres, the second period in Dickens's narrative which demands, not simply an atmospheric background picture of events that were likely to happen over a fairly undefined period—the

1   *TTC*, 216.
2   *FR*, I, 217.
3   *TTC*, 217.
4   *FR*, I, 219.
5   *Ibid.*, 220.
6   *Ibid.*, 14, 79.

firing of châteaux, the persecution of tax collectors and other aristocratic agents, the airy boasting and fruitless plans of the emigrés—
but actual notorious events that happened during a short and clearly
defined period.

Dickens's account of the September Massacres corresponds in many
details with Carlyle's. A notable Dickensian stage-prop,[1] the grindstone which gives its name to Book III, Chapter ii, may have been
suggested by a sentence from Carlyle's relation of the gruesome
events of September 1792: 'Man after man is cut down; *the sabres
need sharpening*, the killers refresh themselves from wine-jugs'.[2]
Dickens once more plunges himself into the scandalised description
of actual events and established both his knowledge of them and his
characters' involvement in them by his use of details. The house of
'Monseigneur' is confiscated on 3 September,[3] Carlyle makes it clear
that the massacres lasted from 2 September until 6 September and
stresses the length of time that they covered: ' "O everlasting infamy",
exclaims Mongaillard, "that Paris stood looking on in stupor for

---

[1] Carlyle seems to have been an important source for such 'stage-props'. As I have
pointed out he supplied the forty-foot high gallows (see p. 65 above); and he very
probably suggested the grindstone that appears here. He also supplied, almost
certainly I think, an even more vital item of stage machinery. We have already
discussed Dickens's use of Dr. Manette's document, the Carlylean derivation of
which is not in doubt. The document itself, which, of course, is the evidence that
finally condemns Darnay to the guillotine, is discovered in Manette's cell where
it is secreted 'in the wall of the chimney, where I have slowly and laboriously made
a place of concealment for it'. (*TTC*, 303.) The evidence which finally
condemned Louis XVI was a collection of secret letters which were hidden in a
wall by Louis and a locksmith who, says Carlyle, 'fabricated an "Iron Press, *Armoire
de Fer*", cunningly inserting the same in a wall of the royal chamber in the Tuil-
leries; invisible under the wainscot . . .'; the locksmith, 'attended by the proper
Authorities . . . discloses the Iron Press—full of Letters and Papers! Roland clutches
them out; conveys them . . . to the fit assiduous Committee, which sits hard by'.
(*FR*, II, 241.)
  The association between Louis and the locksmith, one Gamain, is an interesting
one for us. Perhaps the most brilliant part of Dickens's depiction of the deep-rooted
neurosis implanted in Manette by his imprisonment, is in his use of the 'stage prop'
which conveys to us that he is regressing to his former state. The obsessional activity
that has been Manette's refuge during the long years in the Bastille is that of a shoe-
maker; when Manette receives a severe emotional shock long after his release, he
returns to his last as if his release had never taken place. This is very reminiscent
of a story in Mercier, about an old man who, on his release from the Bastille,
re-creates in a small room the conditions of his cell. But the use of an obsessional
activity as an escape from painful realities may well have grown from a germ in
The French Revolution. Louis XVI, as the situation around him grew more and
more complex and beyond his grasp, would often disappear and, in seclusion from
the world, lose himself in the pretence that he was a locksmith. Louis learned his
trade from the locksmith Gamain, who, as Carlyle tells us, finally betrayed his
hiding place for secret documents. (*FR*, II, 240.) The combination of the idea
of documents hidden in a wall with that of an activity giving release from the
world is present in both cases, and is, surely, unusual enough to justify an assumption
that either Carlyle or (very much less probably) some other writer on the French
Revolution is supplying Dickens's material here.
[2] My emphasis, *FR*, II, 183.
[3] *TTC*, 245.

four days, and did not interfere!" '[1]   When Dr. Manette goes out to
ensure that his son-in-law is not a victim of the 'Septembriseurs', he
is absent for exactly this period: 'Doctor Manette did not return until
the morning of the fourth day of his absence'.[2]   Another detail from
The French Revolution follows: Lucie Manette learns only later that
'eleven hundred defenceless prisoners . . . had been killed by the
populace; that four days and nights had been darkened by this deed
of horror; and that the air around her had been tainted by the slain'.[3]
After discussing various figures, Carlyle accepts the assessment of
Maton de la Varenne, that 'not less than' 'a thousand and eighty-nine'
prisoners were slaughtered.[4]   Dickens's description of the 'trial' and
probable subsequent massacre of the prisoners of La Force[5] (one of the
jails mentioned by Carlyle) corresponds roughly with Carlyle's account,
but is less detailed. Dr. Manette presents himself before the tribunal,
and 'ascertained, through the registers on the table, that his son-in-law
was among the living prisoners'. 'So sit these sudden Courts of Wild
Justice', recounts Carlyle, 'with the Prison-Registers before them . . .'[6]
'The mad joy over the prisoners who were saved' that astounds
Manette 'scarcely less than the mad ferocity against those who were
cut to pieces'[7] corresponds with Carlyle's description of the formula
by which the crowd knew whether or not to massacre someone
emerging from the prison gates: 'A few questions are put; swiftly
this sudden Jury decides: Royalist Plotter or not? Clearly not: in
that case, let the Prisoner be enlarged with *Vive la Nation*. Probably
yea; then still, Let the Prisoner be enlarged, but without *Vive la
Nation* . . . Volunteer Bailiffs seize the doomed man; he is . . . "enlarged"
. . . into a howling sea . . .'[8] This passage might also have been suggested by Carlyle's account of the trial and release of Jourgniac St
Meard. On his release, Carlyle recounts, ' . . . there arose *vivats*
within doors and without: "escort of three", amid shoutings and
embracings: thus Jourgniac escaped from jury-trial and the jaws of
death'.[9]

Darnay is saved from death in the September Massacres, but Manette
finds it impossible to achieve his trial or his release. Time passes, and
Dickens produces a few facts to suggest the historical background.
The King's trial and beheading, the black flag waving from Notre
Dame, the raising of a national army of three hundred thousand men,
the beheading of Marie Antoinette. All these details appear, widely

[1] *FR*, II, 193.
[2] *TTC*, 256.
[3] *Ibid*.
[4] *FR*, II, 194.
[5] *TTC*, 256.
[6] *FR*, II, 182.
[7] *TTC*, 257.
[8] *FR*, II, 182.
[9] *FR*, II, 191.

scattered, in *The French Revolution*,[1] but could have come equally
well from Thiers or from any other history. A closer parallel is
Dickens's 'revolutionary tribunal in the capital, and forty or fifty
thousand revolutionary committees all over the land . . .'[2] with
Carlyle's '*Tribunal Révolutionnaire*', together with his '*Comités Révolu-
tionnaires* . . . some forty-four thousand of them awake and alive over
France . . .'[3] Dickens's nasty jokes about the guillotine[4] are very
reminiscent of Carlyle's comments on the execution of nineteen
Hébertistes:

> They too 'must look through the little window'; they too 'must sneeze into
> the sack' . . . *Sainte-Guillotine*, meseems, is worse than the old Saints of
> Superstition; a man-devouring Saint?[5]

Dickens's references to the 'twenty-two' Girondistes (a figure which
later reappears as the number of those executed before Carton) and
to the name of the executioner Samson (the *Tale*'s 'strong man of
Old Scripture'[6]) are both paralleled in *The French Revolution*[7] as is
that to 'the rivers of the South . . . encumbered with the bodies of
the violently drowned by night, and prisoners . . . shot in lines and
squares under the southern wintry sun'.[8] There is nothing in Dickens's
use of these details that enables us to attribute them with complete
certainty to his reading of *The French Revolution* but one episode which
does seem certain to have Carlyle as its source is that of Darnay's
release, 'one of those extraordinary scenes with which the populace
sometimes gratified their fickleness, or their better impulses towards
generosity and mercy . . .'[9] This reminds us of the fickleness of the
crowds of the September Massacres, and the scene of Darnay's release
is very reminiscent of Carlyle's description of Marat's triumphal
progress after a similar ordeal. Dickens's crowd, as Carlyle's, is 'like
a sea', recalling his own, and Carlyle's, descriptions of the storming
of the Bastille, and it behaves very like Marat's acclaiming mob:

---

1 *FR*, II, 218–64, 282, 284.
2 *TTC*, 259.
3 *FR*, II, 289.
4 *TTC*, 260.
5 *FR*, II, 395.
6 *TTC*, 260.
7 *FR*, II, 261.
8 *FR*, II, 358–67; *TTC*, 260.
9 *TTC*, 271.

They put him into a great chair they had among them . . . Over the chair they had thrown a red flag, and to the back of it they had bound a pike with a red cap on its top. In this car of triumph . . . [he was] carried . . . on men's shoulders, with a confused sea of red caps heaving about him . . . In wild dreamlike procession, embracing whom they met and pointing him out, they carried him on. (272)

And so the eye of History beholds Patriotism . . . break into loud jubilee, embrace its Marat; lift him into a chair of triumph, bear him shoulder-high through the streets. Shoulder-high is the injured People's-Friend . . . amid the wavy sea of red nightcaps, carmagnole jackets, grenadier bonnets and female mob-caps; far-sounding like a sea! (II, 300)

Although the correspondence of such passages and of many details confirms the heavy debt that Dickens owed to Carlyle, a slight complication should be registered here. According to Dickens, Carlyle lent him 'two cartloads' of books from the London Library, which Dickens claimed to have read.[1] Some of Carlyle's own sources, therefore, were available to him. It is difficult to determine how much Dickens derived from them. It we compare, for instance, the storming of the Bastille with the four sources that Carlyle gives for this episode (though there may be more), we can make several points. Firstly, that copies of all of these sources were possessed by the London Library in 1859; they were therefore quite probably among the 'two cartloads'. Nevertheless, it seems fairly clear that Carlyle is a more likely source for Dickens than any of them. Only one of these sources[2] gives a consecutive account of the day's events, and this contains much less information than Carlyle's, or even Dickens's, version, and clearly has little or no literary relationship with either text. This account, like the other three,[3] is unexciting, and they all seem very unlikely to have caught Dickens's attention as strongly as Carlyle's narrative. Furthermore, compared with Carlyle's evocation of these events, not only is the effect of these exciting events as related by these eye-witnesses diffuse and lack-lustre; it is also very noticeable, by contrast, that each writer is too close to his own part in the day's events to give anything like a total picture, or even sense the volcanic energy of the process unleashing itself. This seems to be Carlyle's contribution. Dickens later marvelled at Carlyle's ability to produce such a 'compact result' from such dull and uninspired accounts. This is perhaps the most telling point: it is Carlyle's particular assemblage

---

[1]   *Letters*, III, 97.

[2]   *Histoire Parlementaire*, ed. Buchez, P. et Roux, P., Paris, 1834–8, II, 102–3.

[3]   *Mémoires du Baron de Besenval*, ed. Berville, S. A. et Barrière, J., Bruxelles, 1823, III, 295–300.

   Mémoires de Bailly, ed. Berville et Barrière, Paris, 1821, 18.

   Mémoires de Linguet et de Dusaulx, ed. Berville et Barrière, Paris, 1821, 292–307.

of the confused events of 14 July that Dickens is following here. Dickens, could, for instance, have got the letter which is the source for the final paragraph of Dr. Manette's document, from Carlyle's own source[1] a copy of which was in the London Library. But to find it, Dickens would have had to wade through an appendix of only marginally related material. In *The French Revolution* he found it (in English—Dickens's command of French was not perfect) as a vital and exciting part of the day's action, set in a sequence of events that he himself was, more or less, to follow. Dickens mentions Carlyle's sources only to exclaim at their dryness, and to wonder at Carlyle's genius in producing such a result from such material.

Here, if we are looking for one, is the great link between the *Tale* and its predecessor, *Hard Times*. Dickens, as he put it himself, 'always found himself turning away from the books of reference and re-reading this marvellous new growth from those dry bones with renewed wonder';[2] *The French Revolution* is, above all, a supreme triumph of the Romantic Imagination over 'Hard Facts'. Carlyle's history, for Dickens, was 'the book which always appeared more imaginative in proportion to the fresh imagination he brings to it, a book to be placed for inexhaustiveness before every other book'. The quality of the 'imagination' involved here was, as I have suggested in an earlier chapter, at the root of Carlyle's unique status as a prophetic figure, as a 'man of intuition' who, as Mill confessed, 'saw many things long before me, which I could only when they were pointed out to me, hobble after and prove'.[3] It was Carlyle's imaginative power that provided the driving force behind his great attack on rationalism, and on the associated decline in belief: his romantic insight was seen by the Victorians as being inseparable from his capacity for inspiring 'manliness', for raising 'the moral tone of the age'. Carton and—above all—Harthouse, suggest, I think, how sensitive Dickens was to this facet of Carlyle's influence over his contemporaries. Like almost everyone else, as I now hope to show, Dickens turned to Carlyle for more than pronouncements on social issues, or an exciting and highly coloured prose style.

---

[1] Linguet et Dusaulx, *op. cit.*
[2] De Wolef Howe, 191.
[3] See p. 9 above.

Part III

G

Part III

CHAPTER SIX

Devotion and Belief

'I CANNOT fix my mind', says Sir John Chester, 'for any long period upon one subject'.[1] Chester is the first of a long list of languid, upper-class characters in Dickens's novels, all of whom have one obvious trait in common. Eugene Wrayburn has precisely Chester's problem, though with an added dimension:

> Now, I have been inclined to pursue such a subject; now, I have felt that it was absurd, and that it tired and embarrassed me. Absolutely, I can't say. Frankly and faithfully, I would if I could. . . . You know that when I became enough of a man to find myself an embodied conundrum, I bored myself to the last degree by trying to find out what I meant.[2]

This, in turn, recalls Harthouse, whose clear identity as a Carlylean Dilettante establishes an important analogy, between the meaning for Dickens of these characters, and that of Carlyle's philosophy:

> . . . whither *he* tended, he neither considered nor cared. He had no particular design or plan before him; no energetic wickedness ruffled his lassitude. He was as much amused and interested, at present, as it became so fine a gentleman to be . . .[3]

There are, perhaps, two lists to draw up: characters who belong strictly to the type, and those who belong to it through one or more traits, but are disqualified for other reasons. The first list is obvious enough: Chester himself; James Harthouse; Henry Gowan; Sidney Carton; and Eugene Wrayburn. For the second, among

---

[1] *BR*, 117.
[2] *OMF*, 286.
[3] *HT*, 127.

Dickens's more important characters, we can suggest Arthur Clennam for lack of purpose but not for indifference, and (very different) Steerforth for upper-class self-assurance and lack of fixed purpose, but not for languor. Unlike the inspirational virgins of the complementary Dickensian tradition, most of the members of this one are both interesting in themselves and important to the books in which they appear. We can also say that they had an important personal meaning for Dickens himself, and an only slightly different one for his Victorian readership.

The meaning of these characters for Dickens's first readers can be discussed in terms to which Carlyle is clearly relevant. Both Dickens and Carlyle believed in the gospel of work, and the delineation of his anti-heroes shows Dickens preaching it. Arthur Clennam, despite his obvious dissimilarities with Harthouse and the rest, has a peripheral association with the tradition, but with the inspiration of Little Dorrit, shakes himself free of it completely. The sunshine in which they both stride, at the end of their story, into 'a modest life of usefulness and happiness . . .'[1] illuminates one Victorian ideal, which both Dickens and Carlyle, in their different ways, helped to strengthen. This is obviously more Dickensian than Carlylean: but the weight attached to the word 'usefulness' here has 'been increased by Arthur's steady and idealised work for Clennam and Doyce. Of course, there is an important distinction: it is precisely the unbending rigour of such stern biblical exhortations as Carlyle's obsessive 'Work while it is called To-day; for the Night cometh, wherein no man can work',[2] that (until Little Dorrit reclaims him) has rendered Arthur unfit for sustained effort. Arthur is a victim of the unbending Hebraic strain in nineteenth-century Christianity, of which Carlyle himself was a product and to some extent a vehicle. Nevertheless, Dickens's anti-heroes and Carlyle's dilettantes both nourished the same popular tradition: how closely they antithesised the same ideal can be seen by the ease with which the Dickens stereotype is adapted, in *Hard Times*, to a more precisely Carlylean idiom. Neither Wrayburn at one end of the line, nor Chester at the other, have any strictly Carlylean overtones at all, demonstrating, perhaps, that these characters, even when Carlyle is relevant to their meaning in context, have an independent life for Dickens himself.

The heroines to be found in nearly all the novels fulfil an obviously complementary role, isolated most neatly by the relationship of Sidney Carton and Lucie Darnay. The Dickensian heroine represents most obviously the inspiration of energy and purpose; she steadies the uncertainty stemming from the hero's lack of a fixed centre of belief,

---

[1] *LD*, 826.
[2] *SR*, 149.

and leads him to higher things. To the ennobling influence of Agnes, David Copperfield owes all that he has become:

> She filled my heart with such good resolutions, strengthened my weakness so, by her example, so directed—I know not how, she was too modest and gentle to advise me in many words—the wandering ardour and un-settled purpose within me, that all the little good I have done, and all the harm I have forborne, I solemnly believe I may refer to her.[1]

The phrase 'wandering ardour and unsettled purpose within me' emphasises another aspect of this theme for Dickens himself. The langour of his dilettante figures may partly refer to members of his family;[2] their restlessness reflects his own. The recurrence of Dickens's virginal heroines, though it should obviously enough be discussed in terms of literary convention, must also be explained by his own increasing loneliness and uncertainty. The overwhelming effect of the death of Mary Hogarth lasted for many years; these heroines, without any doubt, represent much of what he felt she had embodied.

Dickens's restlessness is hard to explain, perhaps most obviously because he could not explain it himself. But as for many others, before and since, one answer was clear: he needed the right woman. 'Why is it', he wrote to Forster in 1854, 'that as with poor David, a sense comes always crushing on me now, when I fall into low spirits, as of one happiness I have missed in life, and one friend and com-panion I have never made?'[3] The kind of woman he idealised in his novels (as many writers have suggested) makes it clear enough that, for him, a woman was to be just as much an object of veneration, a rock to cling to in an uncertain world, as a creature of flesh and blood. Dickens's heroines, in the novels at least, up to 1859, mirror exactly one Victorian ideal, an ideal which was—for instance— summed up with appalling clarity in the Rev. James Baldwin Brown's *Home Life* (1866): 'At home for a man', wrote Mr. Brown, 'ought to mean, shut up awhile with truth, purity, dignity, goodness, and charity, zoned with a cestus of beauty, and dressed in a lustre of love'.[4]

In a way, a certain kind of Victorian woman performed a more delicate, but nevertheless (despite obvious reservations) an analogous function to that fulfilled for his age by Carlyle himself; she provided a substitute, or an accessory, for religion; certainty (or its illusion) in an uncertain world; the embodiment of moral stability. This ideal of womanhood, and the popular reaction to the Sage have in common their quasi-religious framework of reference; and Carlyle's most basic tenet is the need of every human being to feel *reverence*: the Victorian

---

[1] *DC*, 519.
[2] See Collins, *Education*, 50.
[3] Forster, 639.
[4] Brown, J. B., *The Home Life*, London, 1866, 19-20.

impulse to tranfigure their women as objects of this instinct can, I am sure, be usefully pointed out when we try to understand Carlyle's influence over his times. Both the teachings of the prophet of Chelsea, and the ideal of womanhood of the age that embraced him as its greatest spiritual leader, owed their potency to something like the same cause: the inability of the Victorian era to evolve a stable corporate ideal, that could fulfil the same function as the Church had done for previous generations, and to which private as well as public uncertainties could be referred.

The analogy becomes more clearly justified if we consider the relevance, both of Carlyle's teaching and of the Victorian ideal of woman, to the ethic of nineteenth-century imperialism. Carlyle's importance here scarcely requires demonstration. 'He has raised the moral tone of the age, and awakened a noble spirit of strength and courage in the young'; his is 'the voice of the trumpet'. How readily this kind of sentiment could be grafted on to the general feeling about the 'truth, purity, dignity, goodness and charity', of womankind can be conveniently observed in the hysterical public reaction evoked by the events of the Indian mutiny. Dickens himself reflected faithfully the general feeling[1] and, in collaboration with Wilkie Collins, wrote a Christmas story entitled *The Perils of Certain English Prisoners*, the aim of which was, as he wrote to Morley, 'to shadow out, in what I do the bravery of our ladies in India'.[2] English women in India earned the worship of their countrymen at home for two reasons; their martyrdom and allegedly violated purity, and their unstinting courage in the face of the enemy, as they joined in the fighting like the men. In the reports that appeared in the papers, British womankind seems to be the object of two distinct kinds of hero-worship, which somehow merge: for the stained-glass madonna, inspiring men by their higher natures, and at the same time, for the heroine of action, who joined in and fought with the men. Like Florence Nightingale in the Crimea, they are both idealised and down to earth. In the *Perils*, two ladies (one of them Dickens's heroine, Marion Maryon) help with the loading of rifles:

> Steady and busy behind where I stood, those two beautiful and delicate young women fell to handling the guns, hammering the flints, looking to the locks, and quietly directing others to pass up powder and bullets from hand to hand, as unflinching as the best of tried soldiers.[3]

Miss Maryon is a heroine of action; she is also as pure and inviolable as Agnes Wickfield herself. Before battle is joined, she makes Gill Davis swear solemnly to kill her rather than allow her to be taken by

---

[1] See my 'Dickens and the Indian Mutiny', *Dickensian*, LXVIII (1972), 3-15.
[2] *Letters*, II, 894.
[3] *PCEP*, 186.

the pirates. 'If you cannot save me from the Pirates, living', she pleads, 'you will save me, dead. Tell me so'.[1] For the rest of the story, Davis devotes himself totally to the idea of her protection. Like Richard Wardour before, and Sidney Carton after him, Gill Davis is redeemed (from a dimly hinted future degeneration) by the love of a shining, unattainable lady. Like Lucie Manette, Marion Maryon is conscious of her role. She gives Gill Davis a ring as reward for his devotion:

> The brave gentlemen of old—but not one of them was braver, or had a nobler nature than you—took such gifts from ladies, and did all their good actions for the givers' sakes. If you will do yours for mine, I shall think with pride that I continue to have some share in the life of a gallant and generous man.[2]

And Gill keeps the memory of her injunction sacred: 'I thought of her last words to me . . . and I never disgraced them. If it had not been for those dear words, I think I should have lost myself in despair and recklessness'.[3]

Davis himself, in part at least, clearly represents Dickens (part of his childhood is spent 'betwixt Chatham and Maidstone;'[4] he is a foundling child who, like Pip, cannot aspire to the hand of his beloved because of his humble origins) and what Marion Maryon represents here has a very clear relevance to Dickens's personal needs, needs which, surely, we can hardly avoid describing as being in some broad sense religious or quasi-religious in character. It is a critical common-place (justified enough) to point out the sentimental prettiness and apparent lack of conviction of 'religious' passages in his novels, and 'What the waves are always saying' in *Dombey and Son*, and 'the star that guided us to our Saviour's home' on which Stephen Blackpool gazes while he is dying in the Old Hell Shaft, are certainly unhappy attempts at conveying transcendent or religious feelings. But senti-mentality and literary failure do not necessarily rule out Dickens's total sincerity, as Stephen Blackpool perhaps indicates. It can, of course, be argued that, apart from its sentimentality, Dickens's religious feeling was both inconsistent and cut off from tradition. Yet, as Professor Fielding points out, 'this would never have been recognised by Dickens himself; it is strongly contradicted by the experience of many who read him; and though it may be that there is sometimes a certain technical superficiality in his art as a novelist in expressing his faith, it is evident that he came to have a deeper concern with the spiritual view of life than many of his more critical readers allow'.[5]

---

[1] *Ibid.*, 185.
[2] *Ibid.*, 206.
[3] *Ibid.*, 207.
[4] *Ibid.*
[5] Fielding, K. J., 'Dickens's Novels and the Discovery of the Soul', *Aryan Path*, XXXIII (1962), 210.

Some entries in the notebook he began keeping in the 'fifties seem to reflect a personal predicament which, though not religious in itself, must, I think, be related to his religious and quasi-religious impulses: he saw himself as

> . . . playing hide-and-seek with the world and never finding what Fortune seems to have hidden when he was born . . .

and as

> . . . the man who is incapable of his own happiness. Result, where is happiness to be found then. Surely not everywhere? . . . Is *this* my experience?[1]

WOMEN
SUPPLY A
NEED FOR
SOMETHING

It is this kind of uncertainty that lies behind his fascination, especially during the 'fifties, with restless characters like Harthouse, and during his whole career up to 1859, with their obverse, represented most clearly by characters like Agnes who, though totally unsatisfactory as women, reveal through their total blankness, more poignantly than anything else could, Dickens's need to fulfil somehow his 'sad unhappy lack or want of something'. The 'something' remains undefined, only half-understood, and the total non-personality of Agnes herself corresponds perfectly with this lack of definition. Her image remains insubstantial but glowing with promise, imagined against the 'tranquil brightness' of 'a stained-glass window in a church'.[2] 'David has that relation to Agnes', thinks Professor Hillis Miller, 'which a devout Christian has to God, the creator of his selfhood, without whom he would be nothing'.[3] Agnes herself (let alone David) is surely not substantial enough to justify this; what we *can* say, though, is that Agnes certainly represents David's (and Dickens's) *need* to define this 'selfhood', if not the real conviction of its attainment.

This need, I tentatively suggest, provides a partial answer to an important question. Why, we have to ask, *should* Dickens have been susceptible to Carlyle's influence in the first place? What did Carlyle supply that Dickens needed? In a way, this is the most vital question of all. On its answer must partly depend the weight we give to Carlyle's influence among all the many others that crowded in on his consciousness, both private and social. Dickens's response to Carlyle is, I think, a complex phenomenon, and it would be naïf to single out any one reason for it more than others. Nevertheless, one partial explanation, I think, may well have something to do with Dickens's uncertainty about himself, about his 'selfhood'. Carlyle, beyond any doubt, was a vague but very powerful influence over many sensitive people who, for a wide variety of reasons, felt unsure about life and about themselves. In 1855, the reviewer of a selection of Carlyle's

---

[1] See *Ibid.*, 211.
[2] *DC*, 223.
[3] Hillis Miller, J., *Charles Dickens: The World of his Novels*, London, 1959, 157.

works scornfully gave a splendid list of various classes of reader to
whom he thought the Sage most appealed. 'The influence of Mr.
Carlyle's writings', he thought, 'and especially of his *Sartor Resartus*,
has been primarily exerted on classes of men most exposed to temptations of egotism and petulance, and least subjected to anything above
them—academics, artists, litératteurs, "debating" youths, Scotchmen
of the phrenological grade and Irishmen of the Young Ireland
School'.   Carlyle appealed to the general doubts of his age, and to the
individual uncertainties of each of his readers. He gained his influence
in what Bulwer Lytton, for instance, called 'an age of visible transition
—an age of disquietude and doubt',[1] to which his message was entirely
appropriate. And his influence, as the list I have just quoted amusingly
suggests, was obviously more powerful for those who were sensitive
to this facet of the period. Certainly, this general 'disquietude' found
an approximate analogue in one aspect of Dickens's situation. Despite
his enormous vitality and joyous sense of fun (which, despite the strong
temptations, must never be lost sight of) he was, at the same time, often
confused and intensely depressed.   And what was involved in this
feeling—one clear expression of which is the 'old unhappy loss or
want of something' that David Copperfield complains of before his
marriage to Agnes[2]—also helps to explain, I think, why Carlyle,
more than anyone else, should have come to exert such an influence
over him.

    The theory, it may be thought, is a crude one to explain such a
phenomenon as the influence of one complex genius over another,
and, it cannot be over-emphasised, certainly covers only part of the
relevant ground. My suggestion is that Dickens was often lonely and
confused, and badly needed a girl (this is beyond dispute); and that
until he had found one and broken the imprisonment of his marriage,
Carlyle's personal prophetic aura made a stronger appeal than it
would normally have done. The inappropriateness of such a substitute
seems the most obvious objection to this. But the tendency of unhappy
people to espouse, in one way or another, some particular 'philosophy
of life' (especially one which offers firm moral authority) in an
unconscious attempt to solve their personal problems, is obvious
enough and widely observable. Part of Dickens's emotional life can
certainly be discussed in these terms, despite his undimmed capacity
for enjoyment and laughter. A signpost to the relationship between
Carlyle's influence on Dickens, and the novelist's private life can, I
think, be found in the characterisation of Stephen Blackpool. Stephen,
I have noted, provides the most unmistakeably Carlylean formulation
in all Dickens's works; and he is, at the same time, a very interesting
example of the obtrusion into Dickens's fictions of his own life. He

    [1] Lytton, E. B., *England and the English*, London, 1874, 281.
    [2] *DC*, 646.

represents not only the Carlylean worker, hungry for just authoritarian government, and release from social isolation and 'mechanism'; he personifies also Dickens himself, longing for a divorce from his wife, and a woman with whom to replace her.   Stephen's obsessive refrain, 'It's aw' a muddle', refers indiscriminately to both rôles. This combination of meanings in one character is, perhaps, curious enough to attract our attention; and Stephen, as I have already asserted, was very much more important for Dickens and to *Hard Times* as a whole than he has seemed to modern critics.   Certainly, he gives a revealing glimpse of one important layer of feeling in Dickens's life when he wrote *Hard Times*. Carlyle provided, I suggest, exactly what someone with such problems as Dickens had to face might respond to; an absence of specifics; vague but powerfully uplifting suggestions which could be ignored if they didn't fit, or subtly altered to reflect the personality of the wearer; and at the same time and above all, the appearance of solidity, of unshakeable moral authority. Carlyle's was the philosophy for those who doubted, and needed a rock, or even a straw, to cling to; precisely what the 'doubt' referred to was not necessarily important. It was enough to have, in some aspect of one's life, 'nothing to steer by but the stars'.   Carlyle's defiance of 'The Everlasting No' could appeal equally to someone who (like Teufelsdröckh) had lost his girl and was nursing a broken heart, or to someone bewildered (perhaps simultaneously) by loss or lack of faith, or, again, to someone simply disoriented by the inhumanity and growing practical influence of modern rationalism, and by the pressures of modern life. And Teufelsdröckh's famous assertion of himself epitomises, not simply the appeal of *Sartor* itself, but also much of the influence of Carlyle's whole *oeuvre*. Teufelsdröckh's defiance can be seen as an amazingly flexible statement. It deals simultaneously, it will be recalled, with the effects of both his personal and his social problems as well as with his relationship with 'The Universe'; it counteracts Blumine (the faithless object of Teufelsdröckh's love), the effects of Benthamite rationalism, and his lack of a sense of existence, all at the same time. It follows hard upon parts of *Sartor* which I have discussed as having probably relevance to *Hard Times*, and for which I have given documentary evidence of Dickens's knowledge, and it is one of the first and most notable examples in modern civilisation of that vague but potent phenomenon, The Power of Positive Thinking:

> Full of such humor, and perhaps the miserablest man in the whole French Capital or Suburbs, was I, one sultry Dog-day, after much perambulation, toiling along the dirty little *Rue Saint-Thomas de l'Enfer*, among civic rubbish enough, in a close atmosphere, and over pavements hot as Nebuchadnezzar's Furnace; whereby doubtless my spirits were little cheered; when, all at once, there rose a Thought in me, and I asked myself: 'What *art* thou afraid

of? Wherefore, like a coward, dost thou forever pip and whimper, and go cowering and trembling? Despicable biped! what is the sum-total of the worst that lies before thee? Death? Well, Death; and say the pangs of Tophet, too, and all that the Devil and Man may, will or can do against thee! Hast thou not a heart; canst thou not suffer whatsoever it be; and, as a Child of Freedom, though outcast, trample Tophet itself under thy feet, while it consumes thee? Let it come, then; I will meet it and defy it!' And as I so thought, there rushed like a stream of fire over my whole soul; and I shook base Fear away from me forever. I was strong, of unknown strength; a spirit, almost a god. Ever from that time, the temper of my misery was changed: not Fear or whining Sorrow was it, but Indignation and grim fire-eyed Defiance.[1]

The intellectual content, function, and adaptability of this famous passage, despite its lofty tone, are about the same as can be observed in that old war-time favourite 'Pack up your troubles in your old kit bag and smile, smile, smile'. And yet, Carlyle's contemporary effectiveness in encouraging positive attitudes and dissipating uncertainty (though perhaps often only temporarily) cannot be questioned. It is Carlyle's own character and personality (which somehow, indefinably, convey themselves in this passage as in all his works) that give Teufelsdröckh's defiance its authority. Carlyle's message must be judged by its effect on his contemporaries, whose witness is overwhelming: 'he incites the mind of others to action'; he has 'infused into the mind of the English nation . . . sincerity, earnestness, healthfulness and courage': these reactions to Carlyle[2] represent the consensus of a vast section of Victorian opinion. Without any doubt, they mirror exactly those of Dickens himself.

[1] *SR*, 128.
[2] See pp. 15-16 above.

CHAPTER SEVEN

The People: Revolution
and Radicalism

IN 1850, Dickens put into the mouth of a character in a *Household Words* story sentiments he would have liked to be sure were typical of working class feeling:

> I am not a Chartist, and I never was. I don't mean to say but what I see a good many public points to complain of, still I don't think that's the way to set them right. If I did think so, I should be a Chartist. But I don't think so, and I am not a Chartist. I read the paper, and hear discussion, at what we call 'a parlor' in Birmingham, and I know many good men and workmen who are Chartists. Note. Not Physical force.[1]

Dickens, though, was not merely opposed to overtly violent proletarian movements but also, as Stephen Blackpool reminds us, to the more peaceful trades unions, which in the 'fifties were beginning to provide a new and more effective focus for working-class aspirations. Stephen, as Dr. Leavis rightly says, 'invites an adaptation of the objection brought, from the negro point of view, against Uncle Tom, which was to the effect that he was a white man's good nigger'.[2] Again, the appropriate Carlylean work establishes a relevant contrast. 'Is the condition of the working people wrong', asks Carlyle in the opening chapter of *Chartism*, 'so wrong that rational working men cannot, will not and even *should not* rest quiet under it?'[3] Carlyle's answers, to this and to the converse of the same question ('or is the discontent itself mad, like the shape it took? Not the condition of the working people that is wrong; but their disposition, their own thoughts, beliefs and feelings that are wrong?') are clear enough. The

---

[1] [Dickens, C.], 'A Poor Man's Tale of a Patent', *HW*, II (1850), 73.
[2] Leavis, F. R. and Q. D., 205.
[3] *Chartism*, 38. My emphasis.

rebellious behaviour of the masses under oppression is not only the inevitable, but the right and just external sign of their lot. Dickens, we might say, is by nature more in sympathy with 'Moral Force' Chartists like William Lovett, while by contrast Carlyle, the philosopher of 'Rights and Mights'—though of course he held that violence should be avoided if possible—shows himself temperamentally more able to understand the forces that gave their influence to Chartist leaders of the 'Physical Force' party, like Lovett's arch-enemy, O'Connor. Dickens's position was that of many middle-class radicals; as Lovett ruefully complained,

. . . we were fast gathering up the favourable opinion of the Middle, as well as of the Working Classes, when the violent ravings about physical force, by O'Connor, Stephens, and Oastler, scared them from our ranks; they, doubtlessly conceiving that they had better put up with known evils, than trust to an unknown remedy purposed to be effected by such desperate means.[1]

There is little evidence of Dickens's contemporary views on actual Chartist disturbances, though a passage from *The Old Curiosity Shop* must be closely related to his idea of what they were like.[2]   Little Nell and her grandfather have left the peace of the countryside, and wandered into the town. Night has fallen:

. . . night . . . when the people near them looked wilder and more savage; when bands of unemployed labourers paraded the roads, or clustered by torch-light round their leaders, who told them, in stern language, of their wrongs, and urged them on to frightful cries and threats; *when maddened men, armed with sword and firebrand, spurning the tears and prayers of women who would restrain them, rushed forth on errands of terror and destruction, to work no ruin half so surely as their own* . . .[3]

[1] Lovett, 143.
[2] Dickens's short description of a Chartist mob in action is recognisable enough; we can compare the short passage in italics with, for instance, an eye-witness report from the trial of Stephens, who 'condemned the practices in the factories, and advised the people to arm themselves. He told them to get their guns or pikes, and have them over their chimney-pieces . . . When the grand attack was to be made, they were to go to the factories with a dagger in one hand and a torch in the other'. Dickens made two visits to Manchester, an important Chartist centre, at the height of the unrest: once in November 1838, just over a month after the mammoth gathering on Kearsal Moor of 24 September, and during a period of regular highly excited torchlight meetings in the area; and again in January 1839, at a time when, to quote Mark Hovell, 'Magistrates trembled and peaceful citizens felt they were living on the edge of a volcano'. Middle-class opinion in Manchester was certainly extremely disturbed by the autumn meetings and by the general unrest, and Dickens's impressions of what Chartists got up to must date from this period; the torchlight meetings were suppressed not long after his first visit. (*Annual Register*, 1838, Chronicle, 161; Hovell, 136-7; *Chartist Studies*, 45.)
[3] *OCS*, 336. My italics.

The passage I have placed in italics contains the most vivid indication of Dickens's feelings, and it is interesting that this short passage does not appear in the manuscript of the novel, and was added at the proof stage.[1] Dickens took some pains in its composition; there are so many alterations and deletions in this fragment of manuscript that he wrote out a fair copy of it on a separate proof sheet. Perhaps this, combined with the fact that he thought it worthwhile to add this clause at all, may indicate that the whole passage as it stood did not fairly represent his attitude to rebellious workers, and that he wished to add something that would strengthen the paragraph's already implicit condemnation of them; without this fragment Dickens's attitude is not as clear as, perhaps, he thought it might be. It may also be significant that a long paragraph describing their plight was deleted in proof from the same number; of course, there could be other reasons for this: the passage is irrelevant to the novel, and Dickens may not have had the space to publish all he had written. Nevertheless, both the proof alterations I have noted have a complementary effect, weakening Dickens's expression of sympathy with the lot of the urban labourer, and strengthening his condemnation of their violence.

In two of Dickens's novels, descriptions of insurrectionary mobs are centrally important; in three more there are brief but convincing scenes involving rioting crowds which, though less important to their context, fit interestingly into an overall pattern. Dickens's literary fascination with crowd behaviour spans a large part of his career; the long period of gestation of *Barnaby Rudge* started around May 1836, and the final number of *A Tale of Two Cities* appeared in *All the Year Round* in November 1859. And during these years, his interest breaks to the surface in short scenes in *Oliver Twist*, *The Old Curiosity Shop*, and *Little Dorrit*. This preoccupation is central to him, for reasons that are fairly clear. The mob, like the prison and the fireside, is a great centralising emblem, enacting in dramatic form and fusing together such Dickensian (and Victorian) preoccupations as the need for order and control; the fear of cruelty; the horror of anarchy and its converse: the belief in 'civilisation' and the values of hearth and home.

Mobs show Dickens emotionally at full stretch; he both fears them and exults in them. 'I have just burst into Newgate, and am going in the next number to tear the prisoners out by the hair of their heads', he wrote excitedly to Forster in December 1841, when his account of the Gordon Riots in the serialisation of *Barnaby Rudge* was reaching its climax.[2] Dickens is carried away by the mob's energy; at the same time, he is terrified by its destructiveness, a terror which he feels in an

---

[1] *OCS* proof sheets, Forster Collection, Victoria and Albert Museum.
[2] Forster, 169.

acutely personal way. The first mob scene in his novels is also a flight from retribution; in *Oliver Twist* it is a mob that hounds Bill Sikes to the garish Nemesis demanded by the conventions of the Victorian 'sensation novel'. The mob's character as a kind of avenging fury clearly contains an important part of its meaning for Dickens. That this is true of *A Tale of Two Cities* scarcely needs underlining; the dark fatefulness of Madame Defarge's knitted blacklist of victims for the vengeance of the people is one of the book's less subtle motifs. And apart from Bill Sikes, Dickens gives us two earlier glimpses of this idea. Neither Barnaby Rudge's father nor Rigaud alias Blandois is psychologically convincing, as Bill Sikes, inside the limitations imposed by his brand of characterisation, obviously is; and neither of them is in any way central to the novel in which he appears. But both of them have at least one moment which carries conviction. Rigaud is in prison, charged with the murder of his wife. Outside, a mob waits for him. The jailer comes to release him, telling him of the hostile crowd:

> He passed on out of sight, and unlocked and unbarred a low door in the corner of the chamber. 'Now', said he, as he opend it and appeared within, 'come out'.
> There is no sort of whiteness in all the hues under the sun at all like the whiteness of Monsieur Rigaud's face as it was then. Neither is there any expression of the human countenance at all like that expression, in every little line of which the frightened heart is seen to beat. Both are conventionally compared with death; but the difference is the whole deep gulf between the struggle done, and the fight at its most desperate extremity.[1]

This ought to be bad writing and yet, once we have penetrated its prosiness, the passage carries conviction. Rigaud, of course, comes well after the heyday of the full-blown Dickensian villain. Rudge comes between Bill Sikes and Quilp, and Jonas Chuzzlewit; and though a less successful character, he still has something of their lurid fascination. It is interesting that Rudge *in extremis* places himself in his diseased imagination in a situation not unlike that of Sikes near his end, or Rigaud as I have just shown him. Rudge has been captured for a murder committed many years before, and when the rioters come to sack Newgate, he is awaiting trial there. He is awakened by 'the roar of voices, and the struggling of a great crowd':

> He started up as these sounds met his ear, and, sitting on his bedstead, listened.
> After a short interval of silence the noise burst out again. Still listening attentively, he made out, in course of time, that the jail was besieged by a furious multitude. His guilty conscience instantly arrayed these men against himself, and brought the fear upon him that he would be singled out, and torn to pieces.

[1] *LD*, 13.

Once impressed with the terror of this conceit, everything tended to
confirm and strengthen it . . . . He was one man against the whole united
concourse; a single, solitary, lonely man, from whom the very captives in
the jail fell off and shrunk appalled . . . .

Every shout they raised, and every sound they made, was a blow upon his
heart. As the attack went on, he grew more wild and frantic in his terror:
tried to pull away the bars that guarded the chimney and prevented him
from climbing up: called loudly on the turnkeys to cluster round the cell
and save him from the fury of the rabble; or put him in some dungeon
underground, no matter of what depth, how dark it was, or loathsome, or
beset with rats and creeping things, so that it hid him and was hard to find.[1]

Any novelist of Dickens's powers might be expected to be able to
imagine such fears and attempt a description of them, but they do
seem to occur to him with what one might think more than usual
readiness. Why is Bill Sikes hounded by a mob at all? Apart from
an exciting scene, the crowd in *Oliver Twist* adds little to the novel.
Even more curiously irrelevant is the short scene from *Little Dorrit*.
And this preoccupation does not belong only to the early part of
Dickens's career: *Oliver Twist* was published in book form in 1838,
Barnaby Rudge in 1841, *Little Dorrit* in 1857; and, of course, the notion
of being 'singled out and torn to pieces' is taken, in *A Tale of Two
Cities* (1859), to a grisly logical conclusion, in its gruesome description
of the massacre of Foulon. This episode, like many others (as I have
shown), follows closely the text of Carlyle's *French Revolution*;[2] but
Dickens could easily have omitted it, as he necessarily omitted most
of the incidents of Carlyle's long history. How much these scenes
reflect emotionally some part of Dickens himself is a question outside
the scope of this inquiry, but we can certainly suggest that he seems
able in them to commit himself imaginatively to what he is depicting
in a way which it may be useful to remember when we consider his
highly emotional later pronouncements on two historical events
involving insurrectionary movements and their victims. The converse
of such terrors is the desire, expressed in the *Tale*, to 'petrify' each
member of the mob 'with a well-aimed gun'. This goes with his
ideas on the revenge to be exacted from the perpetrators of the Indian
Mutiny:

. . . I wish I were Commander-in-Chief in India. The first thing I would
do to strike that oriental race with amazement (not in the least regarding
them as if they lived in the Strand, London, or at Camden Town), should
be to proclaim to them in their language, that I considered my holding
that appointment by the leave of God, to mean that I should do my utmost
to exterminate the Race upon whom the stain of the late cruelties rested;

[1] BR, 496-7.
[2] See pp. 77-8 above.

H

and that I was there for that purpose and no other, and was now proceeding, with all convenient dispatch and merciful swiftness of execution, to blot it out of mankind and raze it off the face of the earth.[1]

Dickens's feelings about the Jamaica Insurrection of 1865 and its aftermath have been apologetically explained away by pointing to his admiration for Carlyle.   There are also, I shall suggest in a later chapter, other and perhaps more fundamental reasons for them.

The mobs in *Barnaby Rudge* allow somewhat more broadly based conjecture about exactly what it is that Dickens feels them to threaten. Hugh, the uncontrolled savage, is their just epitome: he provides a direct antithesis for Chester, whose personality is shown as having suffered an excess of 'reason' and education. Like the crowd, which is manipulated by Gashford for his own ends, Hugh is putty in the hands of Chester; their relationship, like that of Caliban and Prospero, shows the interaction of 'Nature' and 'Nurture' taken to their limits. The crowd represents the breakdown of civilisation, enacting, quite simply, a reversion to barbarism. Unlike Carlyle, who in *The French Revolution* sees the mob as the agent of a necessary historical process, Dickens sees it as the enemy of progress; for him, this key word inevitably includes order and stability, immunity from the primordial cruelties of the past. The crowd in *Barnaby Rudge* is described as being 'like a mad monster',[2] as 'wild and savage, like beasts at the sight of prey'.[3]   In more human, but scarcely less bestial terms, its component members are 'the very scum and refuse of London',[4] more charitably, simply 'idle and profligate persons'.[5]   The mob is a prey to its own appetites, barbarous and animal in its inability to see beyond the moment, incapable of rational thought: 'The great mass never reasoned or thought at all, but were stimulated by their own headlong passions, by poverty, by ignorance, by the love of mischief, and the hope of plunder'.[6]   Like the sea (the image is used repeatedly[7]), the crowd is unstable and dangerous: '. . . the ocean is not more fickle and uncertain, more terrible when roused, more unreasonable, or more cruel'.[8]   The actions of the mob are seen as a simple rape of

---

[1] *Letters*, II, 889.
[2] BR, 375.
[3] *Ibid.*
[4] BR, 374.
[5] *Ibid.*, 396.
[6] *Ibid.*, 402-3.
[7] *Ibid.*, 363, 367, 505, 516. Dickens's use of sea imagery here may conceivably indicate Carlylean influence, particularly when compared with the sea-imagery of the descriptions of mob violence in both *TTC* and *FR* (see chapter V).   I have, however, been unable to find any other textual indications of Carlylean influence over *BR*.
[8] *Ibid.*, 396.

certain ideals of accumulated civilisation, of solidity and slow growth: '. . . worse than all', says Dickens, after describing the destruction of Lord Mansfield's house, furniture, plate, jewels, pictures and manuscripts, 'because nothing could replace this loss, the great Law Library, on almost every page of which were notes in the Judge's own hand, of inestimable value—being the results of the study and experience of his whole life'.[1] Even more terrible, for Dickens, is the violation of the values of hearth and home enacted in the gutting of Haredale's country house, 'the exposure to the coarse, common gaze of every little nook which usages of home had made a sacred place, and the destruction by rude hands of every little household favourite which old associations made a dear and precious thing . . .'[2] For Dickens here, mob rule (real or fictional) means nothing less than the direct confrontation of 'the worst passions of the worst men' and 'all that was good and peaceful in society'.[3]   For Carlyle, even the butchers of the September massacres have their own peculiar justification, their own special kind of order, which springs from the nature of their historic task. 'Fell Slaughter', says Carlyle, 'one of the most authentic products of the Pit you would say, once give it Customs, becomes War, with Laws of War; and is Customary and Moral enough; and red individuals carry the tools of it girt round their haunches, not without an air of pride—which do thou nowise blame'.[4]

For Dickens, the actions of the mob in *Barnaby Rudge* provide one more example of the almost unrelieved nastiness of past ages, and at one point the crowd's excesses are, interestingly, compared with the use of 'the block, the rack, the gibbet, and the stake in cruel Mary's reign'.[5]   This reminds us of the series of false book titles in the Gad's Hill Library, called 'The Wisdom of our Ancestors', and of the doggerel verse Dickens contributed to *The Examiner* in the summer of 1841[6] (when Barnaby Rudge was appearing in *Master Humphrey's Clock*), one line of which ('The good old laws were garnished well with gibbets, whips, and chains . . .') demonstrates its relevance to *Barnaby Rudge*; when the inhabitants of the Newgate death cells plead to be freed from the blazing prison, Dennis, 'who had been bred and matured in the good old school, and had administered the good old laws on the good old plan . . . bore these appeals with a deal of philosophy'.[7]   Dickens's recoil from the violence of the mob stems, obviously enough I think, at least partly from the same root as his hatred of injustice and oppression; the division of Dennis's loyalties between the mob and the 'good old school' is clearly shown as an

---

[1] *Ibid.*, 510.
[2] *Ibid.*, 422-3.
[3] *Ibid.*, 339.
[4] FR, II, 200.
[5] BR, 387.
[6] Forster, 192.
[7] BR, 500.

unreal one. When the oppressed are guilty of destructive violence, they become (as in the *Tale*) the oppressors, the destroyers of the civilised values that guard against anarchy and cruelty: for Dickens, the march of progress means, among other things, ever greater immunity from the barbarism of the past.

Dickens's horror of mob violence indicates the nature of the dilemma posed for him by working class movements. Adult education was one thing, and was bound to lead to greater stability: organised political action was another matter. For Dickens, the fundamental question posed by the opening chapter of *Chartism* had no simple answer, as it had for Carlyle: both the 'condition of the working people' *and* their 'disposition' were wrong. Stephen Blackpool's grotesque resignation in the face of injustice clearly represented for Dickens an ideal reaction. Stephen's supine acceptance of his fate is inadmissible for obvious reasons, though what ought to be stressed is that it is Dickens himself who makes it so by the vividness and the commitment with which he depicts his plight and that of the class he represents. What irritates us is Dickens's failure to draw from his insight the reasonable conclusion; what can scarcely be questioned is the fundamental and passionate nature of the insight itself. Professor Peyrouton may be partly right to suggest that Dickens's radicalism sprang from his fear of the consequences that would follow from a failure to take action;[1] but that it also sprang from Dickens's genuine and deeply felt horror at the condition of the working class is beyond doubt.

I have already quoted a short passage from *The Old Curiosity Shop* which indicates Dickens's feelings about Chartist mobs; a paragraph he deleted from the same number at the proof stage is well worth considering here, if only as a convenient way of representing the ambivalence of Dickens's position. The passage is a long one, but it ought to be quoted at length:

They had been used to stop at cottage doors, and beg a drink of water; and though these cottages were poor and small, they were often shaded by green trees, always in the free air, open to the sun and wind, and gay with the song of birds. How different the stys, in which the working townsmen, women, children, babies—they all worked here—huddled together, and had their sickly homes! In courts so numerous, as to be marked in every street by numbers of their own, for names for them could not be found— in narrow, unpaved ways, exhaling foetid odours, steeped in filth and dirt, reeking with things offensive to sight, smell, hearing, thought; shutting out the light and air; breeding contagious diseases, big with fever, loathsome humours, madness, and a long ghastly train of ills—in places where, let men disguise as they please, no human beings can be clean or good, or sober, or contented—where no child can be born but it is infected and tainted from the hour it draws its miserable breath, and never has its chance of

[1] Peyrouton, N., "Dickens and the Chartists", *Dickensian*, LX(1964).

worth or happiness—in such noisome streets they, the tens of thousands, live and die and give birth to others, tens of thousands more, who live and die again, never growing better, but slowly and surely worse, and whose depraved condition,—whose irreligion, improvidence, drunkenness, degeneracy, and, most unaccountable of all, whose discontent, good gentlemen reprobate in Parliament time till they are hoarse; devising for their reformation Sabbath Bills without end . . . and building up new churches with a zeal whose sacred fervour knows no limits.

'Misery!' said a portly gentleman standing in the best street of the town that very night as he went home from dinner, and looking round him. 'Where is it? A splendid Town Hall—a copy from the antique—the finest organ in Europe, a museum of natural curiosities, a theatre, some capital inns, excellent shops where every luxury may be purchased at very little more than the London price; an elegant market-place, admirably supplied! What would they have? Misery! Pooh pooh! I don't believe a word of it.'[1]

Although Dickens had other reasons for dissatisfaction with Parliament, his attack on it here is a piece of pamphleteering on behalf of a particular bee in the bonnet, which he had already aired in *Sunday Under Three Heads* (1836), as well as a more general statement of principle, like Carlyle's in *Chartism*; he is not uniquely concerned with the government's general failure to remedy the lot of the poor, with 'what Parliament ought to have done in this business, what they will, can or cannot do',[2] though his diatribe against Members of Parliament who 'reprobate' the 'discontent' of the lower classes rather than its cause has a Carlylean overtone. And his attack on the 'portly gentleman' may be just as much a simple satirical statement about the rich and the poor, about Dives and Lazarus, as a general social point, a suggestion that there are 'two nations'. But the whole passage certainly suggests an attitude to the conditions of the urban poor that coincides broadly with Carlyle's. Dickens's description here relies on the contrast between the greenness and freshness of his idealised countryside and the hellishness of his description of the urban worker's lot, a contrast pointed by many at this time and earlier, and one which Carlyle evoked again in *Chartism*:

Is it a green flowery world, with azure everlasting sky stretched over it, the work and government of a God; or a murky-simmering Tophet, of copperas-fumes, cotton-fuzz, gin-riot, wrath and toil, created by a Demon, governed by a Demon? The sum of their wretchedness merited and unmerited welters, huge, dark and baleful, like a Dantean Hell . . .[3]

When did Dickens's concern for the poor begin to be expressed in a coherent and effective way? His determination to 'strike the heaviest

---

[1] Forster Collection, repr. *The Dickensian*, L (1954), 21-2.
[2] *Chartism*, 40.
[3] *Ibid.*, 60.

blow in [his] power for them' dates at least from 1838,[1] and there are other unconnected early examples of a feeling for the conditions of working men, of which the attack on the New Poor Law in *Oliver Twist* is the most famous.   Nevertheless, we can see a deepening understanding of the injustice of working class life, and also a clearer personal engagement in its problems, taking place quite rapidly at a particular period.   In 1840 he could address a Mechanics Institute and give as his main reason for supporting it the increased recognition that would be given to men of letters by creating a wider and better educated public. The speech was intended half humorously, perhaps, and he continued to make the point about the benefits to literature of a more educated public, but the comparison with later speeches to similar institutions is interesting. So too, we might think, is the distinctly double-edged image Dickens chose in his speech, at this time of civil strife, to describe (whether ironically or not) the masses: the spirit behind such institutions, he thought, 'laid a moral foundation calculated to promote the best uses amongst what was styled the "many-headed", but which by the aid of such institutions would soon be designated the "many-thoughted, monster" '.[2] As some of the imagery he uses in *Barnaby Rudge* indicates, 'the people' were, for him, a kind of monster, a Caliban whose violence might be tempered by a little learning, and though Dickens here seems to reject the image of the 'many-headed monster', he later used it himself, in the general context of the *Tale*, interestingly enough in a letter to Carlyle.[3]

Until 1843, most of Dickens's public speeches were to literary bodies, or (in America) at dinners in his honour. In 1843 began the long series of addresses he gave to and for institutions for the relatively under-privileged. In that year, he spoke for (a curious collection) The Printers' Pension Society, the Hospital for Consumption and Diseases of the Chest, the Charitable Society for the Deaf and Dumb, the Sanatorium, founded in 1840 by Dr. Southwood Smith, and the Athenaeum, the Manchester adult education institution, which was then in difficulties. We can, perhaps, see these speeches as extending somewhat the period referred to by Forster as leading up to his departure for Italy in 1844. I have quoted Forster's remarks before, but they are certainly worth presenting again in this slightly different context. 'Several months before he left England', says Forster, 'I had noticed in him the habit of more gravely regarding many things before passed lightly enough; the hopelessness of any true solution of either political or social problems by the ordinary Downing-street methods had been startlingly impressed on him in Carlyle's writings; and in the parliamentary talk of that day he had come to have . . . little

¹   Pilgrim *Letters*, I, 484.
²   *Speeches*, 4.
³   See p. 26 above.

faith'. . . .[1] Dickens was certainly thinking about the shortcomings of action by 'Downing-street methods' before 1844; speaking to a meeting in support of the Sanatorium in June the previous year, he had praised Lord Ashley, the chairman, 'who had sacrificed party spirit and politics that he might advance the cause and interest of the neglected and forlorn—who had boldly stood forward among seven hundred legislators, and maintained that women should not be compelled to do the work of harnessed brutes'.[2]   Ashley, of course, was one of the few contemporary politicians Carlyle ever specifically named as typifying the kind of real, and not sham, aristocracy that was needed to deal with the Condition of England Question. Dickens had his own reasons both for admiring Ashley, and for his disillusionment with parliamentary government, about the daily workings of which he knew, in any case, more at first hand than did Carlyle. Nevertheless, we can probably date a fresh awareness of parliamentary refusal of responsibility from 1843; and we can certainly link this new understanding, at least partly, with Dickens's reading of Carlyle's works, certainly of *Chartism*. A passage from Carlyle's essay, which appears in the chapter entitled 'Laissez-Faire', provides what we can see, I think, as fairly solid evidence of this, which confirms Forster's attribution to Carlyle of Dickens's loss of faith in parliamentary methods, and which dates the birth, or modification of these views from 1843, and not, as Forster might perhaps be supposed to suggest, from 1844. 'Are these millions taught?   Are these millions guided?'[3] asks Carlyle:

> This Church answers: Yes, the people are taught. This Aristocracy, astonishment in every feature, answers: Yes, surely the people are guided! Do we not pass what Acts of Parliament are needful; as many as thirty-nine for the shooting of the partridges alone? Are there not treadmills, gibbets; even hospitals, poor-rates, New Poor-Laws?[4]

This must, surely, be behind one of Dickens's most well-known passages, from *A Christmas Carol* (1843):

> 'Are there no prisons?' asked Scrooge.
> 'Plenty of prisons', said the gentleman, laying down the pen again.
> 'And the Union workhouses?' demanded Scrooge. 'Are they still in operation?'
> 'They are. Still', returned the gentleman, 'I wish I could say they were not'.

---

1 Forster, 347.
2 *Speeches*, 43.
3 *Chartism*, 71.
4 *Ibid.*, 72.

'The Treadmill and the Poor Law are in full vigour, then?' said Scrooge.
'Both very busy, sir'.
'Oh! I was afraid, from what you said at first, that something had occurred
to stop them in their useful course', said Scrooge. 'I'm very glad to hear
it'.[1]

Scrooge's refusal of responsibility, this example of Laissez-Faire in
action must, I think, be seen as Carlylean, despite the obvious way in
which *A Christmas Carol* represents all the qualities which distinguish
Dickens from the Sage. The *Carol* was published for Christmas 1843.
The same month, a passage I have already quoted from *Martin Chuzzlewit* (to illustrate Carlyle's stylistic influence on Dickens) was published
in the novel's twelfth number; the writing of the Christmas book
and this part of *Martin Chuzzlewit* very probably went on together.
What the passage represents, very clearly, is another demonstrably
Carlylean example of Dickens's thinking, at exactly this point in
time, about the refusal of responsibility for the working classes by
the traditional ruling classes. It implies, too, the Carlylean notion
of the necessity of arriving at the root cause of the discontent of
working men, rather than attempting to deal merely with its
symptoms. The whole passage[2] is relevant here, but the last sentence
alone makes the point adequately enough:

Oh magistrate, so rare a country gentleman and brave a squire, had you
no duty to society, before the ricks were blazing and the mob were mad;
or did it spring up, armed and booted from the earth, a corps of yeomanry,
full-grown![3]

The context of the passage from the *Carol* which I have quoted, however, shows, perhaps, that Dickens had still not fully reached an
understanding of one essential notion, so important that it can be
said to distinguish the 'early' from the 'late' Dickens. In *A Christmas
Carol*, Dickens puts this famous speech into Scrooge's mouth to
underline an individual failure of charity: by the conversion to
Benevolence of one person, the gloomy spectres of the *Tale* are quite
banished. A year later, in *The Chimes*, the responsibility has become
diffused throughout the whole of society, and the easy solution has
disappeared altogether. This new depth of understanding was almost
certainly due—partly at least—to Dickens's reading of Carlyle's
works.

[1] *CC*, 12.
[2] Quoted in full on p. 34 above.
[3] *MC*, 497-8.

Dickens's second Christmas story is written, very clearly, I think, under Carlylean influence, though we face many of the same problems as in *Hard Times* in establishing the fact; the insight into his society that Dickens shows in *The Chimes* must be understood as drawing life from a general climate of feeling, which Carlyle nurtured but did not create. Dickens certainly wrote *The Chimes* when Carlyle was at the height of his fame, and this fact alone must emphasise the strong likelihood that what seems Carlylean in *The Chimes* probably is. Nevertheless, *The Chimes* poses a familiar cultural problem. Carlyle's fame depended in the first place on the peculiar disturbed ethos of the late 'thirties and early 'forties; and it is directly to this ethos that we can see Dickens responding, in *The Chimes*, with an immediacy and a strength of feeling that he could never have extended to any merely literary influence. In trying to distinguish what is Carlylean influence and what coincidence of view in *The Chimes* we are to some extent engaged in unravelling a kind of tautology. Certainly, no one notion in *The Chimes* can be seen as peculiarly Carlylean: as in *Hard Times*, it is the *combination* of ideas that suggests Carlyle's influence. The most pervasive idea of *The Chimes*, and the most deeply held by Carlyle himself, for instance, was also the most widely held political truism of the decade: the idea of the 'two nations'. Disraeli's famous phrase was not to become common property until the following year, but the nearness in time of the publication of two such different literary phenomena as *Sybil* and Dickens's second Christmas story emphasises how widely the notion was being discussed, how little Dickens *needed* Carlyle for this idea. Nevertheless, Carlyle does, I think, lie directly behind Dickens's articulation of it in *The Chimes*. The weightiest indication of this, perhaps, lies in the biographical evidence, which I have already discussed, of Dickens's persistent efforts to ensure Carlyle's 'indispensable' presence at the private reading of his Christmas tale. There is little doubt that Dickens, as later in *Hard Times*, expected Carlyle to recognise his own gospel reflected in his story. A comparison with the demonstrably Carlylean articulation of the 'two nations' theme in *Hard Times* helps to confirm that when Dickens thought about the division between rich and poor, Carlyle's warnings on the subject were likely to come to mind. Will Fern's set-piece on the wrongs of the poor, like Stephen's, is a heart-felt plea delivered to a cynical (though rather larger) upper and middle class audience; the poor who happen to be present merely provide a convenient back-drop. His central argument is clear:

> . . . gentlemen, gentlemen, dealing with other men like me, begin at the right end. Give us, in mercy, better homes when we're a-lying in our cradles; give us better food when we're a-working for our lives; give us kinder laws to bring us back when we're a-going wrong; and don't set Iail, Jail, Jail, afore us, everywhere we turn. There an't a condescension you

can show the Labourer then, that he won't take, as ready and as grateful as a man can be; for he has a patient, peaceful, willing heart. But you must put his rightful spirit in him first; for whether he's a wreck and ruin such as me, or is like one of them that stand here now, his spirit is divided from you at this time. Bring it back, gentlefolks, bring it back![1]

Like Stephen Blackpool, Will Fern asks, not for a radical change in the social structure, but for a change of heart in the ruling classes; like Stephen, too, he points out the impossibility of changing the relationship between the rich and the poor unless the root causes of discontent are removed. In both these demands, these two fictional workers are echoing Carlyle.[2] Alderman Cute, who believes that the discontented poor, like Fern, should be put down, owes much, of course, to a real-life prototype, Sir Peter Laurie. But there is little doubt that Dickens's understanding of his creed derives also from Carlyle:

> To believe practically that the poor and luckless are here only as a nuisance to be abraded and abated, and in some permissible manner made away with, and swept out of sight, is not an amiable faith. That the arrangements of good and ill success in this perplexed scramble of a world . . . are in fact the work of a seeing goddess or god, and require only not to be meddled with: what stretch of heroic faculty or inspiration of genius was needed to teach one that? To button your pockets and stand still, is no complex recipe.[3]

This might almost be a direct commentary on Alderman Cute's admonition to Meg:

> Now, I give you fair warning, that I have made up my mind to Put distressed wives Down. So, don't be brought before me. You'll have children —boys. Those boys will grow up bad, of course, and run wild in the streets, without shoes and stockings. Mind, my young friend! I'll convict 'em summarily, every one, for I am determined to Put boys without shoes and stockings Down. Perhaps your husband will die young (most likely) and leave you with a baby. Then you'll be turned out of doors, and wander up and down the streets. Now, don't wander near me, my dear, for I am resolved to Put all wandering mothers Down.[4]

It is this refusal of understanding of the lower classes by the upper which Carlyle, more notably than any other literary figure of the decade, pointed out; the refusal of responsibility he attacked came not simply from a failure to provide the right answers but from an inability even to ask the right questions. For Carlyle, the questions

---

1   *Chimes*, 133.
2   See pp. 47ff above.
3   *Chartism*, 48.
4   *Chimes*, 99.

were simple enough: '. . . Why are the Working Classes discontented; what is their condition, economical, moral, in their houses and their hearts, as it is in reality and as they figure it to themselves to be; what do they complain of; what ought they, and ought they not to complain of?—These are measurable questions; on some of these any common mortal, did he but turn his eyes to them, might throw some light'.[1] Will Fern's and Stephen Blackpool's outbursts are presented as unavailing attempts to resolve the impasse caused by a particular failing of understanding, a problem which Carlyle, like many others, helped to bring into general discussion:

> . . . as is well said, all battle is misunderstanding; did the parties know one another, the battle would cease.[2]

And for Carlyle, it is above all this misunderstanding of 'what it is that the under classes intrinsically mean' that leads to their 'discontent grown fierce and mad'.[3] In *The Chimes*, it is the misunderstanding by Cute and Bowley of Will Fern that drives him, in Trotty's dream, to the incendiary madness of the rick-burner. How far it was natural for Dickens thus to justify working-class violence by pointing to its causes, we have already seen; Dickens's perception here is clearly strengthened by his reading of Carlyle, and probably, specifically, of *Chartism*. 'There'll be a Fire tonight', says Will Fern to Meg, taking his last farewell of her:

> There'll be Fires this winter-time, to light the dark nights, East, West, North, and South. When you see the distant sky red, they'll be blazing. When you see the distant sky red, think of me no more; or, if you do, remember what a Hell was lighted up inside of me, and think you see its flames reflected in the clouds . . .[4]

In some ways, we can see *The Chimes* as a first essay in themes Dickens was to explore more fully in the years to come, above all in *Hard Times*. Will Fern and Stephen Blackpool are similar, and not only in their roles as misunderstood Carlylean Workers, mouth-pieces for the wrongs of the poor. They both end up on the wrong side of the law, as hunted men, and in a way their state is a kind of emblem for the dispossession of the working class from its rightful condition. Two other characters in *Hard Times* seem to have more or less obvious precursors in *The Chimes*. Gradgrind's reliance on statistical truth (if no other aspect of his characterisation) is foreshadowed by Mr. Filer, whose contribution I shall examine in the next chapter. And Sir Joseph Bowley has in common with Josiah Bounderby not only

---

[1] *Chartism*, 41.
[2] *Ibid.*, 40.
[3] *Ibid.*, 37, 40.
[4] *Chimes*, 147.

his initials and his overblown pomposity but his conviction that he knows and understands his employees, and his distrust of anyone showing discontent. Bowley, as Dr. Slater points out, is closely related to Carlyle's Man of Business, and it is above all this relationship that provides his link with Bounderby.

It is difficult, for *The Chimes* as for other works of Dickens in which we can trace Carlylean influence, to identify the specific works to which the novelist was indebted, such is the continuity and self-plagiarism of Carlyle's *oeuvre*. But two works are more clearly involved than others here. We can, I think, be fairly sure that *Chartism*, from which I have already made several relevant quotations, was (as it had been in the *Carol*) in Dickens's mind. The other work, whose influence has been identified by Michael Slater through two similarities in incident, is *Past and Present*. I am indebted to Dr. Slater for much of what follows.[1]

The first incident is that in which Trotty reads in a newspaper account, of a case of infanticide followed by suicide. Trotty takes this as underlining Bowley's remarks on the innate badness of the poor, which in his simplicity he has uncritically accepted:

> A crime so terrible, and so revolting to his soul, dilated with the love of Meg, that he let the journal drop, and fell back in his chair, appalled!
> 'Unnatural and cruel!' Toby cried. 'Unnatural and cruel! None but people who were bad at heart, born bad, who had no business on the earth, could do such deeds. It's too true, all I've heard today; too just, too full of proof. We're Bad!' [2]

This appears to have as its source an incident reported by Carlyle to demonstrate how comfortable middle-class people can distort such tragedies, and fail to grasp their meaning. Carlyle's incident is that in which, in 1841, a mother and father poisoned three of their children 'to defraud a "burial-society" of some £3 8s. due on the death of each child . . .':

> 'Brutal savages, degraded Irish', mutters the idle reader of Newspapers; hardly lingering on this incident.

But, says Carlyle, no matter how brutal their actions, there is more to the case than this:

> Such instances are like the highest mountain apex emerged into view; under which lies a whole mountain region and land, not yet emerged. A human Mother and Father had said to themselves, What shall we do to

[1] Slater, M., "Carlyle and Jerrold into Dickens; a study of *The Chimes*", repr. in *Dickens Centennial Essays*, ed, Nisbet, A. and Nevius, B., London, 1971, 184-204.
[2] *Chimes*, 117. Slater, 195.

escape starvation? We are deep sunk here, in our dark cellar; and help is far.[1]

It is almost certainly this Carlylean insistence on plumbing the causes of such desperate actions to their foundations that is behind the sequal to Trotty's derived middle-class horror at the mother who kills herself and her child: his own daughter is later shown driven by the injustice and inescapability of her lot in a society controlled by the Bowleys and the Cutes, to the very edge of such a crime.

A fainter echo of *Past and Present* is to be found as Meg, on the last day of the old year, mingles

> . . . with an abject crowd, who tarried in the snow, until it pleased some officer appointed to dispense the public charity . . . to call them in, and question them, and say to this one, 'Go to such a place', to that one, 'Come next week'; to make a football of another wretch, and pass him here and there, from hand to hand, from house to house, until he wearied and lay down to die; or started up and robbed, and so became a higher sort of criminal, whose claims allowed of no delay.[2]

Meg's experience here (seen in Trotty's vision) reminds us, perhaps, of that of Jo the crossing sweeper in *Bleak House*, who is also passed about like a football. Jo, unlike Meg, is a carrier of infection, and refusal of charity to him is more costly, but this part of Trotty's dream about Meg is nevertheless reminiscent of Jo's plot, and the two stories may well have as their common source an anecdote from *Past and Present*:

> A poor Irish Widow, her husband having died in one of the Lanes of Edinburgh, went forth with her three children, bare of all resource, to solicit help from the Charitable Establishments of that City. At this Charitable Establishment and then at that she was refused; referred from one to the other, helped by none; till she had exhausted them all; till her strength and heart failed her; she sank down in typhus-fever; died, and infected her Lane with fever, so that 'seventeen other persons' died of fever there in consequence.[3]

Other Carlylean echoes, apart from the condition of the working classes, reverberate through the pages of *The Chimes*; these are examined in other chapters. But it is this part of the Condition of England Question, seen here in an unmistakably Carlylean way, with which Dickens is overwhelmingly concerned in this brief but concentrated story. It is very obviously Carlyle's vision of the consequences of the refusal of responsibility of the Upper classes for the

---

[1] *PP*, 6. Slater, 196.
[2] *Chimes*, 148. Slater, 196.
[3] *PP*, 145.

Lower that dominates Dickens's mind in *The Chimes*. And Trotty's vision of the incendiarism to which Will Fern is driven indicates, perhaps, one consequence that Dickens himself certainly feared, a fear which the pages of *Past and Present* and *Chartism* were not calculated to allay; never far from the thoughts of thinking men during the 'forties were the causes, and the effects, of the first French Revolution. And for Dickens as for Carlyle the answer lay, not in allowing the masses to govern themselves, not in any change in the system, but less tangibly, in a change of heart in the governing classes. Will Fern's cry, like Stephen Blackpool's after him, is 'give me a leader'. Carlyle's simple but powerful diagnosis of the Condition of England Question was certainly, by the time Dickens wrote *The Chimes*, broadly that of the novelist, too:

"*Laissez-faire*, Leave them to do"? the thing they will *do*, if so left, is too frightful to think of! It has been *done* once, in sight of the whole earth, in these generations: can it need to be done a second time?[1]

[1]   *Chartism*, 76.

CHAPTER EIGHT

Mechanism

FOR both Dickens and Carlyle, the symbolism of the machine was immensely powerful. Its fascination was partly due to its ambivalence: the machine was the agent of progress; at the same time, it was, in a fairly obvious way, indifferent to human needs, and could even be destructive of human life and happiness. The railway in *Dombey and Son* certainly represents progress, but at the same time it embodies something less benign, which can destroy the warmth and spontaneity of Stagg's gardens,[1] which can even maim or kill human beings. We can see Carker's death as marginally representing (apart from retribution) the sense of the destructive capacity of the machine that was later to contribute to Dickens's *Household Words* campaign for the protection of workers against dangerous machinery:

> He heard a shout—another—saw the face change from its vindictive passion to a faint sickness and terror—felt the earth tremble—knew in a moment that the rush was come—uttered a shriek—looked round—saw the red eyes, bleared and dim, in the daylight, close upon him—was beaten down, caught up, and whirled away upon a jagged mill, that spun him round and round, and struck him limb from limb, and licked his stream of life up with its fiery heat, and cast his mutilated fragments in the air.[2]

This reminds us, perhaps, of some famous lines from the chapter of *Sartor Resartus* that I have already proposed as having direct relevance to *Hard Times*;[3] Dickens's probable knowledge of it, together with similarities in wording, might even conceivably suggest that this passage played a part in the inspiration of Carker's death, despite the obvious difference in character and purpose of the two extracts:

[1] DS, 779.
[2] Ibid., 779.
[3] See pp. 56–8 above.

To me the Universe was all void of Life, of Purpose, of Volition, even of Hostility: it was one huge, dead, immeasurable *Steam-engine*, rolling on, in its dead indifference, to grind me *limb from limb*. Oh, the vast, gloomy, solitary Golgotha, and *Mill* of Death![1]

For both writers, though, as the context of this passage from *Sartor* underlines, it was not so much the physical reality of machines that was dangerous, but their implications in terms of human behaviour. This passage is an indirect link, through Harthouse, with Gradgrind, and the appearance here of the word 'grind' may conceivably be significant. For both Carlyle and Dickens, it was people who thought like machines, and who behaved towards their fellows with the rigid indifference of the machine, who were the ultimate enemy: for Carlyle, of a society whose life-springs would be reverence for the Immensities; for Dickens, of simple human happiness. And without any doubt, it is Carlyle's critique of a particular human attitude, for which the limitations and the inadaptability of the machine provided the appropriate image, that explains much of his relevance for Dickens, above all for the most Carlylean of all his novels, *Hard Times*.

'Signs of the Times' (1829) is Carlyle's earliest important statement on mechanistic thinking, and it lays down the general lines for much of the Prophet's critique of his age. ' . . . let us observe', he says,

> . . . how the mechanical genius of our time has diffused itself into quite other provinces. Not the external and physical alone is now managed by machinery, but the internal and spiritual also. Here too nothing follows its spontaneous course, nothing is left to be accomplished by old natural methods . . . . Instruction, that mysterious communing of Wisdom with Ignorance, is no longer an indefinable tentative process, requiring a study of individual aptitudes, and a perpetual variation of means and methods, to attain the same end; but a secure, universal, straightforward business, to be conducted in the gross, by proper mechanism, with such intellect as comes to hand.[2]

The great promulgators of this new tendency are the Utilitarians:

> . . . the wise men, who now appear as Political Philosophers, deal exclusively with the Mechanical province; and occupying themselves in counting up and estimating men's motives, strive by curious checking and balancing, and other adjustments of Profit and Loss, to guide them to their true advantage: while, unfortunately, those same 'motives' are so innumerable, and so variable in every individual, that no really useful conclusion can ever be drawn from their enumeration.[3]

---

[1] *SR*, 126. My italics.
[2] 'S of T', 466.
[3] *Ibid.*, 474.

Carlyle's analysis of his age in 'Signs of the Times' is, as can easily be seen, so reminiscent of Dickens's in *Hard Times* that we can easily understand why Mildred Christian should believe that in his novel, Dickens 'shows very full acquaintanceship'[1] with this essay. Nevertheless (so far as I can see) there are no textual indications to confirm Dickens's knowledge of 'Signs of the Times' and its direct contribution to *Hard Times*—as there clearly are for *Chartism* and *Past and Present*—and Carlyle says little in this early essay that he did not say again and again later in his career. 'Signs of the Times' made little public impression on its first publication in *Fraser's Magazine* (Dickens was seventeen at the time) and even when it was reissued, at the height of Carlyle's fame in 1842 as one essay in a retrospective two volume collection, it does not seem, so far as I can discover, to have attracted any very marked attention from reviewers or the general public.

Though Dickens's knowledge of 'Signs of the Times' has yet to be demonstrated, it certainly presents us with a summary of a general attitude to society which strongly attracted Dickens, and which is expressed here in a succinct and coherent way. These are two qualities for which to be profoundly grateful, and this essay provides, without doubt, the best quick briefing on the Carlylean background of the Dickensian attitude we are discussing. One of Carlyle's most influential notions on the evils of a mechanistic society, however—that of the Cash-Nexus—though it is implied here, is not fully expressed. Once a society has been established, says Carlyle, in which mere logic has replaced reverence for the unknowable, then the relations between men are altered accordingly. 'Mechanism' and 'Mammonism' are the twin pillars of such a society. The relations of the 'Under-Classes' to their rulers are now based not on reverence and mutual respect but on material self-interest alone. Laissez-faire, in both economics and government means internecine warfare, refusal of responsibility by the governors, hopelessness for the governed. 'The Gospel of Mammonism', as Carlyle puts it in *Past and Present*, has led to strange conclusions:

> We call it a Society; and go about professing openly the totalest separation, isolation. Our life is not a mutual helpfulness; but rather, cloaked under due laws-of-war, named 'fair competition' and so forth, it is a mutual hostility. We have profoundly forgotten everywhere that *Cash-payment* is not the sole relation of human beings; we think, nothing doubting, that *it* absolves and liquidates all engagements of man.[2]

Mammonism and the Cash-Nexus are the direct consequence, in economic terms, of Mechanism. The corollary of this argument is clear; rationality, if not confined to its proper sphere, destroys the

---

[1] Christian, M., 'Carlyle and Dickens', *Trollopian*, II (1947), 21.
[2] *PP*, 143.

possibility for the spontaneous human relationships on which society should be based, and reduces people to the level of mere statistical items: the Cash-Nexus represents man's reduction to the status of the machine. This aspect of Carlyle's critique of Mechanism clearly had a strong appeal for Dickens. Partly it may lie, I think, behind much of the characterisation of Mr. Dombey, who obviously believes in the Cash-Nexus as a satisfactory basis for the relations between master and servant; the passage I have just quoted from *Past and Present* might almost be seen as a direct commentary on this scene from *Dombey and Son*, which appeared two years later:

> 'Oh, of course', said Mr. Dombey. 'I desire to make it a question of wages, altogether. Now, Richards, if you nurse my bereaved child, I wish you to remember this always. You will receive a liberal stipend in return for the discharge of certain duties, in the performance of which, I wish to see as little of your family as possible. When those duties cease to be required and rendered, and the stipend ceases to be paid, there is an end of all relations between us.... It is not at all in this bargain that you need become attached to my child, or that my child need become attached to you.... When you go away from here, you will have concluded what is a mere matter of bargain and sale, hiring and letting: and will stay away.'[1]

Polly Toodle (whose very name has been changed to a safe mono-chrome) represents spontaneity, warmth, the human inter-reliance of lower-class life, and especially of family life. Her relationship with Dombey looks forward to that of Mr. Gradgrind and Sissy Jupe, and backwards perhaps, to the momentary contact between Mr. Filer and Meg in *The Chimes*. This scene, like the one I have quoted from *Dombey and Son*, depicts a particular antithesis of values, the imaginative importance of which, for Dickens, can scarcely be over-estimated:

> '... Married! Married!! The ignorance of the first principles of political economy on the part of these people; their improvidence; their wickedness; is, by Heavens! enough to—Now look at that couple, will you!' ....
> 'A man may live to be as old as Methuselah', said Mr. Filer, 'and may labour all his life for the benefit of such people as those; and may heap up facts on figures, facts on figures, facts on figures, mountains high and dry; and he can no more hope to persuade 'em that they have no right or business to be married, than he can hope to persuade 'em that they have no earthly right or business to be born. And *that* we know they haven't. We reduced it to a mathematical certainty long ago!'[2]

This confrontation, it will be seen, establishes much the same tension of values as that between Dombey and Polly, or between Louisa Gradgrind and her father, in the famous scene from *Hard Times* we have already discussed. In both *The Chimes* and *Hard Times* this

---

[1] *DS*, 16.
[2] *Chimes*, 97-8.

particular tension is expressed by Dickens in terms of an attack on a branch of knowledge whose growth had been rapid and recent: the science of Statistics.   The sudden rise of statistics and statisticians began in the 'thirties with the burgeoning of the statistical agencies necessary for the implementation of Benthamite legislation such as the New Poor Law.[1]   The new passion was encouraged by the development of the Insurance business, and by the statistical societies that began to emerge everywhere.   The statistical department of the Board of Trade was established in 1832, the Statistical Society of London (later chartered as the Royal Statistical Society) in 1834, the Registrar-General's office in 1838. All over the country statisticians— publicly and independently sponsored—were suddenly at work, collecting and classifying material on nearly every conceivable topic. 'In a few years', as G. M. Young puts it, 'the public mind had been flooded with facts and figures bearing on every branch of public life, except agriculture . . . No community in history had ever been submitted to so searching an examination'.[2]

Carlyle's chapter on statistics in *Chartism*, can be seen as one of the earliest assessments of this new flowering of the Benthamite spirit. His analysis has stood the test of time remarkably well; it is considered and constructive, and its targets are selected with a discrimination all too uncharacteristic of his later works.   His main criticism, one which modern statisticians would accept, was that statistics as then practised was not sufficiently developed as a science to provide useful conclusions on problems of any subtlety: 'Tables are abstractions, and the object a most concrete one, so difficult to read the essence of. There are innumerable circumstances; and one circumstance left out may be the one on which all turned.' 'Statistics', Carlyle continues, 'is a science which ought to be honorable, the basis of many most important sciences . . .'[3]   Carlyle does not dismiss statistics as, if we judge by *Hard Times* or by *The Chimes*, Dickens appears to; he dismisses the man without vision who 'stops your mouth with a figure of arithmetic', to whom 'it seems he has there extracted the elixir of the matter, on which now nothing more can be said.' Above all, what has attracted Carlyle's anger against statistics is the way in which it claims authority to pronounce on such matters as the state of the working classes. The 'Condition-of-England Question' is 'a most complex matter; on which . . . Statistic Inquiry, with its limited means, with its short vision and headlong extensive dogmatism, as yet too often throws not light, but error worse than darkness.' Carlyle's remarks on the inadequacy of blue-book information to convey the labourer's human condition remind us strongly of Stephen Blackpool (Stephen is not a gin-drinker, but his wife is):

[1]   See Schumpeter, J., *History of Economic Analysis*, London, 1954, 52.
[2]   Young, G. M., *Portrait of An Age*, Oxford, 1960, 33.
[3]   *Chartism*, 42.

How is he related to his employer; by bonds of friendliness and mutual help; or by hostility, opposition, and chains of mutual necessity alone? In a word, what degree of contentment can a human creature be supposed to enjoy in that position? . . . The laborer's feelings, his notion of being justly dealt with or unjustly; his wholesome composure, frugality, prosperity in the one case, his acrid unrest, recklessness, gin-drinking, and gradual ruin in the other,—how shall figures of arithmetic represent all this?[1]

Dickens, of course, repeatedly found the idea of 'figures of arithmetic' convenient to symbolise the human malaise of rationalism. Carlyle's phrase is reminiscent of Mr. Filer's 'mathematical certainty', and of some of the alternative titles Dickens considered for *Hard Times: According to Cocker, Prove it, Two and Two are Four, Simple Arithmetic, A Matter of Calculation*, and *A Mere Question of Figures*. The relevance for Dickens of such a Carlylean statement on statistics as I have quoted is clear enough. We are appropriately reminded here of a passage from Mill's famous criticism of *The French Revolution*. Dickens throughout *Hard Times* and Mill here can be seen to be making similar statements inside the same general framework of reference and, it seems to me, to be operating at a similarly profound level of critical insight; 'fancy', here as in *Hard Times*, carries a human meaning that excavates far deeper than the stratum of Dr. Holloway's 'All work and no play':

We at once felt, that what had hitherto been to us mere abstractions, had become realities . . . . Other historians talk to us indeed of human beings; but what do they place before us? Not even stuffed figures of such, but rather their algebraical symbols; a few phrases, which present no image to the fancy . . . [2]

Dickens's views on statistics may (though I doubt it) have been less antagonistic in reality than they appear in *Hard Times*. In a letter to Charles Knight, written the year after the publication of *Hard Times*, Dickens tried to explain them, and his explanation has far more in common with the reasoning of Carlyle's chapter (part of which, incidentally, is an attack on a statistical pamphlet published by Knight in 1836) than with the novel, which is far less discriminating:

My satire is against those who see figures and averages, and nothing else— the representatives of the wickedest and most enormous vice of this time— the men, who, through long years to come, will do more to damage the real useful truths of political economy than I could (if I tried) in my whole life; the addled heads who could take the average of cold in the Crimea during twelve months as a reason for clothing a soldier in nankeens on a night when he would be frozen to death in fur, and who would comfort

[1] *Ibid.*, 44-5.
[2] *Mill's Essays on Literature and Society*, ed. Schneewind, J., New York, 1965, 186-7.

a labourer in travelling twelve miles a day to and from his work, by telling him that the average distance of one inhabited place from another in the whole area of England, is not more than four miles.[1]

The critique of statistics in *Hard Times*, it might be argued, represents (like much of the novel's social criticism) only part of Dickens's views on the subject, and we may think that the selectivity of Dickens's imagination in this novel has the effect of making them less Carlylean (if we are to take this letter at its face value) than they were in reality. How well does the argument of this letter fit other Dickensian statements on statistics? This question leads to another: how Carlylean, in fact, was Dickens's understanding of the implications of the science of statistics? Dickens, it is easy to show, certainly had views on statistics before he could possibly have read *Chartism*. In 1837, he published a satirical description of an imaginary conference of statisticians, one of whom—a Mr. Slug—delivers to the meeting.

> . . . the result of some calculations he had made with great difficulty and labour, regarding the state of infant education among the middle classes of London. He found that, within a circle of three miles from the Elephant and Castle, the following were the names and numbers of children's books principally in circulation:—

Jack the Giant-killer	7,943
Ditto and Bean-stalk	8,621
Ditto and Eleven Brothers	2,845
Ditto and Jill	1,998
Total	21,407

> He found that the proportion of Robinson Crusoes to Phillip Quarlls was as four and a half to one . . . The ignorance that prevailed, was lamentable . . . . a little boy of eight years old, was found to be firmly impressed with a belief in the existence of dragons . . . . They had not the slighest conception of the commonest principles of mathematics, and considered Sinbad the Sailor the most enterprising voyager that the world had ever produced. [2]

Later, delivering his most telling point in a discussion of 'Jack and Jill', Mr. Slug pronounces that 'the whole work had just one great fault, *it was not true.*' The assumptions of this satire remind us, perhaps, of the 'dry Ogre', dragging childhood into 'gloomy statistical dens by the hair'[3] of *Hard Times*, and indicates again a vital general distinction between Carlyle's and Dickens's reactions against mechanism. Rationality implies for Dickens, partly at least, a kind of child's nightmare imprisonment inside a rigid and inhuman world, and fantasy, particularly that available to the child mind, appropriately represents

---

[1] *Letters*, II, 620.
[2] *Mudfog Papers*, London, 1880, 85-6.
[3] *HT*, 7.

the antidote to it. Mr. Slug's reference to 'Sinbad the Sailor' reminds us of the escapist literature (including *The Arabian Nights*) in which David Copperfield loses himself, books which 'kept alive my fancy, and my hope of something beyond that place and time.'[1] Fantastic, non-rational behaviour is, of course, the most obvious hallmark of many of Dickens's comic characters, and one general tendency of Dickens's humour is implicitly to represent logical behaviour as something greatly less endearing than illogical. Dickens's satire on Mr. Slug and his colleagues depends on a simple enough antithesis, between the values of untrammelled fantasy and those of unimaginative rationality. This particular satirical idea was to remain an important part of his own critique of statistics in particular and of rationalism in general. As he wrote in *Household Words* in 1853, 'In a utilitarian age . . . it is a matter of grave importance that Fairy Tales be respected.'[2] Three years after the publication of *Hard Times*, Dickens attacked the kind of school 'where the bright childish imagination is utterly discouraged, and . . . where I have never seen among the pupils . . . anything but little parrots and small calculating machines.' [3] This substantially represents the burden of his satire on statistics in *The Mudfog Papers*. Dickens continued to stress this particular opposition, though his understanding of the science of statistics itself was to become—as was hardly difficult—rather more subtle than it appeared in this early sally. Mr. Filer's diatribe on the economics of eating tripe implies a critical understanding on Dickens's part, of the operations of a certain kind of mind, that is not present in the conception of Mr. Slug, and an understanding, too, of the social consequences of the imaginative failure involved. The criticism of statistics here (as in the grim interview between Gradgrind and Louisa, discussed in an earlier chapter) is obvious enough, and is reminiscent of the central argument of Carlyle's chapter on the subject—'There are innumerable circumstances; and one circumstance left out may be the vital one on which all turned.'[4] It would be foolish to deduce that Dickens owed so simple a perception to Carlyle. But in the direct application of a mistaken statistical premise to the condition of the working class, in such a pervasively Carlylean literary context, there can surely be little doubt that Mr. Filer is reflecting Dickens's reading of Carlyle and probably, specifically, of *Chartism*:

> 'But who eats tripe?' said Mr. Filer, looking round. 'Tripe is without an exception the least economical, and the most wasteful article of consumption that the markets of this country can by possibility produce. The loss upon a pound of tripe has been found to be, in the boiling, seven-eighs of a fifth more than the loss upon a pound of any other animal substance whatever.

---

[1] *DC*, 55.
[2] [Dickens, C.], 'Frauds on the Fairies', *Household Words*, VIII (1853), 97.
[3] *Speeches*, 241.
[4] *Chartism*, 42.

Tripe is more expensive, properly understood, than the hothouse pine-apple. Taking into account the number of animals slaughtered yearly within the bills of mortality alone; and forming a low estimate of the quantity of tripe which the carcases of those animals, reasonably well butchered, would yield; I find that the waste on that amount of tripe, if boiled, would victual a garrison of five hundred men for five months of thirty-one days each, and a Feburary over. The Waste, the Waste!'[1]

The opposition between Fact and Fancy, though explored most fully in *Hard Times*, concerned Dickens from the very beginning of his career, in a fairly obvious way and for fairly obvious reasons. The antithesis formed part of a common tradition of Romanticism, in which Carlyle was an important, but not unique link. More importantly perhaps, Dickens's recoil from one kind of logic has affinities with his reaction against cruelty, especially the cruelty of the adult against the child. Fantasy, for Dickens—above all, perhaps, the fantasy and warmth of his eccentrics, especially his lower-class eccentrics—is the antidote for both. The respective attitudes of Carlyle and Dickens to Mechanism, despite the parallels we have observed, are distinguished clearly, throughout Dickens's career, by what the two writers oppose to it. Carlyle is not worried by mechanistic thinking because it interferes with human happiness; his objection to it is that it attempts to distort something that he takes to be altogether more important:

A SOUL is not like wind . . . contained within a capsule; the ALMIGHTY MAKER is not like a Clock-maker that once, in old immemorial ages, having *made* his Horologe of a Universe, sits ever since and sees it go! . . . . For indeed, as no man ever saw the above-said wind-element enclosed within its capsule, and finds it at bottom more deniable than conceivable; so too he finds . . . your Clock-maker Almighty an entirely questionable affair, a deniable affair . . .[2]

For Carlyle, 'the gleam of . . . eternal Oceans, like the voice of old Eternities, far-sounding through thy heart of hearts'[3]; for Dickens, Sleary's circus and the Toodles.

[1] *Chimes*, 94–5.
[2] *PP*, 144.
[3] *Ibid.*, 142.

CHAPTER NINE

History and Society

B OTH Carlyle and Dickens had strong views about the past, without
which we cannot fully understand their feelings about the present:
for both writers, a distinctive interpretation of history was a vital
shaping force for their personal attitudes to the Victorian age. The
difference between their philosophies of history is fundamental, and
it can be seen broadly to underline the contrast between their
personalities that I have already noted. Carlyle's *Past and Present*
(1843) provides a convenient and obvious starting-point. This work,
I have suggested, is certainly relevant to Dickens's understanding of
his own age, and probably directly inspired parts of *The Chimes*. But
though Dickens's Christmas story undoubtedly shows how similar in
some respects were their views on modern society, it also demonstrates,
equally obviously, how very different they were at the same time.
'I know', says Trotty Veck, in a moment of inspired vision,

> . . . that our inheritance is held in store for us by Time. I know there is a
> sea of Time to rise one day, before which all who wrong us or oppress us
> will be swept away like leaves. I see it, on the flow![1]

This, on the face of it, seems Carlylean enough, with its notion of an
inevitable and finally cataclysmic historical process; and yet, a familiar
difference of emphasis has to be registered. What Dickens, in this
passage, considers to be inevitable is the abolition of 'oppression';
Carlyle throughout his *oeuvre* foresees the unavoidable and explosive
disappearance of 'unreality'. The distinction is vital, and for the
whole period of their literary relationship; I have already drawn it
with particular reference to *A Tale of Two Cities* and *The French*

---

[1] *Chimes*, 151.

Revolution. Past and Present compares the Victorian Age with the twelfth century, and finds the contemporary condition of the English working man inferior, materially and—more important—spiritually, to that of the feudal serf. When Dickens and Carlyle deplore the gulf separating masters and men in the industrial areas, they have a very different alternative ideal in mind, as *Past and Present* makes abundantly clear:

> Gurth with the brass collar round his neck, tending Cedric's pigs in the glades of the wood, is not what I call an exemplar of human felicity : but Gurth, with the sky above him, with the free air and tinted boscage and umbrage round him, and in him at least the certainty of supper and social lodging when he came home; Gurth to me seems happy, in comparison with many a Lancashire and Buckinghamshire man of these days, not born thrall of anybody! Gurth's brass collar did not gall him: Cedric *deserved* to be his master . . . . Liberty, I am told, is a divine thing. Liberty when it becomes the 'Liberty to die by starvation' is not so divine![1]

The 'brass collar' round Gurth's neck is Carlyle's symbol of the just but inflexible authority that he believed in also as the true basis of industrial relations. All this, fairly obviously, is a long way from Dickens's beliefs as we see them in *Hard Times* and elsewhere: though Stephen Blackpool can certainly be seen to echo Carlyle's demand to 'give me a leader', a brass collar is not quite what he has in mind. Though *The Chimes*, for instance, reflects much of Carlyle's analysis in *Past and Present* and *Chartism*, this is one element in it that Dickens emphatically did not accept. Indeed, it may well be, in spite of his rapidly increasing respect for Carlyle at this period, that Dickens's original intention was consciously to mark his dissent, in *The Chimes*, from this part of his creed. Nothing could be better calculated, one would have thought, to confirm Dickens's distrust of the 'Good Old Times', than the spirit of much of the section of *Past and Present* dealing with the twelfth century, and as Dr. Slater has shown, there is an interesting deleted passage from the manuscript of *The Chimes* which may confirm this. The passage is part of a satire on Young England, but at one point at least, sounds rather more like an attack on parts of *Past and Present*. It was to have formed part of Trotty's vision at the beginning of the 'Third Quarter':

> Before one sofa where the youngish sort of gentleman . . . lay dozing, a small party were enjoying rustic sports, while another rather larger party were being hanged on trees in the background and a third were having brazen collars soldered round their necks as the born vassals of an undeniably picturesque Baron; singing at the same time 'Oh the good old times, the grand old times, the glorious old Feudal times, the Genuine Genteel Millenium!'[2]

[1] *PP*, 205.
[2] Penguin *Christmas Books*, Vol. I, Ed. Slater, M., Appendix A, 247-52.

The reference, here, to 'vassals in brazen collars' is very reminiscent of *Past and Present*, and this may explain the opposition from Forster that caused Dickens to delete this passage. One feasible explanation, I think, may be that Dickens, either consciously having intended this as an attack on *Past and Present*, or realising afterwards (with Forster's help) that it seemed very like one, erased the passage to avoid giving offence to Carlyle, to whom, of course, it was his ambition to read the story aloud. Whatever the truth of this, the comparison of these two passages certainly underlines the distinction I have just drawn. Dickens's feelings about 'the good old times' are conveyed, adequately enough, by the titles of a series of false book backs in his library at Gad's Hill entitled 'The Wisdom of our Ancestors—I. Ignorance. II. Superstition. III. The Block. IV. The Stake. V. The Rack. VI. Dirt. VII. Disease.'[1] Dickens believed in the present as necessarily better than the past, and the future as necessarily better than both. This is, in a way, related to the idea of history of the Enlightenment, and Dickens's attitude to the past here has affinities not with Carlyle but with Bentham who, as Humphry House points out, 'had called "Our Wise Ancestors", "the Wisdom of Ages", and "the Wisdom of Old Times", mischievous and absurd fallacies springing from the grossest perversion of the meaning of words.'[2] Carlyle, for all his understanding of the distinctiveness of his own times and his dislike of inappropriate anachronisms, certainly believed in 'The Wisdom of our Ancestors':

How have cunning workmen in all crafts, with their cunning head and right-hand, tamed the Four Elements to be their ministers; yoking the Winds to their Sea-chariot, making the very Stars their Nautical Time-piece;—and written and collected a *Bibliothèque du Roi*; among whose Books is the Hebrew BOOK! a wondrous race of creatures: *these* have been realised, and what of Skill is in these: call not the Past Time, with all its confused wretchednesses, a lost one.[3]

He believed too, not—like Dickens—in a constant, unbroken movement away from the barbarism of the past, but—not unlike the Saint-Simonians—in a series of cycles of growth and decay, of progress and regression:

How . . . Ideals do realise themselves; and grow . . . from amid the . . . ever-fluctuating chaos of the Actual: this is what World-History, if it teach anything, has to teach us. How they grow; and, after long stormy

[1] House, 35.
[2] *Ibid.*
[3] *FR*, I, 10.

growth, bloom out mature, supreme; then quickly (for the blossom is brief) fall into decay; sorrowfully dwindle; and crumble down, or rush down, noisily or noiselessly disappearing.[1]

The cruelty and oppression that Dickens saw when he looked to the past was the factor that determined more than any other his historical philosophy. Carlyle's philosophy of history has fairly obvious affinities with a bewildering variety of sources: Walter Scott; German Romanticism; Scottish Calvinism; the Saint-Simonians.[2] Dickens's is more difficult to pin down in terms of an historical or literary background. He read history, I suspect, mainly for its incident, rather than its 'philosophy'. His view of history is simple enough in all conscience, and it would not, I think, be a fruitful exercise to try to explain it in terms of his reading of historians. When Dickens surveyed the past, he looked for and found the cruelty and oppression he hated in his own age: the past differed from the present for him mainly in the greater scale of its injustice. The *Child's History of England* is a pamphlet against the viciousness and general unpleasantness of preceding ages, and an implied profession of belief in the greater enlightenment (despite their serious and obvious failings) of his own times.

This underlying distinction between the two men's feelings about history seems to me to operate in almost exactly the same way between their specific attitudes to the present. This is clearly not a convenient view; if accepted (as I think it must be on any reasonable reading of the available evidence) two general hypotheses about the Sage's influence on the novelist, which have apparently been widely accepted, must be either rejected or heavily qualified: firstly, that, though Dickens began his career as a humanitarian and a liberal, under Carlyle's shadow he grew increasingly intolerant and reactionary with the years: secondly, that Dickens came to be increasingly depressed by his own times, to see his age overwhelmingly as a kind of diseased and nightmarish prison, and that this totally pessimistic view can be explained, at least partly, by Carlyle's influence. The earliest version of the first of these two general proposals can be observed, in a rudimentary form, as early as 1850, though as we might expect, there is a significant difference of emphasis to be registered here. 1850, of course, is the year of *Latter-Day Pamphlets*, the most shocking of which, an attack on the humane treatment of convicted criminals entitled 'Model Prisons', attracted wide and scandalised public attention. Reviewing *David Copperfield*, *Fraser's Magazine* pointed out certain similarities between the chapter in Dickens's new novel entitled 'I am shown two interesting penitents' and Carlyle's pamphlet, and even reprinted passages from both,

---

[1] *Ibid.*, 11-12.
[2] See Shine, H., *Carlyle and the Saint-Simonians*, London, 1941.

concluding that Dickens 'follows as junior on the same side', with 'an entire condemnation of the whole system'.[1] The apparent agreement was noted as a curiosity, it being clear to the reviewer that they were diametrically opposed on everything else. In this last suggestion, as Professor Collins has pointed out, the writer was certainly badly wrong,[2] and the parallel with 'Model Prisons' has not gone unnoticed by modern scholars. Professor Collins further points out that in an article by Henry Morley, published in *Household Words* in June 1850, 'Model Prisons' is mentioned with approval, an approval which, given Dickens's known editorial habits, he probably shared, and that Dickens 'did not part company with him over *Latter-Day Pamphlets*, as did so many of his thoughtful and decent contemporaries.'[3]

Fraser's Magazine's proposition that 'Dickens follows as junior on the same side' certainly sets up an interesting line of inquiry, the pursuit of which has led at least one writer to claim uncompromisingly that Carlyle's pamphlet 'led directly to Dickens's article "Pet Prisoners" and the satire on the milksop treatment of prisoners in *David Copperfield*.'[4] 'Model Prisons', as I have pointed out, probably horrified Carlyle's audience more than any other of the *Latter-Day Pamphlets* and whether or not Dickens can really be shown to have accepted its more reactionary elements is obviously a question of some importance. What shocked his contemporaries was only partly the matter of Carlyle's doctrines; mainly, it was the unchristian spirit, even the savagery, of his manner. Carlyle's pamphlet can be seen, broadly, to make three points. Firstly, that the conditions of the criminals inside the 'model prison' he visited were better than those to be found in honest working class homes; secondly, that the purpose of a prison sentence is punishment, not reformation; and thirdly, that reformation is, in any case, impossible, and that society should simply put the criminal out of harm's way, and then return to its legitimate concerns:

. . . scoundrel is scoundrel: that remains forever a fact; and there exists not in the earth whitewash that can make the scoundrel a friend of this Universe; he remains an enemy if you spent your life in whitewashing him. He won't whitewash; this one won't. The one method clearly is, That, after fair trial, you dissolve partnership with him; send him, in the name of Heaven, whither *he* is striving all this while, and have done with him. And, in a time like this, I would advise you, see likewise that you be speedy about it! For there is immense work, and of a far hopefuler sort, to be done *elsewhere*.[5]

---

[1] *Fraser's*, XLII (1850), 709.
[2] Collins, *Crime*, 156.
[3] *Ibid.*
[4] Goldberg, 64.
[5] *LDP* 336.

It is difficult to avoid the impression, at times, that Carlyle's feelings about punishment betray a kind of grim satisfaction in the idea of its infliction. At one point, he recounts an ancient German practice, carried out on a man who had committed certain crimes:

> Him once convicted they laid hold of, nothing doubting;—bore him, after judgement, to the deepest convenient Peat-bog; plunged him in there, drove an oaken frame down over him, solemnly in the name of gods and men: 'There, prince of scoundrels, that is what we have had to think of thee, on clear acquaintance; our grim good-night to thee is that! In the name of all the gods lie there, and be our partnership with thee dissolved henceforth. It will be better for us, we imagine!'[1]

The main evidence for or against Dickens's acceptance of this pamphlet is to be found in an article by him, published in *Household Words* (at the end of April 1850, about two months after the publication of 'Model Prisons') entitled 'Pet Prisoners' and in the 'penitents' chapter from the final double number of *David Copperfield*. Both the article and the chapter are explicit attacks on the so-called 'separate' system, whereby, through solitary confinement, contact between prisoners was (or was supposed to be) prevented.[2]   In both, Dickens attacks the system on two main grounds, that the conditions of the prisoners are better than those endured by the poor outside the prison gates, and that the separate system encourages a hypocritical and self-important frame of mind in the prisoner: thus, Uriah Heep is perfectly equipped by nature to thrive under such a system. This, clearly, is no part of Carlyle's complaint, and in any case the jail he attacks in 'Model Prisons' (which has been identified as Coldbath Fields[3]) followed the rival 'silent' system, of which Dickens approved. Nevertheless (like many others at this time) Dickens agrees with Carlyle in his complaint that the poor outside prison fare worse than the criminal inside, and in his view that prisons should punish the criminal; like Carlyle, he complains that the treadmill has been almost abolished[4] and he goes on to recommend that work should be made as uncongenial to the prisoner as possible. Thus, Dickens certainly accepts two of the three main ideas of 'Model Prisons'.

On the face of it, there may seem to be a fairly substantial accumulation of evidence in support of the suggestion that Carlyle's 'Model Prisons' substantially influenced 'Pet Prisoners' and part of *David Copperfield*. Nevertheless there is, I am sure, a far weightier case against this proposition.   Briefly, it is that on the two points in Carlyle's argument on which the two men agreed (the undesirability that the conditions of the criminal should be superior to those of the honest

---

[1] *Ibid.*, 335-6.
[2] See Collins, *Crime*, 54.
[3] *Ibid.*, 64.
[4] *LDP*, 310, and [Dickens, C.], 'Pet Prisoners', *Household Words*, I (1850), 103.

poor, and the necessity for the criminal to be punished) both writers represented a substantial section of public opinion; and that the manner and matter of the most widely attacked parts of 'Model Prisons' are reflected neither in 'Pet Prisoners', in *David Copperfield,* not in Morley's article, 'The Great Penal Experiments'. Nor does Dickens's failure to break with Carlyle over *Latter-Day Pamphlets* imply that he agreed with everything in them. Though, certainly, many did turn against Carlyle over the *Pamphlets,* perhaps a more remarkable feature of the furore over their publication was the number of people who disagreed with all or part of them, but who, nevertheless, continued to admire Carlyle. The dilemma of such readers was summarised by the *North British Review*: 'Even where one differs most strongly from Mr. Carlyle', thought the writer,

... and feels almost constrained to fall out with him absolutely and finally as a teacher of what seems to be false, cruel and mischievous, there is still, we are well aware, one consideration that ought to operate in making one ponder the difference long before expressing it, and in inducing one, if one must express it, to do so as modestly as possible. This is the consideration of Mr. Carlyle's real greatness of intellect, which renders it almost a matter of certainty that you cannot conceive or express any notion in connexion with any of the topics he has formally handled, that he has not himself conceived or expressed before you with far greater clearness and force, and a far more exact appreciation of its real significance and worth.[1]

It was, of course, quite possible to accept much of Carlyle's argument in 'Model Prisons', while wholeheartedly rejecting its barbaric tone. The *Eclectic Review* could quote with approval Carlyle's attacks on the soft treatment of 'The Devil's regiments of the line', and his contrast with the treatment by society of the poor;[2] nevertheless, the writer condemns the peat-bog passage, discussed above, as 'almost too barbarous to be quoted',[3] and concludes that Carlyle cherished 'too much honour for and faith in, mere arbitrary force'.[4] Similarly, *The Dublin Review* agreed with another of Carlyle's arguments, also accepted by Dickens, while rejecting firmly the pamphlet's un-christian tone: Carlyle was right, thought the reviewer, to attack the principle that the idea of punishment was the improvement of the criminal himself. 'Justice', he thought, 'is done by society *as* justice, and in virtue of an inherent or delegated right to visit crime with punishment . . .' And yet, pointed out the writer,

---

[1] 'Latter-Day Pamphlets. Edited by Thomas Carlyle', *North British Review,* **XIII** (1850), 15.
[2] 'Pilgrimage to Utopia', *Eclectic Review,* LXVII (1850), 476.
[3] *Ibid.,* 477.
[4] *Ibid.,* 476.

. . . even this principle, fundamentally true, is dealt with by him in a way to make it even falser and far more hateful than the system it opposes. According to him the scoundrel is unimprovable, irreclaimable,—if he be hastening to the gallows, clear the road for him; if he choose to go to Hell, send him thither with all dispatch, extinguish him at least out of human society as a mutinous wild beast. How abhorrent the spirit of all this is to the teaching of our Lord, and of our Lord's Church, we need scarce observe.[1]

To suggest that this passage from *The Dublin Review* might well be taken as a rough guide to Dickens's probable opinions (if he came to the point of forming any) on the worst excesses of 'Model Prisons', would, I think, be more consistent with what we know of his views and personality, than to argue that he approved of everything in the pamphlet. Morley's reference in his own article on penal experiments to Carlyle's 'graphic but eccentric pen',[2] though approving, is something short of idolatry perhaps, and Morley is in any case referring to Carlyle's physical description of the—to him—palatial Coldbath Fields prison. Morley, furthermore, refers to it to help point the contrast, not with inadequate working class conditions, but with those of another London prison. Though Dickens was more upset by the oppression of the innocent, Carlyle's description of an ancient German public execution is, surely, exactly the kind of thing the novelist was thinking of every time he lambasted 'The Good Old Times', and Carlyle's nostrum of 'A collar round the neck, and a cart-whip flourished over the back', reminds us not only of the 'brass collar' of *Past and Present* but the 'brazen collar' of the deleted passage in the manuscript of *The Chimes*, discussed above. Dickens's hatred of the barbarity of 'The Good Old Times' had not abated since 1844, and an article by Percival Leigh, published in the same issue of *Household Words* as 'Pet Prisoners', makes this clear. Entitled 'A Tale of The Good Old Times', the article is a long catalogue of the nastiness of past ages in which is necessarily included the barbarity of their punishments.[3]   Morley's article, 'The Great Penal Experiments', shows a similar fierceness against unacceptable prison conditions in Dickens's own time. Dickens's views on the treatment of prisoners were certainly reactionary in comparison with the advanced opinion of the day[4]; but then, so were those of a large section of the public. [5] Above all, no matter how illiberal his opinions may seem to the modern reader, they never begin to approach the fatalistic savagery of the most notorious parts of 'Model Prisons'.

Carlyle's complaint that condemned criminals were the object of more philanthropic sympathy than honest, starving workers, brings

---

[1] 'Carlyle's Works', *Dublin Review*, XXIX (1850), 201.
[2] [Morley, H.], 'The Great Penal Experiments', *Household Words*, I (1850), 250.
[3] [Leigh, P.], 'A Tale of the Good Old Times', *Household Words*, I (1850), 104-5.
[4] Collins, *Crime*, 70ff.
[5] *Ibid.*, 17-20.

us to another and larger section of humanity which both men thought attracted philanthropic attention that might have been better directed towards the English working man: the Negro in particular, and dark-skinned races in general. And here, the admirer of Dickens must face the unpalatable fact that his views about black and brown people, though humanitarian at the beginning of his career, grew progressively more illiberal, and that his utterances on the subject on more than one occasion reached depths of savagery never plumbed by Carlyle even in 'Model Prisons'. On his first visit to America, certainly, Dickens felt everything a young liberal should about slavery: 'I don't think I could have borne it any longer', he wrote to Forster, after he had, with relief, left the slave states behind him. [1] He was duly shocked by the treatment of negroes in the South, and in his letters home to Forster, and afterwards in *American Notes*, gave impassioned descriptions of their plight. But years later, in the aftermath of the Jamaican insurrection, he could write about negroes in a far from liberal spirit:

> That platform-sympathy with the black—or the Native, or the Devil—afar off, and that platform indifference to our own countrymen at enormous odds in the midst of bloodshed and savagery, makes me stark wild. Only the other day, here was a meeting of jawbones of asses at Manchester, to censure the Jamaica Governor for his manner of putting down the insurrection! So we are badgered about New Zealanders and Hottentots, as if they were identical with men in clean shirts at Camberwell, and were to be bound by pen and ink accordingly.[2]

I have described his reaction to the Indian Mutiny elsewhere, and there are other evidences of a hardening attitude to coloured races, which I shall discuss. The hysterical tone of Dickens's attitude to negroes later in his life has been ascribed directly to Carlyle's influence, among others by A. A. Adrian, who notes a 'compelling similarity in style and substance' between Dickens's letter to de Cerjat on the Eyre controversy (quoted above) and Carlyle's remarks on emancipated slaves in *Past and Present*:

> O Anti-Slavery Convention, long-sounding long-eared Exeter-Hall—But in thee too is a kind of instinct towards justice, and I will complain of nothing. Only black Quashee over the seas being once sufficiently attended to, wilt thou not perhaps open thy dull sodden eyes to the 'sixty thousand valets in London itself who are yearly dismissed to the streets, to be what they can, when the season ends';—or to the hunger-stricken, pallid, *yellow-colored* 'Free Laborers' in Lancashire, Yorkshire, Buckinghamshire, and all other shires! These Yellow-colored, for the present, absorb all my sympathies.... Quashee has already victuals, clothing; Quashee is not dying of such despair

---

[1] Forster, 240.
[2] *Letters*, III, 445.

as the yellow-colored pale man's . . . . in one of those Lancashire Weavers, dying of hunger, there is more thought and heart, a greater arithmetical amount of misery and desperation, than in whole gangs of Quashees.[1]

Both Carlyle and Dickens attack here Exeter Hall's concern for natives 'at the expense of our own countrymen', as Mr. Adrian points out, and he concludes that 'so alike in texture are the two that they might almost be taken for pieces of the same cloth. It is as though Dickens had woven the fabric of his argument on the loom of his master, Carlyle. With respect to the development of his ideas, about slavery at least, Dickens certainly fulfilled the promise which he had made in his letter to Carlyle in 1863: "I am always reading you carefully and trying to go your way".'[2] Professor Ford underlines this judgement in his assertion that 'Dickens's response to the Eyre case is an indication of the overpowering influence which Carlyle had upon many of his contemporaries. Dickens could well say, as Ruskin once did: "I must follow my great father, Carlyle".'[3]

Both these conclusions, I am certain, illustrate the dangers of too easily discerning the influence of one mind over another. The effect here of completely ignoring the non-Carlylean background to Dickens's feelings about the Eyre controversy in particular and about coloured people in general is, I am sure, to seriously over-emphasise Carlyle's influence on him so far as these topics are concerned. Carlylean influence was certainly, I think, a factor, and Mr. Adrian is right to underline Dickens's suggestively Carlylean style in his letter about the Jamaican insurrection. But Dickens had other reasons for his support of the Eyre committee, one obvious explanation for which is provided by his hysterical attitude, some nine years previously, to the Indian Mutiny. Many people supported Governor Eyre because they felt that he had shown the kind of firmness that might have avoided tragedy in India. As Tennyson wrote to the Eyre committee, 'the outbreak of our Indian Mutiny remains as a warning to all but madmen against want of vigour and swift decisiveness'. Many supporters of Governor Eyre, including Tyndall, made the same point.[4] And though Carlyle certainly gave the Eyre committee a weight and effectiveness it might not otherwise have gained, his real function was not to create a climate of public opinion, but to provide it with an appropriate father figure. Dickens's view on the Eyre controversy was almost certainly strongly influenced by the Indian Mutiny; his views on firm treatment of natives by Europeans, however, go back even further. Carlyle's influence, as I shall argue, may

1 PP, 267.
2 Adrian, A. A., 'Dickens on American Slavery: A Carlylean Slant', PMLA, LXVII (1952), 329.
3 Ford, G. H., 'The Governor Eyre Case in England', UTQ, XVII (1948), 228.
4 Tennyson, H., Alfred, Lord Tennyson, A Memoir, London, 1897, II, 40-1, and Hume, H., The Life of Edward John Eyre, London, 1867, 283.

have been a significant factor in their evolution; but at least as important, I think, was the simple but distinctive view of society and of history that I have already discussed. Dickens's article 'The Noble Savage' has been compared closely with Carlyle's 'Occasional Discourse on the Nigger Question', and one scholar considers that 'it draws a good deal of its illiberal tincture from Carlyle's broadsides in the *Latter-Day Pamphlets*'.[1] I disagree; Dickens's illiberality here is his own, I think, as one passage from his article demonstrates very suggestively. After a long and uncomfortably passionate diatribe on the dirty habits of the 'savage', Dickens arrives at the conclusion that he is 'a wild animal with the questionable gift of boasting; a conceited, tiresome, bloodthirsty, monotonous humbug'. He then comes to what we can see as the irritant activating this rather unpleasant bee-in-the-bonnet. In spite of all his obvious barbarity, says Dickens,

. . . it is extraordinary to observe how some people will talk about him, as they talk about the good old times; how they will regret his disappearance, in the course of this world's development, from such and such lands where his absence is a blessed relief and an indispensable preparation for the sowing of the very first seeds of any influence that can exalt humanity . . .[2]

For Dickens the 'savage' represents, like the mob in *Barnaby Rudge*, the antithesis of civilisation and progress, and though the Indian Mutiny made Dickens's feelings against coloured people more vindictive, it only confirmed what he already thought about their alleged viciousness and brute stupidity. 'The Noble Savage' was an attack on what he thought to be the sentimentality with which some people bewailed the fate of certain primitive races at the hands of 'civilisation'. His wrath was aroused, among other things, by the activities of George Catlin, an ethnologist who attempted to bring the plight of the American Indian to the attention of the world. He did this by touring exhibitions which demonstrated the customs and activities of an actual group of Ojibbeway Indians, and by the publication of his *Letters and Notes on the Manners, Customs and Condition of the North American Indians* (1841). Dickens's article opens with an attack on Red Indians:

His calling rum fire-water, and me a pale face, wholly fail to reconcile me to him. I don't care what he calls me. I call him a savage, and I call a savage a something highly desirable to be civilised off the face of the earth.[3]

[1] Goldberg, 55.
[2] [Dickens, C.], 'The Noble Savage', *Household Words*, VII (1853), 337.
[3] *Ibid.*

Dickens's contemptuous reference to Catlin's activities suggests an unpleasant interpretation of the phrase 'civilised off the face of the earth'. Catlin's tours were more or less explicit propaganda (as were the *Letters and Notes*, to which Dickens refers in his article) against the decimation of the Red Indian people, 'three fourths of whose country', as Catlin wrote in 1841,

> . . . has fallen into the possession of civilised man within the short space of 250 years—twelve millions of whose bodies have fattened the soil in the meantime; who have fallen victims to whiskey, the small-pox and the bayonet; leaving at this time but a meagre proportion to live a short time longer, in the certain apprehension of soon sharing a similar fate.[1]

Carlyle, even in 'The Nigger Question', appears much more benevolent than Dickens about non-whites.[2]   His main argument is that the West Indian negro is inferior to the white man, and that he should not be allowed to sit around eating pumpkins, but should be forced to work in obedience to his white superiors; at the same time, Carlyle suggests that the attention of Exeter Hall philanthropists should be given to the starving poor at home, rather than to the (allegedly) over-fed liberated slaves of Jamaica. Dickens certainly agreed with Carlyle about the inferiority of the blacks, and in 1857 he published in *Household Words* an article by Elizabeth Lynn, called 'Why is the Negro Black', which includes a bizarre 'scientific' explanation for this[3]: interestingly enough, the article at one point refers to the negro as 'Quashie', a variant of Carlyle's contemptuous nickname. Like Miss Lynn, Dickens held that, despite the negro's obvious inferiority, he should be treated humanely, though he felt this considerably less fervently after he knew about the atrocities of the Indian Mutiny. Despite the spirit of the earlier part of 'The Noble Savage', Dickens concludes his article (as perhaps he can hardly avoid) by slightly grudgingly stating this principle:

> We have no greater justification for being cruel to the miserable object, than for being cruel to a WILLIAM SHAKSPEARE or an ISAAC NEWTON; but he passes away before an immeasurably better and higher power than ever ran wild in any earthly woods, and the world will be all the better when his place knows him no more.[4]

---

[1] Catlin, G., *Letters and Notes on the Manners, Customs and Condition of the North American Indians*, London, 1841, 4-5.

[2] Though Dickens's judgement on the possibilities ('under civilised direction') of the African Negro shows some discrimination between negroes and other 'savages', paralleled perhaps by Carlyle's remark in 'The Nigger Question' that 'The black African, alone of wild men, can live among men civilised.   While all manner of Caribs and others pine into annihilation in presence of the pale faces, he contrives to continue . . .' ('NQ', 302).

[3] [Lynn, E.], 'Why is the Negro Black?', *Household Words*, XV (1857), 587.

[4] 'Noble Savage', 339.

A. A. Adrian points out the change in Dickens's view (which he attributes to Carlyle's influence) by comparing the humanity of his horrified attacks on the cruelty of American slavery in *American Notes* with his references (on his second American visit) to a freed negro slave as an 'untidy, incapable, lounging, shambling black'; in fact, as the last paragraph of 'The Noble Savage' seems to show, it was quite possible for Dickens to look down on what he saw as inferior races and still believe that they should be treated properly, though his apparently total lack of sympathy with Catlin's objectives may betray, even at this stage in his career, a curious ambivalence on this point.[1] Whatever the truth of this, however, Dickens certainly thought little of the intelligence of non-white races towards the end of his career or before. He wrote to Forster from America in 1868 that the 'melancholy absurdity of giving these people votes . . . would glare at one out of every roll of their eyes . . . if one did not see . . . that their enfranchisement is a mere party trick to get votes.'[2] Dickens's views on the intrinsic inferiority of liberated slaves and of negroes in general were more respectable and widespread than they are now, and the year after Dickens sent this letter to Forster, Francis Galton, no reactionary, was classifying the negro as being inferior to the caucasian by 'not less than two grades' in his own alphabetic calibration of human intelligence, part of his 'evidence' for this being supplied by the American negro.[3]

Some thirty years before, when Dickens was editor of *Bentley's Miscellany*, he had published an article on American slaves which may be illuminating. *Bentley's*, of course, was far less intimately under Dickens's control than his later periodicals, and is not a sure guide to his views. But the article represents what must have been

---

[1] Dickens's attitude to Catlin suggests, even in the 'forties, a callousness about the plight of certain dark races which it may be as well to remember when we consider the suggestion that Dickens's attitude in the 'sixties, particularly to the Governor Eyre controversy, was largely determined by his respect for Carlyle, and went against his normal liberal and humanitarian feelings. Dickens's attitude during the 'forties to Catlin's activities on behalf of the North American Indians contrasts interestingly with that of the man who was later to become Governor Eyre of Jamaica, who strongly approved of Catlin's campaign, and wrote in a similar vein about the plight of the Australian Aborigine (also an object of Dickens's disgust). He considered their customs worthy of respect, and writes feelingly (and perhaps ironically) on their behalf; the Aborigine, he wrote, might perhaps be considered barbarous; nevertheless, 'could blood answer blood perhaps for every drop of European's shed by natives, a torrent of theirs by European hands would crimson the earth'. (Eyre, E., *Journals of Expeditions of Discovery into Central Australia*, London, 1845, II, 155.)

[2] Forster, 782-3.

[3] Galton, F., *Hereditary Genius*, London, repr. 1962, 395: '. . . the number among the negroes of those whom we should call half-witted men is very large. Every book alluding to negro servants in America is full of instances. I was myself much impressed by this fact during my travels in Africa. The mistakes the negroes made in their own matters were so childish, stupid and simpleton-like, as frequently to make me ashamed of my own species. I do not think it any exaggeration to say, that their c is as low as our e, which would be a difference of two grades . . .'

a perfectly respectable viewpoint throughout the Victorian era, for 'liberals' as well as for reactionaries. 'I never met an Englishman', stated the writer, 'who, after being six months in the States did not agree that the plan of treating the blacks as natural inferiors was unavoidable . . .'¹ Like Carlyle, Dickens thought that negroes could achieve something under a white master, and when he wrote 'The Niger Expedition' (1848) could still feel comparatively benevolent about them. At this stage, Dickens was prepared to accept favourable accounts of them as 'a faithful, cheerful, active, affectionate race', and thought, significantly, that it was 'clear that they, *under civilised direction*, are the only hopeful human agents to whom recourse can ultimately be had for aid in working out the slow and gradual raising up of Africa'.² Dickens's views about black people, though they are not unreminiscent of Carlyle's are, I think, his own. Though his attacks on the cruelty of American slave-owners belong to the early part of his writing life, he never changed his mind about the institution of slavery, and when he switched his support from the North to the South in the American Civil War, it was not on the slavery issue, which—like many others—he had come to believe a Northern pretext.³ In any case we have, I think, no need to go to Carlyle's writings to explain the essential elements in Dickens's feelings about coloured races. His low estimate of their intelligence probably represented the general consensus of middle class opinion, and his aggressiveness towards them in his later years can better be explained by his reaction to the great Victorian trauma of the Indian Mutiny, and to what he had learned over the years about their allegedly barbarous habits,⁴ than ascribed to a slavish acceptance of Carlyle's views. Nevertheless, though Dickens's broad feelings about coloured races were his own, one important specific attitude to their treatment may well have been partly inspired by Carlyle's teachings: his contempt for Exeter Hall. 'It might be laid down as a very good general rule of social and political guidance', he begins 'The Niger Expedition', 'that whatever Exeter Hall champions, is the thing by no means to be done'.⁵ Dickens had probably never been over-enthusiastic about missionary activities, and as Dr. Goldberg reminds us, he had satirised the 'improving handkerchieves' sent (in *Pickwick*) by the Reverend Mr. Stiggins to the West Indies. Given Dickens's feelings about negroes, about evangelical activities, and about Carlyle,

¹ 'American Niggers—Hudson River Steam-Boat Dialogues', *Bentley's Miscellany*, VI (1839), 262.
² *MP*, 111. My italics.
³ Waller, J., 'Charles Dickens and the American Civil War', *Studies in Philosophy*, LVII (1960), 535-48.
⁴ See 'His Sable Majesty's Customs', *AYR*, XII (1864), 414-20, on the savage's barbarous habits, and on the Jamaican insurrection and the inferiority of the Jamaican negro, 'Black is not *quite* White', *AYR*, XV (1866), 173-7.
⁵ *MP*, 108.

it is certainly very likely that he would read Carlyle's diatribes on emancipated Jamaican slaves, and their philanthropic English allies, with attention. Carlyle felt strongly on this subject, and wrote about it on no fewer than three occasions, in *Past and Present*, in *Latter-Day Pamphlets*, and in a *Fraser's Magazine* article published in 1849, the 'Occasional Discourse on the Nigger Question'. Carlyle's attitude to the negro, as to everything else, is shot through by his fatalistic idea of life as a burden to be born stoically, whose main purpose is the work we are set here to do, by 'The Gods', or 'The Immensities'. Since his emancipation, says Carlyle, the West Indian negro has not worked, and the economy of the West Indies is deteriorating. Because he will not work, and recognise his just superiors, his spiritual condition is worse than it was under slavery. The Negro should be justly treated, but if he will not work, then just authority, the 'beneficent whip', must force him to it.[1]

Carlyle's disapproval of slavery, though actually expressed at one point in the essay, is something less than passionate, though he spends some time dealing (no doubt sincerely) with the necessity for the just treatment of the American slave. But if Carlyle does not believe in actual slavery, he certainly believes in what seems something very like it. The negro should obey the white man, just as any inferior should obey his superiors. The emancipated slave too (like all servants) should be bound to his master by a contract for life, or for a very long period. 'You are not "slaves" now', he apostrophises the West Indian negro, 'nor do I wish, if it can be avoided, to see you slaves again: but decidedly you will have to be servants to those that are born *wiser* than you, that are born lords of you; servants to the Whites, if they *are* (as what mortal can doubt that they are?) born wiser than you.' [2] Like most Victorians, as I have pointed out, Dickens agreed with this last conclusion, the acceptance of which certainly contributed to the feelings of both men about the neglect of the white man at home by the Exeter Hall philanthropists who spent so much time thinking about the welfare of distant black people. Carlyle and Dickens were by no means the only people to notice the misplaced attention of some philanthropists, and Mrs. Trollope, for instance, had attacked them in *Michael Armstrong* (1840), some three years before Carlyle in *Past and Present*. Mrs. Trollope describes Mary Brotherton's father as

. . . an anti-(black)-slavery man, who subscribed to the African society, and the Missionary fund; drank Mr. Wilberforce's health after dinner whenever he had company at his table; and while his own mills daily sent millions of groans to be registered in heaven from joyless young hearts and aching infant limbs, he rarely failed to despatch with nearly equal regularity (all booked

[1] 'NQ', 318-9.
[2] *Ibid.*, 321.

for the same region) a plentiful portion of benevolent lamentations over the sable sons of Africa, all uttered comfortably from a soft armchair . . .[1]

Dickens attacked Exeter Hall on the same grounds (as well as for their incompetence) in 'The Niger Expedition' and the diction (as well as the sentiments) of his apostrophe to them indicates clearly, on whatever other information and on whatever private prejudices Dickens may also have based his own attitude to their activities, that Carlyle's views certainly played an important part in its formulation:

> Believe it, African Civilisation, Church of England Missionary, and all other Missionary Societies! The work at home must be completed thoroughly, or there is no hope abroad. To your tents, O Israel! But see they are your own tents! Set *them* in order; Leave nothing to be done *there* . . .[2]

Dickens's best known treatment of this theme is, of course, in the character of Mrs. Jellyby in *Bleak House*. Mrs. Jellyby, though she lets herself live in filth and confusion, and neglects her own family, spends all her time in philanthropic missionary activities. 'It *must* be very good of Mrs. Jellyby to take such pains about a scheme for the benefit of Natives', says Esther Summerson mildly, 'and yet . . . the housekeeping!'[3]   Dickens's examination of this theme in *Bleak House* follows the broad argument of 'The Niger Expedition', and the location of 'Borrioboola-gha', on the left bank of the Niger, points clearly enough to 'The Niger Expedition' as the most direct inspiration of this. Dickens's information about the expedition, of course, came from the narrative of it, written by two of its members, of which his article is partly a review, and this work, as much as Carlyle's views, provided the direct inspiration for Mrs. Jellyby. 'The Niger Expedition' appeared before 'The Nigger Question' or *Latter-Day Pamphlets*, but after *Past and Present*, and it certainly seems possible that this last work contributed to Dickens's awareness of the shortcomings of Exeter Hall: after complaining in *Past and Present* of the activities of 'loud-sounding long-eared Exeter-Hall', Carlyle reminds his readers of the English unemployed; 'if I had a Twenty Millions', he resoundingly asserts, 'with Model-Farms and Niger expeditions, it is to these that I would give it!'[4]

Implicit in Carlyle's criticisms of Exeter Hall is the wider question of his views about the government, or non-government of the lower classes by the upper. The tale of Jo the crossing sweeper, and its moral, are probably partly inspired by a passage from *Past and Present*.[5]

---

[1]   Trollope, F., *Life and Adventures of Michael Armstrong*, London, 1840, 67-8.
[2]   *The Examiner*, 19 August, 1848; *MP*, 123.
[3]   *BH*, 42.
[4]   *PP*, 267.
[5]   See p. 115, above. One immediate source for Jo was a boy named George Ruby (see House, 32), but the passage from *Past and Present* clearly contributes his infectious illness and its results.

The context in which I have already quoted this passage, in tracing Carlyle's influence on *The Chimes*, indicates again, I think, the seminal nature of Dickens's second Christmas Story, and suggests, too, that the Carlylean roots of the social concern demonstrated by Dickens's novels of the 1850's are nourished as much (and probably more) by *Past and Present* and by *Chartism*, as by *Latter-Day Pamphlets*. Dickens's imaginative insight into the plight of the helpless and illiterate Jo has a strong affinity with the following passage from *Chartism*, and Carlyle's reference in it to Chancery may be suggestive:

Bleak House	*Chartism*
It must be a strange state to be like Jo! To shuffle through the streets, unfamiliar with the shapes, and in utter darkness as to the meaning, of those mysterious symbols, so abundant over the shops, and at the corners of streets, and on the doors, and in the windows! To see people read, and to see people write, and to see the postman deliver letters, and not to have the least idea of all that language—to be, to every scrap of it, stone blind and dumb! .... To see the horses, dogs, and cattle, go by me, and to know that in ignorance I belong to them, and not to the superior beings in my shape, whose delicacy I offend! Jo's ideas of a Criminal Trial, or a Judge, or a Bishop, or a Government, . . . should be strange! (220-1).	. . . to this man it is all as if it had not been. The four-and-twenty letters of the Alphabet are still Runic enigmas to him. He passes by on the other side; and that great Spiritual Kingdom, the toil-won conquest of his own brothers . . . is a thing non-extant for him . . . . Baleful enchantment lies over him, from generation to generation; he knows not that such an empire is his . . . Oh, what are bills of rights, emancipations of black slaves into black apprentices, lawsuits in chancery for some short usufruct of a bit of land? (106)

Bleak House brings us to a second general proposition about the nature of Carlyle's influence upon Dickens, that has been advanced and to some extent accepted. Carlyle, it has been claimed, was responsible for Dickens's increasing adoption of a certain view of society, perhaps best summarised by George Bernard Shaw's reading of *Hard Times*. 'This', wrote Shaw, 'is Karl Marx, Carlyle, Ruskin, Morris . . . rising up against civilisation itself as against a disease and declaring that it is not our disorder but our order that is horrible; that it is not our criminals but our magnates that are robbing and murdering us'.[1] Dickens's view of society is fairly obviously not Marx's, as his view of Physical Force Chartism, if nothing else, confirms. And Ruskin discourages comparison with himself (and by the same token with Morris) by his own assessment of Dickens's social philosophy. As he wrote, shortly after the novelist's death, Dickens 'was a pure modernist —a leader of the steam-whistle party *par excellence*. His hero is essentially the ironmaster; in spite of *Hard Times*, he has advanced by his influence every principle that makes them harder.'[2]   *Hard Times* certainly conveys only part of Dickens's view of his world, and so do *Bleak House* and *Little Dorrit*. It is tempting, though beyond any doubt quite wrong, to think of the Court of Chancery, the Circumlocution Office, and the Marshalsea as emblems, for Dickens, of a whole society. The delay, stagnation and hopelessness of these institutions correspond, it cannot be overemphasised, with only part of Dickens's social vision. And though Dickens does not dilate on the hopeful elements in these novels, they are there: Arthur Clennam shakes off the lethargy of his youth, and breaks out of his own private imprisonment to a more useful and fulfilled existence. The point should not be overstressed, of course; nevertheless, when Dickens describes him, at the end of the book, walking into 'a modest life of usefulness and happiness', he is not providing a merely conventional ending, but hinting that the Marshalsea and the Circumlocution Office embody human tendencies which have their natural obverse, which is capable, by perseverance and hard work, of triumphing over the stagnation they represent. The various dilettantisms (the Carlylean term is appropriate here) of Richard Carstone, Skimpole, and Sir Leicester Dedlock and his guests, parallel the elaborate uselessness of the Court of Chancery, and are similarly shown as embodying social tendencies for which there are powerful countervailing forces. Mr. Rouncewell is not a prominent character in *Bleak House*, but his type was responsible for many of the achievements of what this Dickensian ironmaster himself calls 'these busy times, when so many great undertakings are in progress . . .'[3]   Dickens, without any doubt, accepted the spirit of this characterisation of his age, and there are many examples in the pages of *Household Words* of his excitement over 'great undertakings'. The late novels give a gloomier picture of his age than the journalism that Dickens closely supervised over the same period, perhaps most obviously because corruption, the law's delays, and the shortcomings of the ruling class were (and always have been) meatier subjects for fiction than achievement and

[1]   Shaw, G. B., Introduction to *Hard Times*, London, 1912, repr. in *The Dickens Critics*, ed. Ford, G. and Lane, L., New York, 1961, 127-8.
[2]   *The Works of John Ruskin*, Ed. Cooke, E. and Wedderburn, A., London, 1909 XXXVII, 7.
[3]   *BH*, 394.

progress. Carlyle too—though more obviously before the *Latter-Day Pamphlets*—was excited by the pioneering spirit that was abroad, and Rouncewell fairly obviously represents an ideal that he himself propagated. The implied contrast of the direct practicality of Rouncewell with the useless lassitude of the Dedlock circle, and (though not directly) with the wordy and materialist hypocrisy of Mr. Chadband, is also a Carlylean one:

> Looking at the kind of most noble Corn-Law Dukes . . . and also of right reverend Soul-Overseers, Christian Spiritual *Duces* 'on a minimum of four thousand five hundred', one's hopes are a little chilled. Courage, nevertheless; there are many brave men in England! My indomitable Plugson,—nay is there not even in thee some hope? Thou art hitherto a Bucanier, as it was written and prescribed for thee by an evil world: but in that grim brow, in that indomitable heart which *can* conquer Cotton do there not perhaps lie other ten-times nobler conquests?[1]

Rouncewell, of course, conquers iron and not cotton. Dickens's description of his factory radiates an excitement in its abundance, a sense, almost, of organic foison; to compare the luxuriant fantasy of this exuberant celebration of the raw materials of the iron age with the mechanistic soul-destruction of the factories of Coketown is surely effectively to destroy the notion that Dickens's target in *Hard Times* is industrial society *as such*. Industrialism, in this glimpse from *Bleak House*, is on the side of Life, of 'Fancy', rather than of merely statistical truth, of Hard Fact. Rouncewell's brother

> . . . comes to a gateway in the brick wall, looks in, and sees a great perplexity of iron lying about, in every stage, and in a vast variety of shapes; in bars, in wedges, in sheets; in tanks, in boilers, in axles, in wheels, in cogs, in cranks, in rails; twisted and wrenched into eccentric and perverse forms, as separate parts of machinery; mountains of it broken up, and rusty in its age; distant furnaces of it glowing and bubbling in its youth; bright fireworks of it showering about, under the blows of the steam hammer; red-hot iron, white-hot iron, cold-black iron; an iron taste, an iron smell, and a Babel of iron sounds.[2]

'It is impossible', as H. L. Sussman points out, 'for the modern mind, so accustomed to accelerating technological change, to recapture the wonder that the new technology created in the eighteen-twenties, 'thirties and 'forties. This awe Carlyle could not help but share'.[3] The freshness and sense of almost terrified wonder of Dickens's description, in *Dombey and Son*, of Carker's last train-ride, conveys something of this feeling, and it compares interestingly with Carlyle's

---

[1] *PP*, 189.
[2] *BH*, 846.
[3] Sussman, *Victorians and the Machine*, London, 1968, 24.

description of his own first railway journey in 1839. 'The whirl through the confused darkness, on those steam wings', he wrote to his brother John

> . . . was one of the strangest things I have experienced—hissing and dashing on, one knew not whither. We saw the gleam of towns in the distance—unknown towns. We went over the tops of houses—one town or village I saw clearly, with its chimney heads vainly stretching up towards us—*under* the stars; not under the clouds, but among them. Out of one vehicle into another, snorting, roaring we flew : the likest thing to a Faust's flight on the Devil's mantle; or as if some huge steam night-bird had flung you on its back, and was sweeping through unknown space with you, most probably towards London.[1]

Though Carlyle later became increasingly disenchanted with the implications of scientific and industrial progress, in the 'forties he still believed that it was to the Captain of Industry that society must look for its regeneration. *Chartism* and *Past and Present* are not entirely despairing documents; rather are they manifestoes for a new society, and only with *Latter-Day Pamphlets* does Carlyle's view of his age become predominantly pessimistic.

It is the coincidences of view between *Latter-Day Pamphlets* and certain of Dickens's writings of the 1850's that lead Dr. Goldberg to portray a totally disillusioned Dickens, heavily influenced by the cynicism of Carlyle's bitter declining years. The Carlylean phrase Dr. Goldberg gives to the chapter in which he propounds his view ('The Universal Social Gangrene') conveys this reading of Dickens clearly enough. As I have argued, on at least two subjects discussed in the *Pamphlets*—Prisons and Negroes—Dickens's views, though apparently rather like Carlyle's, were nevertheless firmly grounded in his own experience. The pessimism of *Latter-Day Pamphlets* does, nevertheless, correspond, in both its tone and its specific concerns, with one side of Dickens's attitude to society. Though Dickens did accept the broad tendency of his times, he observed at the same time the persistence in the age of progress of the increasingly obsolete practices of 'the good old times' (the Court of Chancery, the Circumlocution Office), and also the rise of a new breed who could, like Rouncewell, be agents of justice and progress, but might equally well be their enemies. Rouncewell, the Carlylean Captain of Industry, is an industrialist and a banker; but so is Bounderby. Though the New Man might represent energy and vitality, he might also, like the financier Merdle, embody its opposite tendency, the paralysis and aimlessness that Dickens hated so much. The Circumlocution Office and the Marshal-sea are in different ways the institutional embodiments of these tendencies. The Circumlocution Office, of course, elicited from

---

[1] *Life in London*, I, 167.

Carlyle the one comment that (so far as I know) has come down to us expressing his approval of the social criticism of one of Dickens's works, as well as of its entertainment value. Carlyle's comments on administrative inefficiency in *Latter-Day Pamphlets*, I have argued, may have been directly relevant to Dickens's attacks on the unheroic addiction to red tape of the Government of India during the Mutiny, and—given Dickens's views on Carlyle—it certainly seems highly likely that his attack on the combination of aristocratic dilettantism and red tape embodied by the Circumlocution Office was, at least partly, inspired by Carlyle's 'Downing-street' pamphlets. When Arthur Clennam visits Mr. Tite Barnacle's mews house, Dickens comments on 'the number of Barnacle families within the bills of mortality who lived in such hutches of their own free flunkey choice'.[1] The term 'flunkey' of course, is a distinctively Carlylean one, and the broad lines of Dickens's chapter on 'The Whole Art of Government' coincide with Carlyle's attack in *Latter-Day Pamphlets*. Dickens's onslaught in *Little Dorrit*, like Carlyle's in the *Pamphlets* (and, of course, elsewhere) is on the institution of Parliament itself and not merely on bureaucracy, on what Carlyle calls 'our "red-tape" establishments, our Government Offices, Colonial Office, Foreign Office, and the others, in Downing Street and the neighbourhood.' Dickens's satire on the Circumlocution Office also includes an attack on the Houses of Parliament. Since Dickens had more actual experience of the daily workings of Parliament, this was certainly based at least as much on personal experience as on Carlyle's teachings:

> It is true that How not to do it was the great study and object of all public departments and professional politicians all round the Circumlocution Office. It is true that every new premier and every new government, coming in because they had upheld a certain thing as necessary to be done, were no sooner come in than they applied their utmost faculties to discovering How not to do it . . . . It is true that the debates of both Houses of Parliament the whole session through, uniformly tended to the protracted deliberation, How not to do it . . . . All this is true, but the Circumlocution Office went beyond it.[2]

The title of the Circumlocution Office, and its goal, 'HOW NOT TO DO IT', imply together a distinctively Carlylean criticism, and the virtues of practicality, inventiveness, and persistence of the firm of Clennam and Doyce embody the appropriate Carlylean antithesis. What we need, says Carlyle, is 'Not a better Talking-Apparatus . . . but an infinitely better Acting-Apparatus . . .'[3] The qualities needed for such an acting apparatus, he continues, are 'industry, energy [and]

---

[1]   *LD*, 111.
[2]   *LD*, 104-5.
[3]   *LDP*, 345.

utmost expenditure of human ingenuity'. To say that these qualities, precisely those that Dickens admired most, were the foundation of the colossal—and for him intensely exciting—achievement of the Victorian age is to state the obvious. The Circumlocution Office and the firm of Clennam and Doyce, set up a tension which represents the struggle between established and increasingly obsolete forms, and expansive new life, that characterises any rapidly evolving civilisation. And though it is usually interpreted symbolically, the Circumlocution Office constitutes almost as much a localised topical satire as, say, the 'Gradgrind School' of *Hard Times*. Dickens was, in fact, isolating well-known administrative inadequacies that were, even as he wrote, being remedied. The Civil Service was still based on the network of hereditary privilege of which the labyrinthine family structure of the Barnacles is a satire. In 1853, the report of Northcote and Trevelyan on the Civil Service was presented, and its most important suggestion, that recruitment should be by competitive examination, was later applied to all aspiring bureaucrats.[1]   The question posed by the Circumlocution Office, as Dr. Holloway suggests, 'is in the end that of the whole transformation of English public life which became both possible and unavoidable, as England developed into an advanced industrial and commercial society.'[2]

[1] See Holloway, J., Introduction to *Little Dorrit*, London, 1967, 17-18.
[2] *Ibid.*, 17.

CHAPTER TEN

Conclusion

THE assertion that Dickens was influenced by Carlyle depends for its credibility on what is claimed for the word 'influence', and on how we establish it. To compare either the whole 'social theory', or the attitude to specific issues, of the two men, to produce the biographical evidence of Dickens's admiration for the Sage of Chelsea, and then to arrive at the looked-for conclusion, is not a productive procedure. As much as the existence of the phenomenon, we need to know its character. What, precisely, are we claiming, when we say that in certain of his works, and during a certain period of his life, Dickens was influenced by the works of Thomas Carlyle?

One thesis can, I am sure, be dismissed, despite what might be considered as evidence to the contrary: the notion that Dickens was a humble disciple of Carlyle, who sat at his master's feet, and carefully evolved his own view of society from a study of the Sage's social theory. Curiously enough, this is a view that Dickens himself can be seen to foster, and his own professions of faith to the master—'No man knows your books better than I' (1854); 'I am always reading you and trying to go your way' (1863)—certainly seem to confirm it. But we should, I think, treat these professions with caution. Dickens certainly admired Carlyle, and was anxious for his approval. But reverence for the Sage of Chelsea did not always, for Dickens as for his age, imply the adoption, or even the approval of his views. Few people admired, and many disliked, the *Latter-Day Pamphlets*; but public respect for Carlyle, nevertheless, remained remarkably unshaken after their publication. The statement of Dickens's allegiance to 'your way', made in 1863,[1] comes between *Great Expectations* and *Our Mutual Friend*, neither of which (like his final novel, *Edwin Drood*),

---

[1] *Letters*, III, 348.

it seems to me, suggest any compelling reason why Carlyle's influence should be invoked as a significant part of their ideological background.

If we can rule out the more or less direct transference of ideas from one mind to another that is implied by the notion of a master-disciple relationship, how, then, can we identify the operation of Carlyle's influence over Dickens? The answer to this question, I think, is difficult to give in an organised way. Though we can produce a list of Carlylean headings that seem to contain much of Dickens's response to his world (the fear of Mechanism, mistrust of Parliamentary Government, impatience with administrative inefficiency, contempt for Mammonism, concern with the Condition of England Question, hostility to negroes, awareness of the potential destructiveness of the mob), the primary sources in Dickens's topical reactions and emotional life of all these notions are, nevertheless, scattered and various; we form them into a coherent body of opinion at our peril. It is also important to note that, in establishing the various primary reasons why Dickens should respond to different areas of Carlyle's ideology, it has frequently been possible, even necessary, to do so without actually referring to Carlyle's works. What we can say, I think, is that Carlyle offered an imprecise but consistent structure of ideas and opinions that happened to overlap (given a little unconscious adaptation) with many of Dickens's disparate and disorganised feelings about particular issues and about life in general. Backed by a personality that Dickens found worthy of admiration and respect and by Carlyle's massive reputation, this structure of ideas presented him with a nucleus around which his own ideas could form and also, perhaps, with a mirror by which he could recognise their shape.

The influence of Carlyle over Dickens thus presents a microcosm of the Sage's influence over his times. Carlyle did not present new ideas; he articulated what many already felt, in 'a living form'. The wide range and the lack of precise definition of his ideas, or of their relative importance, combined with his eminence and his personal magnetism, allowed his admirers (consciously or unconsciously) to seek and often to find their own feelings in his works, and as a result to embrace them once more with a new certainty; what Carlyle's admirers disagreed with in his writings could be, and frequently was, conveniently ignored. Hence, Kingsley could invoke Carlyle's name, in *Alton Locke*, in support of his own plea for a regeneration of the clergy:

> When will the clergy learn that their strength is in action, and not in argument? If they are to reconvert the masses, it must be by noble deeds, as Carlyle says; 'not by noisy theoretic laudation of *a* Church, but by silent practical demonstration of *the* Church'[1]

---

[1]   Kingsley, C., *Alton Locke*, London, 1878, 322.

This is hardly more than an incidental theme in Carlyle's works, but Kingsley calls explicitly on Carlyle's name at least twice in *Alton Locke*—and implicitly throughout the novel—to strengthen his own articulation of it. Carlyle's religious position is discussed in this novel at one point in a way which supports Kingsley's purpose rather more neatly than the reality of Carlyle's doctrine; if the Sage's views were not quite convenient, they could always be bent slightly:

'Mr. Carlyle', said Miss Staunton, in her abrupt way, 'can see that the God of Nature is the God of man'.

'Nobody denies that, my dear.'

'Except in every word and action; else why do they not write about Nature as if it was the expression of a living, loving spirit, not merely a dead machine?'

'It may be very easy, my dear, for a Deist like Mr. Carlyle to see *his* God in Nature; but if he would accept the truths of Christianity, he would find that there were deeper mysteries in them than trees and animals can explain'

. . . .

'Mr. Carlyle is no Deist', said Miss Staunton; 'and I am sure, that unless the truths of Christianity contrive soon to get themselves justified by the laws of science, the higher orders will believe in them as little as Mr. Locke informs us that the working classes do'.[1]

Alton Locke proclaims an explicit debt to Carlyle, and the way in which it does so suggests two things about his influence, on Dickens and others, as well as on Kingsley. Firstly, despite Dickens's admiration for Carlyle, and the frequent similarity of his ideas with those of the Prophet, nowhere in his fiction does he approach such a profession of allegiance as this novel constitutes. Kingsley actually mentions Carlyle's name in *Alton Locke* no fewer than twenty times, and either quotes or paraphrases him on at least thirteen of these occasions. Nowhere in Dickens's novels (as we would expect) is Carlyle's name explicitly mentioned, and the nearest he comes to actually quoting him is in the rare and unacknowledged use of such standard items of Carlylean vocabulary as 'flunkey'[2] or 'unreality'.[3] Even in *Hard Times*, dedicated to Carlyle as it is, and containing as it does a recognisably (and probably consciously) Carlylean structure of ideas, the Master's Voice is heard as a pervasive and potent, but nevertheless secondary, resonance rather than—as in *Alton Locke*—an openly presented propagandist's boom.

Carlyle's message was an essentially flexible one, a chameleon that tended to fit the colouring of an admirer's existing prejudice or insight. Dickens, for instance, saw in *The French Revolution* (particularly in the crowd scenes) an intensely exciting narrative, and a sense

---

1 *Ibid.*, 186–7.
2 See p. 147 above.
3 *TTC*, 100.

of vitality and seething movement akin to his own; he did not, except in the most general way, see a philosophy of history—despite his own assertion in the *Tale*'s preface—with which he could identify. And, as I have argued, though Carton himself eventually embodies a sense of duty and sacrifice which has easily discernible affinities with part of Carlyle's historical thesis, the Carlylean connection with a wider historical process is never made. More directly relevant to Carton's story was a general current of imperialist and Christian sentiment, akin to that aroused by the Indian Mutiny: devotion and sacrifice were the appropriate weapons with which to triumph over savagery and chaos. Carlyle's doctrine can be seen to parallel and to underpin this kind of sentiment, but it had little to do with its creation. Alton Locke's reaction to *The French Revolution*, in contrast with Dickens's, is that it embodies precisely the sense of history that the novelist never ceased to anathematise. 'I know no book', Locke says,

> . . . which at once so quickened and exalted my poetical view of man and his history, as that great prose poem, the single epic of modern days, Thomas Carlyle's 'French Revolution'. Of the general effect which his works had on me, I shall say nothing: it was the same as they have had, thank God, on thousands of my class and of every other. But that book above all first recalled me to the overwhelming and yet ennobling knowledge that there was such a thing as Duty; *first taught me to see in history not the mere farce-tragedy of man's crimes and follies, but the dealings of a righteous Ruler of the universe*, whose ways are in the great deep, and whom the sins and errors, as well as the virtues and discoveries of man, must obey and justify.[1]

Dickens's reverence for Carlyle, then, is explained not by his acceptance of Carlyle's teachings as a body, but by his local response to certain sub-headings of Carlylean doctrine, taken separately and out of context. And his response to Carlyle was always pre-conditioned: Carlyle can be shown to have been a primary source for few of Dickens's feelings or opinions. Thus, he responded to Carlyle's anti-Mechanism, only partly because he accepted its natural corollary, that Mechanism destroys the capacity for assent. Certainly, this notion was important for Dickens, especially in *Hard Times*, and we miss a vital part of this novel's meaning if we ignore it; but Mechanism for him was always a more deadly foe of laughter and human spontaneity, than of belief.

The question of 'belief' nevertheless, is not irrelevant, I am sure, to Carlyle's influence over Dickens at its height, during the late 'forties and 'fifties. Carlyle's influence began at a period when Dickens's uncertainty about himself and his world was increasing, an uncertainty, as Forster himself pointed out, that was at least partly 'religious' in character. Dickens's religious problem was that of many of his

---

[1] *Alton Locke*, 104. My italics.

contemporaries; he felt the need for some form of religious or quasi-religious expression, but could accept fully neither the social mani-festation, nor the doctrine, of the Church herself. And Dickens's religious feelings, as Forster illuminatingly remarks, rested on 'depth of sentiment rather than clearness of faith'.[1] If Dickens's religious feelings cannot be seen as an explanation of Carlyle's appeal for him, they certainly form an important predisposing factor: when Dickens read Carlyle's writings about his age, he was not simply addressing himself to the works of a social critic, no matter how eminent, but to the almost magical pronouncements of a prophetic figure, 'whose kingdom is not of this world', who was seen by his contemporaries as the vehicle of a special kind of revelation. All the biographical evidence we have of their relationship supports this view. Dickens regarded Carlyle and his works, not simply with interest and respect, but with reverence, even awe.

When Dickens opened himself to the Sage's revelation, however, he was not discovering any new and unsuspected external truths; he was discovering himself. He responded to no part of Carlyle's doctrine that did not find an echo—sometimes slightly distorted—in his own heart. He followed Carlyle's lead over the Governor Eyre controversy, not reluctantly—as Professor Johnson would like to believe[2]—but because it corresponded with his own deepest con-victions, both about mobs and about non-whites. He responded to Carlyle's hatred of mechanistic thinking, not simply because Mechan-ism destroyed belief, but because it destroyed colour and human eccentricity too. He accepted Carlyle's attacks on Parliament and the law, because his own greater experience of them confirmed Carlyle's views. He accepted Carlyle's views on the condition of the working class and on Mammonism because he hated injustice, and on Exeter Hall because he hated humbug. Whether or not Dickens would have responded in the same way to all these separate questions without Carlyle's intervention is impossible to establish with complete certainty: what is almost certain is that his view of society as a whole would have been less coherent. It is in the various social inter-connections of his novels that we see Carlyle's essential contribution. He would still have distrusted Exeter Hall, despised a do-nothing aristocracy, felt pity for the plight of the under-privileged and the uneducated in a ruthless and competitive world, hated the cant and lack of charity of some ministers of the gospel, and admired the energy and initiative of the enlightened Captain of Industry; but he would almost certainly not have drawn the same connections of cause and and effect, and established the same antitheses between them, as he did in *Bleak House*. He would still have distrusted Benthamite political

---

[1] Forster, 348.
[2] Johnson, II, 1065.

economy, current trends in education, and the Department of Practical Art; he would still have felt compassion for the lot of the operative, and deplored his lack of contact with his master; he might even have connected the inhuman regularity of the machine, and the emotional sterility of some Benthamite thinking, with contemporary difficulties in embracing any satisfying and consistent philosophy of life. He might still have understood all these things, but we can say, with complete confidence, that without Carlyle, *Hard Times* would have been a very different novel, and almost certainly a less successful one. In the chemistry of Dickens's development as a novelist, Carlyle's was not the contribution of the element that changes, qualitatively, the course of the reaction; rather, he was the catalyst, without which if it comes into being at all, the new compound is formed only slowly and incompletely. Dickens partly misinterpreted Carlyle for his own ends; certainly, he ignored essential parts of his message. Nevertheless, Carlyle's personality and doctrine together provided a strategic contribution, both emotional and intellectual, to his growth as an artist. If Carlyle had not existed, it would have been necessary—for Dickens as for his age—to invent him. Partly, perhaps, they did.

THE END

Abbreviations

The following abbreviations are used for the titles of works by Carlyle and Dickens:

CARLYLE

Ch	Chartism	PP	Past and Present
FR	The French Revolution	L-DP	Latter-day Pamphlets
JS	The Life of John Sterling	"S of T"	"Signs of the Times"

References to these and other works by Carlyle, unless otherwise stated, are to the Cambridge University Press edition, Boston, 1884, and not to the rare and annoyingly expensive Centenary edition. The former, though somewhat less complete, seems to me in every other way as satisfactory, and I have found it to be widely and cheaply available.

DICKENS

AN	American Notes	LD	Little Dorrit
BH	Bleak House	MC	Martin Chuzzlewit
BR	Barnaby Rudge	OCS	The Old Curiosity Shop
Chimes	The Chimes	OT	Oliver Twist
DC	David Copperfield	RP	Reprinted Pieces
DS	Dombey and Son	TTC	A Tale of Two Cities
ED	The Mystery of Edwin Drood	UCT	The Uncommercial Traveller
GE	Great Expectations	PCEP	The Perils of Certain English
HT	Hard Times		Prisoners

All these works are cited in the *New Oxford Illustrated Dickens* edition, except for *Hard Times*, which is cited in the edition of Professors G. H. Ford and Sylvère Monod, New York, 1966. Abbreviations for Dicken's Letters, Journalism, and speeches are as follows:

AYR	All the Year Round
HW	Household Words
HN	The Household Narrative of Current Events
Letters	The Letters of Charles Dickens, ed. Dexter, W. Bloomsbury, 1938
Pilgrim Letters	The Letters of Charles Dickens, ed. House and Storey, Oxford, 1965
MP	Miscellaneous Papers, London, 1914
Speeches	The Speeches of Charles Dickens, ed. Fielding, K., Oxford, 1960

Bibliography

This bibliography, though it contains some writings not directly quoted or cited, is intended mainly as a guide to work to which direct reference is made in the text, and not as a complete or balanced list of material relevant to the subject.

ADRIAN, A., "Dickens on American Slavery: A Carlylean Slant", PMLA LXVII (1952).
ARNOLD, M., *Essays*, London, 1914.
—— *Letters to Clough*, ed. Lowry, H., Oxford, 1932.
ARONTSEIN, P., "Dickens und Carlyle", *Anglia*, XVIII (1896)
BEN-ISRAEL, H., *English Historians on the French Revolution*, Cambridge, 1968.
—— "Carlyle and the French Revolution", *Historical Journal*, II (1958).
BÖTTGER, C., *Dickens' Historischer Roman A Tale of Two Cities und Seine Quellen*, Königsberg, 1913.
BRIGGS, A., ed., *Chartist Studies*, London, 1959.
BROWN, J. B., *The Home Life*, London, 1866.
BUTT, J., and TILLOTSON, K., *Dickens at Work*, London, 1963.
CATLIN, G., *Letters and Notes on the Manners, Customs and Condition of the North American Indians*, London, 1841.
CARLYLE, T., *Letters to Mill, Sterling and Browning*, London, 1923.
—— *Letters to his Wife*, London, 1953.
—— and Emerson, R., *Correspondence*, London, 1964.
CARNALL, G., "Dickens, Mrs. Gaskell, and the Preston Strike", *Victorian Studies*, VIII (1964).
CAZAMIAN, E., *Le Roman Social en Angleterre*, 1830–1850, Paris, 1928.
CHADWICK, D., "On the Rate of Wages in Manchester and Salford, and the manufacturing districts of Lancashire, 1839–59", *Journal of the Statistical Society of London*, XXIII (1860).
CHRISTIAN, M., "Carlyle's Influence upon the Social Theory of Dickens", *Trollopian* (1947).
COLE, H., and REDGRAVE, R., *Addresses of the Superintendents of the Department of Practical Art*, London, 1853.
COLE, H. and A., *Fifty Years of Public Life of Sir Henry Cole, K.B.*, London, 1884.
COLEMAN, J., "The Truth about *The Dead Heart* and *A Tale of Two Cities*", *New Review*, I, (1889).

COLLINS, P., *Dickens and Crime*, London, 1962.
—— *Dickens and Education*, London, 1963.
—— "Keep Household Words Imaginative", *Dickensian*, LII (1956).
—— "Queen Mab's Chariot among the Steam Engines", *English Studies*, XLII (1961).
—— "The Significance of Dickens's Periodicals", *REL*, II (1961).
DAVIS, E., *The Flint and the Flame*, London, 1964.
DEWOLFE HOWE, M., *Memories of a Hostess*, Boston, 1922.
DICKENS, C., "A Poor Man's Tale of a Patent", *HW*, II (1850).
—— "Pet Prisoners", *HW*, I (1850).
—— "The Noble Savage", *HW*, VII (1853).
—— "Frauds on the Fairies", *HW*, VIII (1853).
—— "The Late Mr. Justice Talfourd", *HW*, IX (1854).
DICKENS, H., "A Chat about Charles Dickens", *Harper's Magazine* (European Edition), LXVIII (1914).
DOLMETSCH, C., "Dickens and *The Dead Heart*", Dickensian, LV (1959).
DUFFY, SIR C. G., *Conversations with Carlyle*, London, 1892.
ELIOT, G., *Essays of George Eliot*, ed. Pinney, T., London, 1963.
ESPINASSE, F., *Literary Recollections*, London, 1893.
EYRE, E., *Journals of Expeditions of Discovery into Central Australia*, London, 1845.
FALCONER, A., "The Sources of *A Tale of Two Cities*", MLN, XXXVI (1921).
FIELDING, K., *Charles Dickens: A Critical Introduction*, London, 1965.
—— "Dickens and the Department of Practical Art", *MLR*, XLVIII (1953).
—— "Mill and Gradgrind", *Nineteenth Century Fiction*, XI (1957).
—— "Dickens's Novels and the Discovery of the Soul", *Aryan Path*, XXXIII (1962).
—— "The Battle for Preston", *Dickensian*, L (1954).
FITZGERALD, E., *Letters and Literary Remains*, London, 1889.
FITZGERALD, P., *Memories of Charles Dickens*, London, 1913.
FORD, G., *Dickens and his Readers*, London, 1955.
—— "The Governor Eyre Case in England", *UTQ*, XVII (1948).
—— and Lane, L., ed., *The Dickens Critics*, New York, 1961.
FOX, C., *Memories of Old Friends*, London, 1882.
FROUDE, J. A., *Thomas Carlyle: A History of the first forty years of his Life*, London 1882.
—— *Thomas Carlyle: A History of his Life in London*, London, 1884.
GALTON, F., *Hereditary Genius*, London, Repr, 1962.
GOLDBERG, M., *Dr. Pessimist Anticant and Mr. Popular Sentiment: The Influence of Carlyle on Dickens*, University microfilms, 1966.
GROSS, J., and PEARSON, G., ed., *Dickens and the Twentieth Century*, London, 1962.
HOLLOWAY, J., *The Victorian Sage*, London, 1953.
—— Introduction to *Little Dorrit*, London, 1967.
HORNE, R., *A New Spirit of the Age*, London, 1844.
HOUGHTON, W., *The Victorian Frame of Mind*, Yale, 1957.
HOUSE, H., *The Dickens World*, London, 1960.
HOVELL, M., *History of the Chartist Movement*, London, 1925.
HUME, H., *The Life of Edward John Eyre*, London, 1867.
JOHNSON, E., *Charles Dickens: His Tragedy and Triumph*, New York, 1952.
—— ed., *Letters from Charles Dickens to Angela Burdett-Coutts*, London, 1953.

LEAVIS, F. R., *The Great Tradition*, London, rpr. 1962.
—— Introduction to *Mill on Bentham and Coleridge*, London, 1950.
and Q .D., *Dickens the Novelist*, London, 1970.
LOVETT, W., *The Life and Struggles of William Lovett*, London, repr. 1967.
MARCUS, S., *Dickens from Pickwick to Dombey*, London, 1965.
MARTINEAU, H., *Autobiography*, London, 1884.
MASSON, D., *Carlyle personally and in his writings*, London, 1885.
—— *British Novelists and their styles*, London, 1859.
MERCIER, L. S., *Tableau de Paris*, Amsterdam, 1782.
MILL, J. S., *Autobiography*, Oxford, 1924.
—— *Mill's Essays on Literature and Society*, ed. Schneewind, J., New York, 1965.
MILLER, J. HILLIS, *Charles Dickens: The World of his Novels*, London, 1959.
MONOD, S., *Dickens Romancier*, Paris, 1953.
MORLEY, H., "The Great Penal Experiments", *HW*, I (1850).
MORLEY, J., *Critical Miscellanies*, first series, London, 1871.
PHILLIPS, H. W., WATTS PHILLIPS, *Author and Playwright*, London, 1891.
PHILLIPS, W., *The Dead Heart*, London, 1855.
PIKE, J. S., "Dickens, Carlyle and Tennyson", *Atlantic Monthly*, CLXIV (1939).
POPE-HENNESSY, U., *Charles Dickens*, London, 1946.
POWELL, T., *The Living Authors of England*, New York, 1849.
RUSKIN, J., *Works*, ed. Cooke, E., and Wedderburn, A., London, 1909.
SAINTSBURY, G., *Corrected Impressions*, London, 1895.
SANDERS, C., ed., "Carlyle's Letters", *Bulletin of the John Rylands Library*, XXXVIII (1956).
SCHUMPETER, J., *History of Economic Analysis*, London, 1954.
SHAIRP, J. C., *Aspects of Poetry*, Oxford, 1881.
SHINE, H., *Carlyle and the Saint-Simonians*, Baltimore, 1941.
SLATER, M., "Carlyle and Jerrold into Dickens; a study of *The Chimes*", repr. *Dickens Centennial Essays*, ed. Nisbet, A., and Nevius, B., London, 1971.
—— Introduction and Appendix to the Penguin *Christmas Books*, Vol. I, London, 1971.
STEPHEN, L., "Thomas Carlyle", *Cornhill Magazine*, XLIII (1881).
STRACHEY. L., *Portraits in Miniature*, London, 1931.
SUSSMAN, H., *Victorians and theMachine*, London, 1968.
THIERS, M. A., *History of the French Revolution*, trans. Redhead, T., London, 1845, and trans. Schoberl, F., London, 1838.
TILLOTSON, G. and K., *Mid-Victorian Studies*, London, 1965.
TILLOTSON, K., *Novels of the Eighteen-forties*, London, 1961.
TROLLOPE, A., *The Warden*, Oxford, 1952.
TROLLOPE, F., *Life and Adventures of Michael Armstrong*, London, 1840.
WALLER, J., "Charles Dickens and the American Civil War", *Studies in American Philology*, LVII (1960).
WILSON, D. A., *Carlyle Till Marriage*, London, 1923.
—— *Carlyle to the French Revolution*, London, 1924.
—— *Carlyle on Cromwell and others*, London, 1925.
—— *Carlyle at his Zenith*, London, 1927.
—— *Carlyle to Threescore and Ten*, London, 1929.
—— *Carlyle in Old Age*, London, 1934.

WOOLNER, A., *Thomas Woolner, R.A., Sculptor and Poet*, London, 1917.
WORDSWORTH, W., *Poetical Works*, ed., de Selincourt, E., and Darbishire, H., Oxford, 1947.
YOUNG, G. M., *Portrait of an Age*, London, 1964.
YATES, E., *Recollections and Experiences*, London, 1884.
——   and BROUGH, R., "*Hard Times* (refinished), by Charles Diggins", *Our Miscellany*, London, 1857.

Index

REVIEW:
DSN V, No. 1, (MARCH 1974) pp. 24-28